BRETHREN SPIRITUALITY

BRETHREN SPIRITUALITY

HOW BRETHREN CONCEIVE OF AND PRACTICE THE SPIRITUAL LIFE

*Proceedings of the
Fifth Brethren World Assembly*

*Sponsored by
Brethren Encyclopedia, Inc.*

James E. Miller, *general editor*

Brethren Heritage Center
Brookville, Ohio
July 11-14, 2013

Brethren Spirituality
How Brethren Conceive of and Practice the Spiritual Life
Proceedings of the Fifth Brethren World Assembly
Brookville, Ohio, July 11-14, 2013

© 2015 Brethren Encyclopedia Inc.

ISBN: 978-0-936693-53-8

RELIGION / Institutions & Organizations

Published by Brethren Encyclopedia, Inc.

www.brethrenencyclopedia.org

All Rights Reserved

Information on the book's cover photo:
In the cover photo Nigerian and American Brethren visited the barn and farm of Abraham Landis on Diamond Mill Road about a mile north of US Rt. 40 in southern Ohio. Here the meeting took place on Nov. 25, 1881, where the decision was made to withdraw from the main body of the German Baptist Brethren and form the group called Old German Baptist Brethren. About 25 percent (1,000) of the members of the Miami Valley joined this new group. An equal number soon followed from other states, so that by May of 1882 there were between 4,000 and 5,000 who identified themselves with the Old German Baptist. *(Dale Ulrich photo)*

Table Of Contents

Introduction i
Program iii
Greetings From Schwarzenau, Germany vii
Leadership xi

Plenary Presentations

Brethren Spirituality in the 18th Century, *Jeff Bach* 3
Brethren Spirituality in the 19th Century, *Dale Stoffer* 25
Brethren Spirituality in the 20th Century, *Bill Kostlevy* 53
The Place of Jesus in Brethren Spirituality, *Brian Moore* 67
Word and Spirit in Brethren Spirituality, *Brenda Colijn* 83
Community, Family, and Individual in Brethren Spirituality, *Jared Burkholder* 103
Brethren Ordinances, *Denise Kettering-Lane* 117

Photos 139

Seminars

The Spiritual Writings of Alexander Mack, Jr., *Aaron Jerviss* 149
Brethren Hymnody, *Peter Roussakis* 161
Separation from the World and Engagement with the World, *Carl Bowman* 183
Brethren Devotional Literature and Poetry, *Karen Garrett* 199
Spiritual Formation Practices, *Christy Hill* 219

Worship Messages

Prayer, *Roger Peugh* 231
Missions and Evangelism as Brethren Spirituality, *Fred Miller* 245
Brethren Spirituality for the Future, *Robert Alley* 253
Youth Panel, *Michael Miller* 261

Introduction

BRETHREN ENCYCLOPEDIA, INC., FOUNDED IN 1977, IS A COOPERATIVE venture of the seven main Brethren groups that have descended from the German Anabaptist/Radical Pietist religious leader, Alexander Mack. Mack's group of eight believers began the Brethren movement with baptisms in the Eder River near Schwarzenau, Germany, in 1708.

Among the cooperative ventures have been the publishing of a four-volume encyclopedia that is useful to all who are interested in Brethren history and genealogy, and the publishing of monographs and materials reflective of the history of the Brethren movement.

The Brethren Encyclopedia board sponsored a Brethren World Assembly which was held at Elizabethtown College in Pennsylvania in 1992. It commemorated the 250th anniversary of the first known Brethren Annual Meeting in America.

Subsequently, world assemblies were held at Bridgewater College in Virginia (1998), Grace College in Indiana (2003) and a grand celebration of the 300th anniversary of the founding of the movement held in Schwarzenau, Germany, in 2008. Approximately 600 Brethren from all the cooperating groups and 18 countries plus about 400 German participants met on August 2 and 3 of that year.

This volume contains the papers and proceedings from the Fifth Brethren World Assembly, held in Brookville, Ohio, July 11-14, 2013. The general theme was "Brethren Spirituality," and the speakers and presenters explored various facets of this theme. A planning committee, under the leadership of Robert E. Alley from the Church of the Brethren, worked for several years to clarify details, coordinating their efforts with those of the sponsoring group, Brethren Encyclopedia, Inc.

THE PURPOSES OF THE BRETHREN WORLD ASSEMBLIES ARE TO:

1. Gather in conversation around a common theme;
2. Share study and worship;
3. Enhance dialogue among the Brethren bodies;
4. Acquaint Brethren with their historic roots.

By God's grace and under His guidance, we believe each of these purposes was achieved in the Brookville meeting. Preserved here is much of the scholarship and exploration from that event. Planning is currently underway for the Sixth Brethren World Assembly, to be held the summer of 2018, likely in Winona Lake, Indiana.

Program

Thursday July 11

9:00 am – 1:45 pm	Registration at the Heritage Center
1:45 – 5:15 pm	Opening Sessions
	Brethren Spirituality in the 18th Century – Jeff Bach (Church of the Brethren)
	Brethren Spirituality in the 19th Century – Dale Stoffer (The Brethren Church)
	Brethren Spirituality in the 20th Century – Bill Kostlevy (Church of the Brethren)
6:00 pm	Catered Dinner at Brookville Grace Brethren Church
7:30 – 9:00 pm	Worship at Brookville Grace Brethren Church
	Host Pastor – Rick Hartley
	Prayer – Roger Peugh (Fellowship of Grace Brethren Churches)
9:00 pm	Ice Cream Social & Fellowship

Friday July 12

8:30 am – noon	Morning Sessions
	The Place of Jesus in Brethren Spirituality – Brian Moore (The Brethren Church)
	Word and Spirit in Brethren Spirituality – Brenda Colijn (The Brethren Church)
	Community, Family, and Individual in Brethren Spirituality – Jared Burkholder (Fellowship of Grace Brethren Churches)
12:00 – 1:30 pm	Lunch
1:30 – 5:30 pm	Afternoon Sessions
1:30 – 5:30 pm	Tour of Brethren Sites
1:30 - 2:30 pm	Concurrent Sessions
	The Bible in Brethren Spirituality – Panel Presentations
	The Spiritual Writings of Alexander Mack, Jr. – Aaron Jerviss (The Brethren Church)
	Tour of Brethren Heritage Center

2:30 – 3:30 pm	Concurrent Sessions
	Brethren Hymnody – Peter Roussakis (The Brethren Church)
	Separation from the World and Engagement with the World – Carl Bowman (Church of the Brethren)
3:30 – 4:30 pm	Concurrent Sessions
	Brethren Devotional Literature and Poetry – Karen Garrett (Church of the Brethren)
	Spiritual Formation Practices – Christy Hill (Fellowship of Grace Brethren Churches)
	Tour of Brethren Heritage Center
4:30 – 5:30 pm	*Brethren Worship Practices* – Panel Presentations
6:00 pm	Catered Dinner at Salem Church of the Brethren
7:30 – 9:00 pm	Worship at Salem Church of the Brethren
	Host Pastor – Michael Hostetter
	Missions and Evangelism as Brethren Spirituality – Fred Miller (The Brethren Church)
9:00 pm	Ice Cream Social & Fellowship

SATURDAY JULY 13

8:30 am – noon	Morning Sessions
	Brethren Ordinances – Denise Kettering Lane (Church of the Brethren)
	Brethren Ordinances – Panel Presentations
	Brethren Spirituality as Witness to the World: International Perspectives I
	Panel Presentations from Church of the Brethren, Old German Baptist Brethren, New Conference, Conservative Grace Brethren Churches International, and Ekklesiyar Yan'uwa a Nigeria.

12:00 – 1:30 pm	Lunch
1:30 – 5:30 pm	Afternoon Sessions
1:30 – 5:30 pm	Tour of Brethren Sites
1:30 – 2:30 pm	Concurrent Sessions
	The Bible in Brethren Spirituality – Panel Presentations
	The Spiritual Writings of Alexander Mack, Jr. – Aaron Jerviss (The Brethren Church)
	Tour of Brethren Heritage Center
2:30 – 3:30 pm	Concurrent Sessions
	Brethren Hymnody – Peter Roussakis (The Brethren Church)
	Separation from the World and Engagement with the World – Carl Bowman (Church of the Brethren)
3:30 – 4:30 pm	*Brethren Spirituality as Witness to the World: International Perspectives II* – Panel Presentations from The Brethren Church, Dunkard Brethren Church, and Fellowship of Grace Brethren Churches
4:30 – 5:30 pm	Youth Responses – Panel Presentations
6:00 pm	Catered Dinner at Salem Church of the Brethren
7:30 – 9:00 pm	Worship at Salem Church of the Brethren
	Host Pastor – Michael Hostetter
	Brethren Spirituality for the Future – Robert Alley (Church of the Brethren)
9:00 pm	Ice Cream Social & Fellowship

SUNDAY JULY 14

Worship at a Brethren church not of one's usual Sunday attendance

Greetings From Schwarzenau, Germany

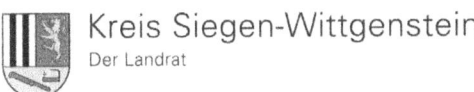 Kreis Siegen-Wittgenstein
Der Landrat

Dear members of the Church of Brethren
and of the Brethren Churches,

I am very glad to greet you with this letter. It is nice that Bernd Julius from Schwarzenau is taking part in the festivity of the 5.th Brethren World Assembly here in Brookville, Ohio.

I fondly remember the 3rd August 2008 when the Brethren World Assembly took place in Schwarzenau in the Siegen-Wittgenstein district. We celebrated then the 300th anniversary of a historical event that continues to have an effect in our times. In the month of August in 1708 five men and three women were baptized in the river Eder by immersion: the first one was Alexander Mack who subsequently baptized the others. That was the hour of birth of the "Schwarzenauer Tunker" ("Dunkards of Schwarzenau") and at the same time that of the current Brethren Churches.

I was born in the Wittgenstein region myself and as the head of the Siegen-Wittgenstein district I am very proud of my home district and its eventful history. The German Baptists could follow their beliefs without being prosecuted because of the tolerance of the former Wittgenstein sovereigns. But the climate changed gradually and in 1720 a big group of German Baptists lead by Alexander Mack left the Wittgenstein region and, after they had spent nine years in Holland, emigrated to the United States.

Today the Churches of the Brethren have developed into a worldwide movement with several hundred thousand members. Because of my own personal roots I am very pleased that many members of your churches are in close contact to the home district of their ancestors. Every year visitors from all over the world come to the Siegerland and visit the Alexander-Mack-Museum in Schwarzenau to find out about the origins and the history of their church.

 Südwestfalen
Regionale 2013

 Siegen-Wittgenstein
Die Menschen sind unser Kapital

Koblenzer Straße 73 · 57072 Siegen · Telefon: 0271 333-2000 · Telefax: 0271 333-2350 · E-Mail: p.breuer@siegen-wittgenstein.de

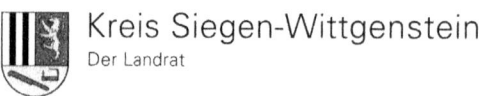

Kreis Siegen-Wittgenstein
Der Landrat

Up to now the Siegen-Wittgenstein district has been a vivid center of Christian faith in Germany. The variety of the vital Christian communities is a strong foundation for the social interaction in our region. At the same time the churches and communities are actively involved in social activities: they take responsibility for child care facilities, for schools or for the care of old and handicapped people. Because of these committed people our region is pleasant to live in.

I hope you will be spending some interesting and beneficial days at the 5th Brethren World Assembly and I would be delighted to see you again in the Siegen-Wittgenstein district.

Best regards,

yours Hallvily

Paul Breuer
District Administrator

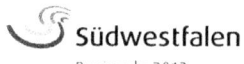

Südwestfalen
Regionale 2013

Siegen-Wittgenstein
Die Menschen sind unser Kapital

Koblenzer Straße 73 · 57072 Siegen · Telefon: 0271 333-2000 · Telefax: 0271 333-2350 · E-Mail: p.breuer@siegen-wittgenstein.de

Stadt Bad Berleburg
Der Bürgermeister

To all members and visitors
of the "Fifth Brethren World Assembly"
c/o Brethren Heritage Center
428 Wolf Creek St.
Suite No. H1
Brookville, DH 453109-1297
USA

July, 2013

Dear members and visitors of the Fifth Brethren World Assembly,

I am pleased to have the opportunity to send you the best greetings from Bad Berleburg-Schwarzenau in Germany, the hometown of Alexander Mack, who performed the act of adult babtism in the Eder River in August 1708. To celebrate this 300th anniversary of the Church of the Brethren the last Brethren World Assembly came back to its roots. With more than 1.000 persons from 18 nations they gathered in Bad Berleburg-Schwarzenau in August 2008.

I love to remember these celebration-days in our city five years ago. I met people with complete different cultures, but the same strong trust in God, who strives for acceptance of the other also in kind of different looks, different traditions and different thoughts. Central beliefs of the Church of the Brethren are peace and tolerance which are also the essential base for a good coexistence within the Brethren family all over the world in former times as well as today. This peaceful living and working together with the acceptance that the other may be different would be a good example for all the countries which are in war.

I wish all members and visitors of the Fifth Brethren World Assembly a good, interesting and peaceful time in Brookville, with the possibility to meet a lot of friends.

Yours faithfully

Bernd Fuhrmann
Mayor of the town
of Bad Berleburg

Rathaus . Poststraße 42 . 57319 Bad Berleburg
Telefon (02751)923-100 . Telefax (02751)923-102
Internet: www.bad-berleburg.de
E-Mail: b.fuhrmann@bad-berleburg.de

Südwestfalen

Speech by the president of the Schwarzenau Heritage Society (Heimatverein) on occasion of the Fifth Brethren World Assembly in Brookville, OH, USA (12.07.2013)

Bernd Julius

Dear participants of the fifth Brethren World Assembly,
Dear international guests and
Dear members of the Planning Team,

First of all I wish to say a cordial thank you very much for having the possibility to attend this assembly. It is for me a special honour to share in this important event among the Brethren.

When I say now a few words to you as a resident from the village of the foundation of the Brethren Movement, Schwarzenau in Germany, I remember immediately with great pleasure the Fourth Brethren World Assembly in August 2008 in Schwarzenau during the 300th anniversary of Alexander Mack's Eder River baptism. At this time I was the chair of the German planning team, and we had a very good and fruitful co-operation with Dale Ulrich from Brethren Encyclopedia. One difference between today and five years ago is that I now am not on duty; so I can relax while following the assembly. I would like to have many meetings and good conversations in the sense of your faith. I already meet with many good friends.

Being also the president of the Schwarzenau Heritage Society (We say in German, "Heimatverein".), I say many thanks for the financial support to the Alexander Mack Museum, especially in the last two years. It helps very much, to maintain the museum in future. The interest rates on investments at this time in Germany are very low. The town of Bad Berleburg already closed because of the costs "Heimathaus" in the rear of the Berleburg-castle and sold the building.

In this way I transmit the best greetings and wishes from all of the Schwarzenau inhabitants to the assembly, especially from the German planning-committee 2008 with Karin Zacharias, Bodo Huester, Peter Kanstein and Otto Marburger. I also will present to you letters of greetings from the mayor of the town Bad Berleburg, Bernd Fuhrmann, as well as the District Administrator of the county Siegen-Wittgenstein, Paul Breuer. Both representatives of the Siegen / Wittgenstein area expressed greetings to the Brethren in the riding hall in 2008 in Schwarzenau.

Finally, I wish all participants of the Fifth Brethren World Assembly God's rich blessings. I certainly will take with me many good impressions across the Atlantic Ocean back to Europe to your roots and my lovely homeland Schwarzenau at the Eder-River in Germany.

Thanks again for the opportunity to be with you here in Brookville.

Leadership

Brethren Encyclopedia, Inc. – Board of Directors & Associates

Robert S. Lehigh, *president* – Dunkard Brethren Church
Dale R. Stoffer, *vice president* – The Brethren Church
Dale V. Ulrich, *secretary* – Church of the Brethren
Terry D. White, *treasurer* – Fellowship of Grace Brethren Churches
Michael Miller – Old German Baptist Brethren Church, New Conference
David E. Miller – Old German Baptist Brethren Church
Gary Kochheiser – Conservative Grace Brethren Churches, International
James C. Gibbel, *assistant treasurer* – Church of the Brethren
Jeffrey A. Bach, *director* – Young Center for Anabaptist and Pietistic Studies Church of the Brethren
John R. Gibbel, *attorney* – Church of the Brethren

Planning Team for Brethren World Assembly

Robert E. Alley, *chair* – Church of the Brethren
Jeff Bach – Church of the Brethren
Brenda Colijn – The Brethren Church
Milton Cook – Dunkard Brethren Church
Tom Julien – Fellowship of Grace Brethren Churches
Gary Kochheiser – Conservative Grace Brethren Churches, International
Michael Miller – Old German Baptist Brethren Church, New Conference

Brethren Heritage Center

Larry Heisey, *Secretary, Board of Directors*

Program Personnel

Robert E. Alley is a retired pastor in the Church of the Brethren and former Annual Conference Moderator (2011). He retired in 2009 after 20-year tenure at the Bridgewater (VA) Church of the Brethren and prior to that served the Everett (PA) Church of the Brethren and the Fellowship Church of the Brethren near Martinsburg, WV. He graduated from Bridgewater College (VA) with a B.A. degree in Philosophy and Religion. He attended Bethany Theological Seminary and earned his M.Div. degree from Eastern Mennonite Seminary in Harrisonburg, VA. He is currently a member of the Board of Directors of the Valley Brethren-Mennonite Heritage Center in Harrisonburg and for Bridgewater Healthcare, Inc.

Jeff Bach is director of the Young Center for Anabaptist and Pietist Studies at Elizabethtown College and also teaches in the Department of Religious Studies. He taught at Bethany Theological Seminary in Richmond, IN, from 1994-2007. An ordained minister, he also pastored Prairie City Church of the Brethren in Prairie City, Iowa 1983-1990. He earned a Ph.D. in religion from Duke University in 1997 and has degrees from Bethany Theological Seminary (1983) and McPherson College in Kansas (1979). He has written *Voices of the Turtledoves: The Sacred World of Ephrata* about the religious thought and practice of the Ephrata Cloister.

Carl Desportes Bowman is perhaps best known as the author of *Brethren Society: The Cultural Transformation of a Peculiar People*. He also co-authored *On The Backroad To Heaven: Old Order Hutterites, Mennonites, Amish, and Brethren*. His most recent Brethren-related work was *Portrait of a People: The Church of the Brethren at 300*, published for the Brethren tricentennial. Additionally, he served as contributing editor to *The Brethren Encyclopedia*, Volume IV. Bowman currently is Director of Survey Research for the university of Virginia's Institute for Advanced Studies in Culture.

Jared S. Burkholder is Associate professor of History at Grace College in Winona Lake, IN. He is a specialist in American Religious History with an emphasis on Pietism, Anabaptism, and Evangelicalism. He has co-edited *The Activist Impulse: Essays on the Intersection of Anabaptism and Evangelicalism* (Wipf and Stock, 2012) as well as a forthcoming collection of essays on the history of Grace College and Theological Seminary (BMH). He has written for the *Pennsylvania Magazine of History and Biography, Fides et Historia*, and the *Journal of Moravian History*. Burkholder blogs at www.hermeneuticcircle.com.

Brenda B. Colijn is a Brethren elder, denominational leader, and professor of Biblical Interpretation and Theology at Ashland Theological Seminary. She is the author of *Images of Salvation in the New Testament*, as well as articles on Brethren interpretation of scripture and Brethren beliefs.

Karen Garrett is a member of Bear Creek Church of the Brethren near Dayton, OH. She was a public school teacher for 30 years. In addition to her M.Ed. degree from Wright State University, she is a 2009 graduate of Bethany Theological Seminary. Her Master's thesis research focused on the Brethren poetry and hymn texts of the nineteenth century. She is currently employed part-time as managing editor of the journal, *Brethren Life & Thought*, and as Coordinator of Assessment for Bethany Theological Seminary.

Christy Hill studied Christian Education at Wheaton College and Talbot School of Theology, eventually receiving her Ph.D. in Educational Studies. She has worked with underprivileged families in Mexico, has discipled junior higher and adult singles in CA, and she equips women for ministry in the local church. She currently teaches undergraduate and graduate students in the School of Ministry Studies at Grace College and Seminary.

Aaron Jerviss is a doctoral candidate in history at the University of Tennessee, with a special interest in the history of peace churches. His dissertation focuses on the experience of Brethren and Quakers during and after the Civil War.

Denise Kettering-Lane is Assistant Professor of Brethren Studies at Bethany Theological Seminary. She holds an undergraduate degree in religion from Ashland University, an MTS from Candler School of Theology at Emory University and a Ph.D. in Religious Studies from The University of Iowa. She has formerly served as the archival assistant at the Brethren Historical Library and Archives in Elgin, Illinois. Particularly interested in women's history, the transatlantic Pietist movement, and Christina devotional practices, she is a licensed Church of the Brethren minister and currently lives in Franklin, Louisiana, with her husband Calvin.

William Kostlevy is Director of the Brethren Historical Library and Archives, Elgin, IL. He formerly was Professor of History and Political Science at Tabor College, Hillsboro, KS and was archivist and special collections librarian at Asbury Theological Seminary and Fuller Theological Seminary. He is an ordained minister in the Church of the Brethren, serving as the pastor of the Florence Church of the Brethren 1982-1988. He has served on the Brethren Historical Committee, and was the primary author of the centennial history of Bethany Theological Seminary. He is also the author of *Holy Jumpers: Evangelicals and Radicals in Progressive Era America*, Oxford University Press (2010).

Fred Miller is a Brethren elder, pastor, and leader in The Brethren Church, having served on the national Mission Board and Executive Board. He has provided leadership in the areas of preaching, leadership development, outreach, and missions at the local, district, and national levels. He is currently pastor of Mount Olive Brethren Church at McGaheysville, east of Harrisonburg, VA.

Brian Moore is a Brethren elder, long-time pastor (retired 2012), and two-time national moderator of The Brethren Church. He is the author of *A Brethren Witness for the 21st Century* as well as articles on Brethren beliefs and practices.
NOTE: Brian Moore, who struggled to make this presentation even though suffering with advanced ALS, passed away January 26, 2015. He retained a vibrant, powerful faith until the end, ministering to hundreds of people on Facebook as he reflected on his spiritual journey through his "valley of the shadow of death."

Roger Peugh, a native of Washington State, started his studies at Grace College in the fall of 1961, went on a YFC Teen Team to Germany fall 1962, and served in Berlin, Germany YFC Spring 1963. He graduated with a B.A. in History in 1965 and a week later married Nancy, and that fall started M.Div. studies at Grace Seminary, from which he graduated in 1968. They moved to Germany in 1969 to begin a church-planting ministry in Stuttgart. In 1989, with four children, they moved back to Indiana where Roger began teaching missions at Grace College & Seminary. Over the years, he also served in various capacities on Grace campus, for nine years as Chaplain.

Peter S. Roussakis is a Brethren elder, pastor, and former Assistant Professor of Church Music at Southwestern University. With training in both theology and music, he has written *Classic Worship: With Brethren in Mind, United in Prayer: Understanding and Praying the Lord's Prayer* and numerous articles on music and worship.

Dale R. Stoffer is a Brethren elder, church planter, Professor of Historical Theology and former Academic Dean at Ashland Theological Seminary. He is active in leadership positions at the local, district, and national levels of The Brethren Church. He is the author of *Background and Development of Brethren Doctrines 1650-1987, A Gleam of Shining Hope,* and numerous articles on Brethren history and theology. He serves on the board of Brethren Encyclopedia, Inc.

Plenary Presentations

Brethren Spirituality in the 18th Century

Jeff Bach

BRETHREN ARE A DEEPLY SPIRITUAL PEOPLE, EVEN IF THEY HAVE BEEN slow or reluctant to write about it. One could say that Brethren saw an intimate connection between spirituality and life-style, adding to Dale Stoffer's comments about Brethren seeing theology or doctrine intimately connected to life-style. Indeed, as Stoffer introduced his treatment of Brethren doctrines, he defined Brethren theology as reflecting "an edifying and devotional biblical spirituality."[1] An example of this combination of scripture, reflection on belief, and central importance of spirituality will come later in this paper.

A good working definition for spirituality comes from Philip Sheldrake in the *Westminster Dictionary of Christianity* (2005). Christian spirituality "refers to the ways in which the particularities of Christian belief about God, the material world and human identity find expression in basic values, lifestyles and spiritual practices. To put matters more classically, Christian spirituality embodies a conscious relationship with God, in Jesus Christ, through the indwelling of the Spirit, in the context of a community of believers."[2]

Sheldrake helpfully points out that "There is no such thing as 'generic spirituality' because spirituality is always particular--that is, grounded in historical and cultural contexts."[3] It "reflects underlying beliefs about human existence even if these are only implicit." Thus, for the purposes of this paper, the term "spirituality" assumes a location within the Christian faith.

Brethren in the eighteenth century could never have imagined a spirituality that was not religious, Christian, and part of a gathered body of believers.

Spirituality was important to the early Brethren, but their guide for the spiritual life came from the scripture, which is a higher authority than any devotional writings. In Alexander Mack Sr.'s *Rights and Ordinances*, the question on "Human Testimony" sheds light on the Brethren view of counsel from spiritual writers. The "son" mentions many who appeal to the saints such as Tauler, Thomas à Kempis and others, who have written such beautiful and gifted books, but have not recorded anything about observing the outward teachings of Christ.[4]

Clearly the early Brethren were aware of and influenced by the widely popular "sermons" of Johannes Tauler, the fourteenth century Dominican mystic, and of Kempis' *Imitation of Christ*. These two books were frequently printed in German and widely read among Pietists. At the same time, Mack counseled against appealing to holy men. He warned against agreeing with writers who "were still in monasteries and under the papal dogma."[5] Mack did not dismiss the value of the spiritual life, but cautioned against making any one writer a guide above the gospel.

In addition to devotional sources widely popular at the time, such as Tauler and Kempis, the early Brethren knew of van Braght's *Martyrs Mirror* and an anonymous Anabaptist book, *Golden Apples in Silver Bowls*, published probably in 1702, and then again at Ephrata in 1745. Marcus Meier has pointed out how both of these books served Mack and Andreas Boni as they argued for the necessity of adult baptism by immersion. So interestingly, at least two Brethren members put these Anabaptist sources of devotion to the purpose of defending doctrine and practice.[6]

The use of books of prayer and devotion was common among Lutherans and the Reformed in the later seventeenth and in the eighteenth century. Brethren did not create forms for prayer in Europe, but they prayed frequently. Some Brethren also fasted at times as a part of their spiritual lives. Like many Pietists, they also sang and read hymn texts as part of their devotional activity. However, the Brethren seemed not to create fixed forms or patterns for all to follow in the eighteenth century. A few particular individuals and their writings provide insight into Brethren spirituality in the eighteenth century.

CHRIST'S SUFFERING, LOVE FOR ENEMY: JOHN LOBACH

John Lobach (1683-1750) was from Solingen/Wald on the lower Rhine and joined the Brethren in Krefeld. In an autobiography written in his later years, Lobach commented on how as a child he had learned formulaic prayers from a Reformed prayer book and felt guilty when he did not recite them.[7] He also recounted spending Sunday afternoons reading the gospel upon the request of his mother. However, he admitted that sometimes he faked reading, or turned two pages at once, in order to finish sooner.[8] As an apprentice under his father, he read the Bible and prayed with his father in the mornings before work. However, even these efforts were fruitless.[9]

Lobach came to a new, vivid spiritual life through a personal experience of conversion sometime before 1713. Painfully aware of his sin and need for forgiveness, Lobach had drifted along with immoral companions and outward pretenses to religiosity. He described a breakthrough in awareness that the "Word of the loving God" touched his heart, so that he could believe that "Jesus Christ was the Savior of all men, especially of those who believe in Him."[10] After the conversion, he continued reading the Bible even more avidly and meeting with a small groups of fellow believers for edification.[11] In counterbalance to the small group context, Lobach also described times of solitude soon after his conversion when his "heart was pierced and smitten by the arrow of the love of God" as he reflected on his sins and God's grace. Lobach recounted being alone in the small yard of his home, reading the second, third and fourth stanzas of Joachim Neander's hymn, "*So soll ich denn noch mehr ausstehen*" ("So must I then endure still more"). He wept over his sins and poured out his heart to God.[12] In the wake of this spiritual struggle, Lobach described experiencing "a living solace and assurance" in his soul.

In some ways, Lobach carried on with devotional practices that he had learned and earlier found empty. He prayed, sometimes in solitude, and read the Bible. He used hymn texts as guides for prayers of confession and assurance of pardon. The new spiritual practice that he picked up was the help of small groups, a hallmark of Pietism. Lobach had used many of these practices prior to his conversion. However, the personal, relational awareness of Christ's forgiveness was the turning point by which the practices took on new meaning to enrich his spiritual life.

Lobach's spirituality continued to develop after he met the Brethren and was baptized in 1716. After his arrest with five other Brethren in 1717, Lobach's letters from prison show a deepening identification with Christ's suffering, a dimension that was likely present after his conversion. He wrote to his mother in 1717, amid rumors in prison that three of the Brethren, including himself, would be executed. Suffering marked an important way that Lobach identified with Christ. He wrote, "For whoever does not take Christ's shame and cross upon himself, even though he may speak in the tongues of angels and give his belongings to the poor, there is no love of Jesus in him."[13] Lobach assured his mother that "Jesus will reassure me through the joyousness of His Spirit with His promise and transfer me to the place of bliss through His crucifixion." Clearly, Lobach's relational identification with Jesus Christ at his conversion and sense of forgiveness now extended to a personal identification with Christ's suffering as Lobach faced the possibility of death. This letter from prison also reveals that the identification with Christ's suffering moved Lobach to a deeper sense of love for enemies as he poured out intercession for forgiveness and blessings to his captors and tormentors. For Lobach, peace in the form of love for enemy was inseparably linked to an experiential awareness of the love of Jesus Christ.

It is fascinating that Lobach chose standard practices of spirituality, such as writing an autobiography of his spiritual life, writing letters of spiritual counsel, reading the Bible, using hymn texts as a spiritual guide, praying in solitude and in small groups. These were all hallmarks of Pietism and reflect some of the disciplines for spirituality that early Brethren used. The new spiritual developments after Lobach joined the Brethren circles were a deeper spiritual identification with the suffering of Jesus and a desire to forgive and love enemies.

After his release, Lobach taught children in a Brethren school in Krefeld. For a while he lived a monastic life with Luther Stetius in a small house, devoting their days to manual labor and prayer,[14] like their friend, Gerhard Tersteegen, the noted Reformed Pietist and mystic. John Lobach is a leading example of the importance of spirituality for Brethren in the eighteenth century.

HYMNS

As the story of John Lobach and the Brethren prisoners at Jülich makes clear, early Brethren eagerly used hymn texts and singing to express and deepen their spiritual awareness of God. William Knepper, one of the Brethren at Jülich, wrote some four hundred hymn texts during his imprisonment. About one hundred of them appeared in the first Brethren hymnal, *Geistreiches Gesangbuch* (*Spiritual Hymnal*), published in Berleburg in 1720. A hymn by Alexander Mack Sr. also appeared in this hymnal. Some of these early hymns made it into *Das Kleine Davidische Psalterspiel*, published on Christopher Sauer's press first in 1744. Due to the limits of time and space, the role of hymns in Brethren spirituality in the eighteenth century will not be covered here. Hedda Durnaugh's excellent study of the German hymnody of the Brethren provides valuable insight into the spiritual themes of Brethren German hymns in the eighteenth century, and the broader Pietist and Anabaptist contexts in which they emerged.[15]

EXAMINATION AND DESIRE FOR CHRIST: MICHAEL FRANTZ

In the New World, the spirituality of the Brethren generated new expressions and directions. The biggest challenge to the spirituality of the Brethren in the eighteenth century was Conrad Beissel's speculative spiritual views about celibacy and the male and female identities of people, even of God. Beissel drew heavily on the views of Jakob Boehme, while the Brethren turned away from the Boehmist influence in Radical Pietism. The Brethren avoided the allegorical reading of scripture that Beissel endorsed. Scripture also served to delimit the excesses of asceticism, improvised ritual and the role of personal prophecy that Beissel endorsed. Because the Ephrata community ultimately grounded their spirituality in sources that the Brethren did not use, Beissel's community will be excluded from this discussion of Brethren spirituality.[16]

The Conestoga congregation was the center of Beissel's separation from the Brethren, beginning in 1728. After Beissel formed his celibate community at Ephrata, about ten miles away from the Conestoga congregation, the Brethren had to defend their theological and spiritual views against the influence of Beissel and shore up the corporate dimension of their spirituality in contrast to Beissel's charismatic persona. Although few printed works came from these Brethren efforts, the most important volume features spirituality as an integral component along with its doctrinal and ecclesiological dimensions.

Michael Frantz (1687-1748) wrote his *Einfältige Lehr-Betrachtungen, und kurtzgefaßtes Glaubens-Bekäntniß* (*Simple Doctrinal Considerations and brief Confession of Faith*) sometime before his death in 1748. However, it was not published until 1770. Frantz became the elder at Conestoga in 1735 at the age of forty-eight, about a year after his baptism into the Brethren faith. Little detail is known about his life. During the thirteen years of his ministry, the Conestoga congregation grew and recovered from its earlier loss of members.

Frantz's confession of faith is rhymed and presents distinctive Brethren beliefs in addition to the general Christian faith that Brethren held. The confession opens with an article on faith in Jesus Christ and his saving grace and covenant and an article on the gathered church.[17] Then Frantz takes up believers' baptism by immersion, footwashing, communion (breadbreaking), and the office of shepherds or ministers.[18] Later in the document, Frantz presents several points on spiritual citizenship, revenge and retaliation, and avoiding human war and oaths, while engaging in spiritual warfare.[19] Two distinctive themes reveal Frantz's refutation of Beissel and Ephrata. He raises points about celibacy, marriage and spiritual marriage to Christ, as well as observance of the Sabbath.[20] Frantz addressed the incarnation of Jesus Christ,[21] affirming that Christ is uniquely fully human and divine in one person, but avoiding the Boehmist androgyny that Beissel adopted. Following the rhymed doctrinal statement, Frantz described the Church as both an inward and an outward fellowship (*Gemeinschaft*). This section on the Church has been translated and published in Durnbaugh's *Brethren in Colonial America*, while the other two portions have not been translated.

The most amazing feature of Frantz's confession of faith is the opening section, a spiritual self-examination, which Frantz calls a "Mirror and Examiner of One's Self." It is only vaguely reminiscent of the Roman Catholic practice of *examen*. The self-examination takes up six pages, with one hundred short, rhymed paragraphs. The paragraphs represent multiple themes, including confession of faults, desire to be conformed to the likeness of Christ, love for Christ, mixed with practical comments regarding respect for marriage and celibacy, for spiritual disciplines such as fasting and prayer, respect for discipline among brothers and sisters in the church, and even a comment about wearing a beard.[22]

The self-examination begins by naming Jesus as the Alpha and Omega, and Frantz's acknowledgement that he must first begin by confessing himself as he truly is. He prays for illumined and purified eyes and ears, and a tongue to praise God, rather than speak carelessly. He even asks for a nose to sniff out what is good and evil within himself.[23] After using the bodily senses metaphorically for spiritual improvement, Frantz turns to virtues that he lacks, and for which he prays, such as gentleness, forbearance, patience, and humility. Ten paragraphs take up the theme of losing self-will to be brought into the likeness of the mind of Christ. Frantz prays to be loosed from self-will so that his heart may belong to Christ alone. Acknowledging the weakness of his own nature, Frantz prays to Christ "to be minded like you," who was of divine nature and pure heart.[24] Even as he prays to be fully given to Christ, he acknowledges hindrances in his life. These paragraphs reflect the common theme in Christian spirituality of surrender to God's will, a theme that traces to Jesus' prayer in the Garden of Gethsemane in the gospels. It is somewhat reminiscent of cataphatic Christian spirituality, seeking to lose self in order to be filled by Christ's presence spiritually.

Frantz employed an unusual device beginning with the thirty-second paragraph, continuing his self-examination. In the thirty-second through the forty-eighth paragraph, Frantz opened each paragraph with the phrase, "I have made myself an image." With this phrase he meant that he had constructed a mental or spiritual image of either a fault or something he lacked, or an image of a spiritual attribute he desired. Frantz did not imply that he was making an idol or a literal image. Rather, he suggested that he was viewing something like an image in a figurative, or spiritual mirror, as he titled this section. Initially after the thirty-second paragraph, Frantz dealt with the spiritual implications of wealth, greed, pride in clothing, and even shaving off the beard as signs of loving other things in the world more than God. Frantz also saw an "image" or reflection in which taking pride in simple clothing may be the worst arrogance of all.[25]

In the self-examination, Frantz acknowledged the importance of spiritual practices such as fasting, praying and giving alms. However, he noted that it is good when it is done "before God in silence," alluding to Jesus' counsel not to call attention to praying and fasting (Mt. 6:1-7). Similarly, Frantz acknowledged that it was an error to despise the single state, which is crowned with honor when maintained in humility with Jesus. Frantz found it equally wrong to despise the married state, which God instituted, and as such is pure.

Here Frantz offered a counterpoint to Ephrata's widely recognized habits of prolonged fasting, dedicated hours of prayers, and orders of celibate men and women. Frantz taught that all of these practices, such as fasting, praying, and celibacy, are not to be despised but observed humbly. Likewise he held that marriage can be a pure state for spiritual people when it is held in honor.

Frantz concluded this section with additional paragraphs invoking the mystical imagery dating back to the New Testament, popular in the Middle Ages, and cherished anew in Pietism. What is unusual is Frantz's application of the metaphor of spiritual marriage not only to the soul's desire for Christ, but also the soul's desire to be joined to the Church, the body of Christ. Frantz expressed a desire to be "married" to Christ and to the Church (*gemein*).

In the forty-ninth paragraph, Frantz abandoned the literary device of an "image," but continued with the metaphor of spiritual marriage. "No life is sweet or better than to have only you, Jesus Christ," he wrote. Both the state of marriage and the state of singleness are "nothing without Your bond of love."[26] Then in a distinctively Brethren move, he links spiritual espousal with Christ to water baptism as a believer.

> You have received me to Yourself, Jesus,
> In water baptism, as your bride and spouse,
> When I renounce all other images and false lovers.[27]

Frantz extends the metaphor as part of his self-examination by asking Jesus to help him test himself, to see if he will serve and be subject to him as a bride was expected to be subject to her husband in that time and culture. He prayed for Jesus to examine his (Frantz's) heart and kidneys, to see if he was indeed Christ's bride and Christ was his husband. Here, Frantz echoed a thought expressed in an Ephrata writing by Johannes Hildebrand. The booklet was an attack on the Moravian views of marriage. In it, Hildebrand, who left the Brethren to join Ephrata, spoke of the kidneys as the "second heart" where spiritual rebirth takes place.[28] This comment reflected a view among some Pietists that the kidneys were like a second heart because their shape resembled that of the heart. Frantz focused on love for Christ, hoping that his conscience would be pure, his faith unstained, and that we would be "like a dove, without false love."[29]

Frantz made no implication of homoerotic allusions in his desire to be a bride to Christ. Rather, he drew on a familiar medieval metaphor revived for Protestants by the Pietists, namely the concept of the soul as bride to Christ. However, Frantz set the marriage with Christ into both a personal relationship with Christ and a shared relationship with the Church, the body of Christ. This spiritual condition, in Frantz's view, was best characterized by humble submission and genuine love for Christ in the context of the Church. Frantz created a distinctively Brethren appropriation of this metaphor by linking spiritual marriage to water baptism of an adult believer. In medieval and early modern mysticism, the Eucharist was the ritual of the church more typically linked to bridal mysticism. Frantz also illustrates well how Brethren spirituality in the eighteenth century is grounded in the gathered community, while having an individual dimension. Frantz's attention to ordinances such as communion, footwashing, and baptism reveals that these practices are equally important for Brethren spirituality, formed in the life of the gathered church.

VISIONS AND VOICES: CATHERINE HUMMER

Catherine Hummer's visions and messages from angels represent a dimension of spirituality that was not unknown among the Brethren, although Brethren regarded them with more questioning, even criticism. Perhaps this suspicion was due to the strong reputation that Conrad Beissel claimed as a prophet and man of visions. Indeed, Ephrata's internal history, the *Chronicon Ephratense*, published in 1786, gave extensive coverage to Hummer. However, Brethren did not dismiss completely the role of dreams or visions for spirituality. Stephan Koch, a Brethren leader in Europe and good friend of Alexander Mack Jr., and later celibate brother at Ephrata, reported dreams of Hochmann and of the Brethren widow Bentz. These were later published on the Sauer press.

Catherine Hummer claimed visions of an angel visiting her and reporting that love had diminished among the brothers (meaning Brethren).[30] During her first vision, the angel also sang to her. For the first hymn, Hummer did not report the text or identify the title. Hummer did cite the lyrics of the second song that the angel sang, "*Wie wohl ist mir.*" As Hedda Durnbaugh was able to identify in 1986, this hymn was composed by William Knepper during the imprisonment of the six Brethren in the Jülich fortress.[31] It was published in the 1720 Brethren hymnal, *Geistreiches Gesangbuch.*[32] This particular stanza speaks of the inward feeling of well-being and praise that the soul feels, even if the mouth is silent. Later in the vision, the angel sang about the end times, assuring her that even though God's children sow now in tears, at the harvest time of the Last Day, their sorrow and suffering will become joy and laughter. The source of this stanza cannot yet be identified, according to Hedda Durnbaugh.[33]

The angel sang a fourth time during the vision. This stanza assured Catherine that whatever may happen, the Lord will take his own to himself, as a chaste bride in honor.[34] The stanza could refer collectively to the Church as the bride of Christ but might imply that Catherine's soul is like a bride to Christ. Hedda Durnbaugh pointed out that this is the seventh stanza of the Knepper hymn, "*Wie wohl ist mir.*"[35]

The angel sang twice more during this particular vision. The fifth song that the angel sang was a stanza that Hedda Durnbaugh has identified as coming from a hymn by an unknown author, "*Wann ich es recht betracht*" ("When I consider it rightly").[36] This hymn first appeared in *Das Kleine davidische Psalterspiel* (*The Small Davidic Psaltery*), first published by Christopher Sauer in 1744. It was the first hymnal of the Brethren in America. The text proclaims that those who can enter the realm of joy will be blessed, and, in order to do so, they should prepare themselves thoroughly in this world (amid presumed trials and suffering).

On the last occasion of singing in the vision, the angel sang the twelfth stanza of the same hymn, "*Wann ich es recht betracht,*" according to the research of Hedda Durnbaugh.[37] This stanza also promises that those who prepare will look on the kingdom of heaven with joy and the entire throng will go pair by pair into the heavenly Zion's meadows.

In subsequent visions between 1762-1765, Catherine Hummer reported out-of-body, trance-like experiences in which she was transported to heaven. She saw believers baptized again as God and Jesus preached to them and also to the unconverted, who had a chance to be baptized. According to Hummer, baptism needed to take place in eternity, to match the physical baptism in the visible world in which we live. She also described a Trinitarian God Abraham, God Isaac and God Jacob. These visions probably reflect some of the mystical views of Conrad Beissel. Certainly, the concept that baptism would be repeated in eternity was consistent with Beissel's view of the dichotomy of the present world and the eternal world.

In her first vision of the angel who sang, Hummer reported devotional activities that were entirely consistent with the Brethren, even if the claim to a visionary revelation to a woman was not typical of the Brethren. Hummer's angelic visitor sang Radical Pietist hymns that were well known to her, one even by a Brethren author. The angel invited her to sing with him, and also to kneel and pray, all typical devotional practices of Brethren at the time. The messages of the cited stanzas are very typical of the Brethren, encouraging preparation and faithfulness in this world in spite of adversity, and promising great joy in the heavenly realm. Although the claim of a personal visionary experience was atypical, even suspicious, for the spirituality of the Brethren in the eighteenth century, the content of the first vision and the spiritual practices it featured were entirely consistent with the Brethren. Only in the subsequent visions did Hummer move farther away from Brethren spirituality, both in the trance-like experiences and doctrinally in the scenes she described.

Catherine Hummer's visions, although reported by the Ephrata chronicler, demonstrate again the central importance of hymns and singing as a vital source for Brethren spirituality. Quoting passages from hymn texts and singing together gave shape to ways that Brethren were aware of God's presence. Hummer's visions also illustrate the central importance of prayer, and with it, the posture of kneeling as formative for spiritual life. Finally, Hummer's contemplative reflection with her messengers and individually illustrates an important role for devotional reflection in Brethren spirituality. The themes of urgent preparation for the end time, perseverance in suffering and the magnificent joys of the heavenly realm, and allusions to metaphors of spiritual espousal are typical for Brethren of the time, as well as for many Pietists. What is unusual for the Brethren is her testimony to personal, individual revelation as her source of inspiration. Nevertheless, when Annual Meeting addressed this phenomenon in 1763, they could not completely object to what Hummer reported, perhaps in part because many of the spiritual themes she expressed were close to those of other Brethren, such as Michael Frantz. Ministers at Annual Meeting in 1763 did criticize her father, Peter Hummer, for sensationalizing her experience in his preaching. The pride that could be generated by so much attention on the one receiving the vision was perhaps as troubling to the Brethren as the phenomenon of visions.

Poet and Pastor: Alexander Mack Jr. and Brethren Spirituality

Alexander Mack Jr., or Sander Mack, was the most prolific Brethren poet in North America in the eighteenth century (the most prolific overall was Wm. Knepper, if he wrote fully 400 hymns). Mack was also the most prolific Brethren writer in the eighteenth century. While some of his work are doctrinal polemics, and much of his writing survives in his letters, his poetry opens an important window onto Brethren understandings of spirituality.

As seen through his poems, Mack's shaping of Brethren contours of spirituality continue the strong roots in the Bible and a personalized focus on Jesus Christ, with awareness of his love revealed in his uniquely redemptive suffering, his call to repentance, and the life of discipleship as a way of recognizing Christ's presence in the world. Related to the theme of repentance are Sander Mack's frequent dire warnings of God's judgment, the seductive power of Satan, and hellfire that follows judgment of unbelievers. The ordinances are opportunities to apprehend the spiritual presence of Christ inwardly while participating outwardly with the gathered body of believers. Throughout Mack's poetic path of spirituality is a deep, at times dark, awareness of the frailty and brevity of life and the wrong directions in which bodily desires can lead. Mack's more somber reflections on life, death, and sorrow are easy to understand, given that he lost his mother and both his sisters within a few years of turning eight. Similarly, he lost three of his daughters (two in childbirth) and a son who died in infancy. He lost some grandchildren to death at young ages. Death had cast a shadow across his family since childhood.

Sander Mack's poems can be roughly organized by groups. First are five poems of some length that are paraphrases of biblical texts, specifically Psalm 67, Psalm 119, Psalm 139, Matthew 25, and a partial poem that apparently was a much longer setting of the stories of Elijah and Elisha from I and II Kings. A few shorter poems are allegories on biblical topics, such as two poems of one stanza each about Esther and one about Rachel. Another large group of poems are the poems written on his birthday, numbering twenty-four poems from 1772-1802, with one of these poems marking the end of a calendar year. Another group of poems are his ten poems for youth, built around various virtues or aspirations. Each of these poems is ten stanzas long. A group of long poems might be designated programmatic poems. These work many themes around a central focus. One of these is his poem that addresses his fellow Germans and exhorts them to obedience to God and humility. Two poems deal with the powers and temptations of Satan. One very long poem (78 stanzas) warns of the end times and God's impending judgment. Another lengthy poem about judgment and repentance focuses on "the big difference" between God's grace and the world's temptations. Another lengthy poem warns that seeming "free thinking" can lead to atheism and a kind of bondage.

Mack's other poems do not fit any particular grouping. Two of them focus on the suffering of Jesus on the cross, including a lengthy hymn of 110 stanzas about the crucifixion and the redemptive significance of Christ's death. Mack's hymn of praise to Jesus Christ ("Jesus Christ, God's Only Son") fits the Christ-centered focus of Mack's spirituality. One text is a hymn about baptism. Other miscellaneous short poems include one about the soul beloved by God, the soul of weak faith whom God helps, a poem on God's love, one on how to win the spiritual prize, one on wealthy poverty, a funeral poem to honor Christopher Sauer II, and one on faith, love, and hope.

The intent in this section of the paper is not to analyze Sander Mack's poetry in detail nor all of his theology or religious themes. Rather this brief look at his poetry will suggest ways that he gives shape to spirituality in a Brethren perspective.

The poems that are biblical paraphrases do not all offer specific insights on spiritual life. Two paraphrases from psalms, Psalm 67 and Psalm 139, deal with the personalized relationship with God, also the themes of those two psalms. The paraphrase of Matthew 25 does not emphasize service to the needy for the sake of service, but the reality of judgment, and the importance of recognizing Christ present in this world, while acting on that awareness through acts of service and mercy.

Interestingly, Mack uses an allegorical approach in two different stanzas about Esther. One stanza deals with her as queen and her power and love for her people. The other stanza describes the "Wise Virgin." Because Mack spent seven years at Conrad Beissel's Ephrata, one might expect these two poems, one on "the Queen" and one on "the Wise Virgin" to allude to the Holy Virgin Sophia, Beissel's personification of the female aspect of God. Mack shows that his break away from Ephrata and its androgynous spirituality was complete. He identified the queen and the wise virgin with

Esther as a model of spiritual virtue and gentle power. Similarly, an allegorical stanza on the beautiful Rachel avoids the Ephrata associations of Rachel as an allegorical figure for celibacy. Instead, Sander Mack praised Rachel as a model of the spiritual beauty of trusting God.

Sander Mack's grounding in Jesus Christ for the spiritual life is most evident in his two poems about the suffering of Christ. One is incomplete, and rehearses the different events of Christ's suffering throughout the day of his crucifixion, highlighting the uniquely redemptive effect of his innocent death on the cross. The other, longer poem was probably intended as a hymn text, and likewise is devoted to the passion of Christ. "*Wo bleiben meine Sinnen*" ("Where have my senses flown") puts the writer into the scenes of Christ's arrest, trial, judgment, punishment, and crucifixion. Reflecting much Baroque poetry devoted to Christ's suffering, Mack's hymn of 110 stanzas invites readers (singers) to identify with the poet and consider their relationship with Christ, their apprehension of God's merciful forgiveness through Christ's suffering, and their own state of repentance and faith.

The last judgment, the punishment of hell for sinners, warnings against Satan's temptations, and a call to repentance feature prominently in Mack's spirituality. These would not be elements unique to Brethren. They reflect other dimensions of the call to repentance. In addition to affirming the positive draw of God's forgiving love, Mack also warns of the negative outcome for those who take judgment lightly or indifferently.

Some of Mack's poetry utilized imagery related to the ordinances for spirituality. In a short poem or hymn text to encourage weak souls, he alluded to the wedding banquet of the Lamb as a hope for persevering in the faith.

(1) Finally every soul that loves God will succeed
God can indeed defeat the enemy
That presses the weak heart;
In distress- even in death
God grants his bread of heaven.

(4) Finally I will be received
Into the pure wedding hall
Where people come together at the Lamb's supper
And there will be the wine of comfort,
Which one pours with water here.[38]

In a lengthy poem about the difference between God's ways and the world's ways, Mack referred metaphorically to the joyful cup that Christ offers, contrasted with what Mack called literally the slop of the world.

> Jesus himself, as our best Friend, will pour out to us the best
> grape juice, the new wine of joy, full of power.
>
> Think about it, you poor sinner: How have you dissipated
> yourself? Every day one diminishes by eating from the hog
> trough of refined vanity. Does this food taste so good to you? Ah,
> think about Christ's blood.[39]

In a poem on baptism, Mack referred to union with Christ in baptism, somewhat as Michael Frantz had done.

> Can the water flow over our body in baptism?
> So then Jesus can take from us all evil so that nothing remains.
> Jesus can purify us and unite us with Himself.
> Whoever can give himself into Christ's death
> Can live with Him eternally.[40]

Alexander Mack Jr. wrote numerous poems and hymn texts reflecting spirituality from a Brethren perspective. He underscored a personalized, relational identification with Christ, who remained the center of spirituality for Mack, as was the case for Lobach, Frantz, and Hummer. Identification with the suffering and the love of Jesus extended the references to this dimension of spirituality found in Lobach and echoed in the spirituality of renunciation in Frantz. Also, the ordinances play an important role in Mack's spirituality. Communion seems to play a stronger role for Mack than was the case for Frantz, but for both, baptism is associated with the spiritual rebirth. The use and creation of hymn texts for devotion remained important for Sander Mack. In his extensive poetic writings, Alexander Mack Jr. further developed themes for spirituality that the Brethren had embraced throughout the century.

INTENSE ILLUMINATION: JACOB STOLL

A fitting conclusion to Brethren spirituality in the eighteenth century was actually published in 1806, shortly after the nineteenth century began. Jacob Stoll (1731-1822), a long-time pastor of the Conestoga congregation, published his *Geistliches Gewürz-Gärtlein heilsuchender Seelen* (*Spiritual*

Spice Garden of Souls Seeking Salvation) in 1806.[41] Johannes Baumann of Ephrata was the printer. Although the publication date was 1806, the spirituality it reflects is vintage eighteenth century pietistic devotion. Already seventy-five when the book was published, Stoll's religious life was formed by influences at their peak in the middle of the eighteenth century.

The *Spiritual Spice Garden* strongly reflects the piety of Gerhard Tersteegen, the Reformed separatist and mystic. Tersteegen was acquainted with Brethren members John Lobach and Luther Stetius, as well as Johann Conrad Rissmann (Bro. Philemon), a member at Germantown who joined the Ephrata community. The *Spiritual Spice Garden* consists of a preface, and then 113 devotional poems based on short passages from the Bible. Eighty-one devotions are based on Old Testament verses and thirty-two on the New Testament. This figure might surprise some modern Brethren who speak of the Brethren as a New Testament church. The Brethren of the eighteenth century held all of the Bible to be inspired, but the New Testament to be the fulfillment of the Old Testament. Following the biblical devotional texts are twenty-five hymns, most likely composed by Stoll himself. The book concludes with nineteen pages of poetic devotions (*Andachten*) by Stoll. The influence of Tersteegen is clear in the format of Bible verses paired with devotional poems. Tersteegen did this in his earlier and widely popular book, *Geistliches Blumen-Gärtlein Inniger Seelen* (*Spiritual Little Flower Garden of Inward Souls*), first published in 1744, and frequently reprinted in Pennsylvania well into the nineteenth century.[42] Even the title of Stoll's work shows the influence of Tersteegen. However, Tersteegen's work contains much more poetry that is not linked directly to scripture. Tersteegen's section of poetry related to Bible verses made use entirely of Old Testament texts. Stoll did not choose any of the same texts that Tersteegen used.

The Old Testament passages come from all of the major sections (Law, Prophets, Writings), including several devotions based on the minor prophets, such as Habakkuk and Haggai. Seventeen of the thirty-two New Testament devotions come from the gospels, with John and Matthew most frequently cited. Five devotions come from John, only six from Matthew. The Matthew passages draw on the Sermon on the Mount only twice. Only one poem relates to Matthew 18, specifically the first two verses about becoming like a child to enter the Kingdom of Heaven, not about church discipline. The one devotion based on the beatitudes deals with only the first four beatitudes, omitting the blessing for peacemakers. Stoll's choice of gospel passages demonstrates that Brethren in the eighteenth century were not so overly focused on Matthew as some scholars in the twentieth century have suggested. Indeed, the Gospel of John is equally as important as Matthew for Stoll.

One passage for devotion is taken each from the book of James, Hebrews, 2 Peter, Jude, and Revelation, as well as passages from other New Testament books. The broad spectrum of verses that Stoll used suggests that Brethren gladly read from the breadth of the Bible.

Many of Stoll's devotions speak of reverence for God, God's mercy and the need for obedience. A poem based on Jeremiah 17:9-10 warns that the heart is deceitful.[43] Stoll counsels inward humility. A devotion on Jeremiah 51:6 warns believers to "flee Babel" and to trust in Jesus and his glory.[44] Here Stoll echoes the old refrain from Radical Pietists, to leave the established churches. This devotion broadens the understanding of Babel to sinful people in general. A poem for Ezekiel 33:11 assures seekers that God has no pleasure in the death of the godless, but desires their conversion.[45]

Many of Stoll's New Testament devotions focus on Christ as the only way to salvation, the model of humility, and the source of love. This continues the same Christ-centered approach to spirituality and the importance of Christ's love that appears in Brethren spirituality throughout the eighteenth century. A devotion on John 7:38 emphasizes a lively faith in the heart that learns to know Jesus personally, a quality of spirituality already seen in Lobach, Frantz and Alexander Mack Jr., and common in Pietism.[46] A devotion based on John 18:10-11 asserts Jesus' authority to banish the use of the sword and to command peace and love for neighbor.[47]

Several of the devotional hymns focus on love for Jesus, the role of Jesus as sacrificial lamb and good shepherd, as well as offer praise to Jesus Christ. One of Stoll's hymns is "*Wie ist die Zeit so wichtig*" ("O How is the time so urgent"), which appeared in the 1951 Brethren hymnal attributed to Alexander Mack Sr. Hedda Durnbaugh first identified this hymn as the work of Stoll.[48]

The devotional poetry in the concluding section of the *Spice Garden* reflects Stoll's most mystical inclinations. A poem of one stanza, "Marriage with Jesus" ("*Sich mit Jesum Vermählen*") asks Jesus to free the author from all sin and wed himself to Jesus, so that he may belong eternally to Jesus.[49] Again, this poem makes no homoerotic implications, rather asks for freedom from all other desires and bonds. In another poem, "The Silent Nothing" ("*Das stille Nichts*"), the author seeks the silent nothing where everything is lost and forgotten, where the ground of the soul is opened and one finds the Eternal One and is lifted up to the One. The author asks Jesus to take his heart and create a new life in it. Here Stoll's devotion resembles some of the counsel of Johannes Tauler from the fourteenth century to forsake all personal interest and become like nothing in order to be filled with God's presence.[50] This counsel was reworked by writers such as Johann Arndt and Jakob Boehme and then reappropriated by various Pietist writers. The focus on the heart as the locus of being joined with Christ reflects the Radical Pietist strains of mysticism. The heart is the way one is joined to Christ, rather than a change in actual being, as some medieval mystics advocated.

Stoll further explored the union with God in a hymn near the end of the *Spiritual Spice Garden*. In the hymn, "O Gentle Savior, Jesus Christ" ("*O Milder Heiland, Jesus Christ*"), he wrote:

> Ah draw me into your Ground
> Where there will be nothing created anymore;
> There speak and make Yourself known to me,
> So will my entire heart by made healthy.[51]

In a poem on the rest of the soul, he wrote:

> Therefore close up, O heart, ear and eyes,
> And turn inward into the Ground.
> There you will find in God rest,
> In Nothing it will first be made known.
> In the Nothing you will find the true One, the essential good:
> With whom you can be eternally one; therefore have good
> courage [for the spiritual journey].[52]

Stoll's *Spiritual Spice Garden* is thoroughly Brethren in its Christ-centered spirituality and in its insistence on the inspiration and authority of the Bible as the locus for finding one's spiritual path through this world. Stoll did not focus on the ordinances but did advocate obedience born of faith and love as central to the spiritual life. While the *Spiritual Spice Garden* is very personal, a guide for individual believers, the community of believers is never forgotten. The gathered church remains the significant setting for pursuing spirituality, as demonstrated in numerous references to the flock of the Good Shepherd, to the apostles, and to obedience. In this sense,

Stoll differed markedly from Tersteegen, who remained loosely attached to the Reformed Church, while advocating the devotional life for individuals. Stoll's book was the last publication of Brethren writers that so intensely mirrored the spiritual vocabulary of the Brethren of the eighteenth century in their love for Jesus, even to the point of using spousal metaphors. While love for Jesus would remain a theme for Brethren in the nineteenth century, the bridal imagery decreased markedly. Similarly, the sense of emptying one's self, or becoming as nothing, in order to be filled with Christ faded from the Brethren of the nineteenth century.

CONCLUSION

Brethren in the eighteenth century tended to be intensely spiritual and religious people, grounding their spirituality in Jesus Christ as the sole source of redemption, and rooting their devotional life in the Bible. In this respect, they were not different from the Radical Pietist context in which they formed. While probably not every Brethren person was intense in their devotional life, one could expect that many Brethren read scripture and prayed. Sometimes the Brethren fasted. Singing and the prayerful reading of hymn texts were popular expressions of spirituality for the Brethren and other Pietists. The eighteenth century was rich in the amount of hymn texts or poetic texts that Brethren composed, although not as prolific as the Ephrata community or writers like Tersteegen.

What is uniquely Brethren is the connection of spirituality to ordinances (practices) of the church, especially in connecting baptism to the union of the soul to Christ. Equally true for the Brethren is the constant role of the community of believers as the context in which individual spirituality developed. Both were important in the eighteenth century Brethren spirituality, just as inner spiritual apprehension of the significance of outward devotional practice were important. The Brethren were not highly unique in their spirituality, although they contributed some unique strains to pietistic spirituality in the eighteenth century. The Brethren were never fully mystics, but they brought to their spirituality a dynamic grounding of the subjective spiritual life in the context of a gathered body of spiritually devoted believers.

Notes

1 Dale R. Stoffer, *Background and Development of Brethren Doctrines 1650-1987* (Philadelphia: Brethren Encyclopedia, Inc., 1989), 4.

2 Philip Sheldrake, *Westminster Dictionary of Christian Spirituality*, (Westminster John Knox Press, 2005), vii.

3 Sheldrake, *Dictionary*, vii. See also Bernard McGinn, John Meyendorff and Jean Leclercq, eds., *Christian Spirituality: Origins to the Twelfth Century*, vol. 16 in *World Spirituality: An Encyclopedic History of the Religious Quest*, ed. Bernard McGinn and others (New York: Crossroad Press, 1985), xv-xvi. Some articles and theses have been written on spirituality from a Brethren perspective, but none have explored the Brethren writers of the eighteenth century in depth in the primary sources.

4 Alexander Mack, Sr., "Rights and Ordinances," in William R. Eberly, ed., *The Complete Writings of Alexander Mack, Sr. 1679-1735* (Winona Lake, IN: BMH Books 1993), 94.

5 Ibid.

6 Marcus Meier, *The Origins of the Schwarzenau Brethren* (Philadelphia: Brethren Encyclopedia, Inc, 2008), 23, 71. Meier points out how Gottfried Arnold's uncited borrowing from *Martyrs Mirror* contributed to Andreas Boni's argument for adult baptism. The influence of *Martyrs Mirror* came through a Radical Pietist channel, as well as representing its own Anabaptist origins.

7 Johannes Lobach's unpublished autobiography, "Ein Neues Merckmahl der Göttlichen Liebes-Wunder dieser Zeit," published in Donald F. Durnbaugh, trans. and ed., *European Origins of the Brethren* (Elgin, IL: Brethren Press, 1958), 190-91

8 Ibid., 192.

9 Ibid., 193.

10 Ibid. 195.

11 Ibid., 200-201.

12 Ibid., 196.

13 Ibid., 270.

14 Ibid., 317.

15 Hedwig T. Durnbaugh, *The German Hymnody of the Brethren 1720-1903* (Philadelphia: Brethren Encyclopedia, Inc., 1986), 20-34, 49-55, 63-66.

16 See Jeff Bach, *Voices of the Turtledoves: The Sacred World of Ephrata* (University Park, PA: Penn State University Press, 2003), 25-95 for an introduction to Ephrata's spirituality and its sources.

17 Michael Frantz, *Einfältige Lehr-Betrachtungen, und kurtzgefaβtes Glaubens-Bekäntniβ* (Germantown: Christopher Sauer, 1770), 9-10.

18 Ibid., 10-12.

19 Ibid., 19-26.

20 Ibid., 13-17, 28-30.

21 Ibid., 12-13.

22 Ibid., 5. The comment on the beard appears in paragraph 34, saying that Frantz would make himself like the god of the world if he would shave off his beard and so "disgrace the image of God."

23 Ibid., 3.

24 Ibid., 6. Paragraphs sixteen through twenty-five focus on self-will.

25 Ibid., 5. The passage related to pride about simplicity reads: I have made an image, in clothing of the simple dress, if I am proud of appearing humble, this could well be the greatest arrogance. (Paragraph 36).

26 Ibid., 6.

27 Ibid.

28 Johannes Hildebrand, *Schrifftmässiges Zeuchüuß von dem Himmlischen und Jungfräulichen Gebährungs-Werck* [n.p., n.d.], 15. The publication is attributed to the Sauer press in Germantown based on type evidence. The date can be set from a comment about the death of a widow on the first day of "February of this year," meaning the year after the conferences with Zinzendorf and the Moravians, which took place in 1742. Thus the year is 1743. See p. 6 of the booklet.

29 Ibid.

30 Lamech and Agrippa, *Chronicon Ephratense* (Ephrata: [Drucks der Brüderschaft], 1786), 232. It is important to note that in the German text, the angel says that love has diminished ("*die Liebe hat sich gemindert*"), not that "love has grown cold," as J. Max Hark translated it in the English translation of the *Chronicon*. For the context of Ephrata's spirituality, this difference is important.

31 Durnbaugh, *German Hymnody*, 145, 20. See also Lamech and Agrippa, *Chronicon*, 232.

32 *Geistreiches Gesangbuch*, (Berleburg: Christoph Konert, 1720), 342.

33 Hedwig T. Durnbaugh, correspondence with author, 8 July 2013. The German text of the hymn stanza is: "Gottes Kinder säen zwar traurig und mit Thränen; aber endlich gibt das Jahr, wornach sie sich sehnen: dann es kommt die Erndte-zeit, daß sie Garben machen, da wird all ihr Gram und Leid lauter Freud und Lachen.» See Lamech and Agrippa, *Chronicon*, 232.

34 Lamech and Agrippa, *Chronicon*, 232. The German text is: "Wer weiß was kommt, was ist bestimmt,wann einst der Herr die Seinen nimmt, die keusche Braut in Ehren: er hat sie schon im Geist erkannt, sie geht ihm auch genau zur Hand, und thut sein Lob vermehren.»

35 *Geistreiches Gesangbuch*, 343. Hedwig T. Durnbaugh, correspondence with author, 8 July 2013.

36 *Das Kleine davidische Psalterspiel der Kinder Zions* (Germantown: Christoph Sauer, 1764), 453 (hymn 457), stanza 7. The hymn has fourteen stanzas. Identification is thanks to Hedda Durnbaugh, correspondence with author, 8 July 2013. The German text is: "O selig wird der seyn, der mit kan gehen ein ins Reich der Freuden, billig solt man allhier sich schicken für und für und wohl bereiten.» It is cited in Lamech and Agrippa, *Chronicon*, 232-233.

37 *Das Kleine davidische Psalterspiel*, 343, stanza 12. Hedwig T. Durnbaugh, correspondence with the author, 8 July 2013. See Lamech and Agrippa, *Chronicon*, 233. The German text is: "Die werden allzugleich das schöne Himmelreich mit Freuden schauen: es wird die schöne Schaar dann gehen Paar bey Paar auf Zions Auen."

38 Samuel B. Heckman, *The Religious Poetry of Alexander Mack, Jr.* (Elgin, IL: Brethren Publishing House, 1912), 112. The translations of the Mack Jr. texts are my own, not Heckman's.

39 Heckman, *Religious Poetry*, 214

40 Heckman, *Religious Poetry*, 114-116.

41 Jacob Stoll, *Geistliches Gewürz-Gärtlein Heilsuchender Seelen* (Ephrata: Johannes Baumann, 1806).

42 Gerhard Tersteegen, *Geistliches Blumen-Gärtlein Inniger Seelen* (Germantown: Peter Leibert, 1791), first published in Germany in 1744.

43 Stoll, *Gärtlein*, 49.

44 Stoll, *Gärtlein*, 53-4.

45 Stoll, *Gärtlein*, 57.

46 Stoll, *Gärtlein*, 110-11.

47 Stoll, *Gärtlein*, 114.

48 Durnbaugh, *German Hymnody*, 127.

49 Stoll, *Gärtlein*, 178.

50 Johannes Tauler, *Predigten*, vol. 2, ed. Georg Hoffman (Einsiedeln: Johannes Verlag, 1961, 1987), 392-94.

51 Stoll, *Gärtlein*, 170.

52 Stoll, *Gärtlein*, 179.

Brethren Spirituality in the 19th Century

Dale R. Stoffer

SPIRITUALITY IS NOT A TOPIC THAT YOU CAN CONSIDER FROM ONLY A SINGLE vantage point, especially among the Brethren. Like a precious gem, it has many facets that need to be analyzed and appreciated to arrive at a complete picture of its intricacies and beauty. I want to take a multifaceted look, therefore, at Brethren spirituality in the nineteenth century in order to gain the fullest perspective possible. I will be looking through various lenses at the spiritual lives of the Brethren during this period: their use of Scripture, their hymnody, their devotional literature, the themes in Brethren periodicals, and the life and ministry of one of the outstanding spiritual guides in all Brethren history, Christian H. Balsbaugh. I will also address the private and corporate lives of the Brethren and their commitment to spiritual formation in their families. The paper will conclude with various observations about the gains and losses with regards to spirituality that the Brethren experienced during the century and offer a tentative description of Brethren spirituality drawn from the paper's insights.

Description of Anabaptist Spirituality

One of the most significant books that I read in preparation for this presentation was a recent work by the Mennonite author, John Driver, entitled *Life Together in the Spirit: A Radical Spirituality for the Twenty-First Century*. In this work Driver argues that Anabaptist spirituality is radically different from Catholic and classical Protestant spirituality. While Catholic spirituality, especially among the Catholic orders, all too often expressed itself in a contemplative, even mystical, approach to God, Protestant spirituality tended to reflect their penchant for correct doctrine, seen especially in their catechetical literature. Likewise, much of Protestant spirituality up through the present has been inward, highly abstract, individual, and essentially private.[1] In contrast, Anabaptist spirituality was marked by the practical concern of how to be obedient to the gospel of Jesus Christ. Anabaptists emphasized the regenerative work of the Holy Spirit that led to a new way of life as Christ's disciples who integrated faith and works, the individual and the community, and service and witness. They sought to order all of life under Christ's lordship and gave special emphasis to the formative work of the visible church and the family in shaping people's lives. Such an approach yielded a spirituality that was Christ-centered, empowered by the Spirit, oriented toward Scripture, consciously corporate, and characterized by commitment to peace and justice and to God's saving mission in the world.[2]

Brethren spirituality is very similar to this depiction of Anabaptist spirituality. Even when the influence of Pietism on the Brethren is added to the mix, the resulting spirituality differs only in emphasis from an Anabaptist perspective. Pietism, especially in its radical form, placed more stress on the individual, valued the mystical and immediate working of the Spirit more highly, was more open culturally and ecumenically, and was more cautious of ritual, form, and externals. The Brethren were moving away from the more radicalized expressions of these tendencies toward more of an Anabaptist perspective even while they were still in Germany. As we will be noting, this trend away from Radical Pietist spirituality was nearly complete by the first third of the 19th century.

DEVOTIONAL AIDS AND PRACTICES IN BRETHREN SPIRITUALITY

The Brethren utilized a variety of resources and devotional practices during the 19th century for their spiritual development. Without doubt, Scripture was the most significant resource that guided the spiritual lives of the Brethren. One need only read Peter Nead's theological writings, or the periodical literature of the last half of the 19th century, or any of the published sermons from this period to realize how Brethren thought was informed and formed by the Bible. During the 19th century the Brethren, for the most part, read the Bible devotionally; the critical, rational, scholarly approach that we often use today did not begin to affect some branches of the Brethren until the 20th century.

Elder James Quinter wrote an article for the *Gospel Visitor* in 1865 that depicts quite accurately the devotional use of the Bible among the Brethren during the 19th century. He noted that "Love to the Scriptures is a characteristic of a Christian character, and may be regarded as a test of genuine piety."[3] He then lists nine suggestions for reading Scripture in an intelligent and profitable manner. First, "*The Scriptures should be read with a devotional state of mind*"; this state of mind is marked by such qualities as "reverence, adoration, respect, and solemnity." Second, "*In approaching the Scriptures to read or study them, it will be greatly to our advantage, and tend much to our proficiency and success in our pursuit of divine knowledge, to have the mind impressed with the divine character of the Author.*" Third, "*An humble and teachable spirit is absolutely necessary if we would study the Scriptures successfully.*" Fourth, "*A deep consciousness of our need of all the instruction contained in the Scriptures is necessary for a profitable reading of them.*" Fifth, "*To read the Scriptures profitably, we should read them under a sense of responsibility*"; that is, those who read God's Word become responsible for living its truth. Sixth, "*The light should be improved as it is obtained*"; in other words, we should put into practice what we know. Seventh, "*We should read with diligence and perseverance.*" Eighth, "*We should study the Scriptures prayerfully, if we would study them successfully.*" Finally, "*we would recommend the reading of the Scripture in regular order.*" Quinter then encouraged his readers to read the entire Bible through in the coming year and even provided a plan for how to do this.[4]

Note how all of Quinter's suggestions have an intentional purpose of forming his readers spiritually through a regular, devotional reading of the Bible. He emphasized the attitudes that we need to bring to Scripture as well the spirit of receptivity and humble obedience that should characterize our approach to the Word. The goal of this process is to allow "the Holy Spirit to humble our hearts, subdue our prejudices, and to work in us that childlike simplicity, without which we cannot effect to make much proficiency in studying the Scriptures."[5]

The Brethren were actually people of two books, the Bible of course, but also the hymnbook. This point is underscored by the fact that over half of the publications by the Brethren between 1790 and 1845 were hymnbooks or devotional literature that contained some hymns.[6] Though the

Brethren never questioned which of these two books had primary authority, they used both in their worship, not just in their Sunday meetings, but also in their private and family devotions. Many Brethren, if they owned any books, possessed at least these two books. James Quinter, in his preface to the 1867 *The Brethren's Hymn Book,* reinforces these points:

> The relation that the Hymn Book stands in to singing in the Church, is such, that gives it a place next in importance to the Bible, among Christians. . . .
>
> . . . when it is remembered that the Bible and Hymn Book constitute the library of some Christians; that the latter is the only book of sacred poetry they possess; that it is not only used as a book to sing from, but it is also read and studied with pleasure and profit, the propriety of having some hymns beside those that are popular in the congregations, will be acknowledged.[7]

Singing is mentioned in Brethren periodical literature as part of family devotions[8] and some Brethren listed singing along with Bible reading and prayer as the most spiritually formative practices for the Christian life.[9] This emphasis on singing is not surprising, given the importance of singing in both the Anabaptist and Pietist movements. The Brethren, as would have been true also of these two other movements, insisted that singing must be more than simply joining text and melody. As the first English-language hymnbook of the Brethren stated in its preface, "My brethren, in the performance of this noble part of worship, we should have our minds devoutly fixed on God, who heareth prayer, and inhabiteth the praises of Israel; not raising our voices only but endeavoring to sing with the spirit, and with the understanding also . . ."[10] Singing that is pleasing to God and edifies the believer involves both head and heart, understanding and spirit, and keeps its focus on God, the object of its worship.

I should note a tangential point that is important with regard to both the Bible and hymnbook. Obviously, utilization of both of these resources meant that one needed to be able to read. Brethren of the 19th century valued a common school education, the equivalent of an eighth grade education. Reinforcing the importance of a literate community of faith is the fact that a number of Brethren elders taught in the public schools up through the mid-century, including Henry Kurtz, James Quinter, Peter Nead, Isaac Price, John Wise, Enoch Eby, and others.[11]

The Brethren also had several other devotional resources at their disposal that enhanced their spiritual formation. Especially for those who could read German, the Sauer and Ephrata presses had made available a wide variety of devotional works, especially of a pietist and mystical flavor. These works were drawn from medieval mystical, Lutheran, Mennonite, English Puritan, Boehmist, Philadelphian, Radical Pietist, and Quietist traditions and even included two New Testament Apocryphal writings, the Gospel of Nicodemus and the Apostolic History of Abdias. This literature created for the Brethren and other German sectarians a devotional, semi-mystical religious atmosphere that framed how they viewed their responsibilities to God and neighbor and their life in this world and the next.[12]

As the Brethren made the transition from German to English especially in the 1830s and 40s, there was an increasing need for devotional literature in the English language. The German-language devotional literature as well as the German-language hymnody of the Brethren was almost completely left behind when the Brethren adopted English as their dominant language. I will address the issue of how this change affected the devotional worldview of the Brethren later in this paper. In April 1851 Henry Kurtz launched *The Monthly Gospel-Visiter*, which became the first of many periodicals that sought to communicate the values of the Brethren and often the agenda of the editors to the church. One of the primary purposes of Kurtz's paper was "To strengthen us and our fellow believers in the faith once delivered to the saints, to the confirming of our hope, and perfecting us in love, so that we may more fully realize our Gospel-privileges."[13] The majority of the articles that appeared in this and other Brethren periodicals were of a devotional nature, though as the church approached the divisions of the 1880s, the periodicals assumed a more doctrinaire and apologetic character. At their best, then, the periodical literature of the Brethren provided them with a devotional literature drawn from not only Brethren writers but also a wide variety of other evangelical traditions, both British and American.

Based on evidence from their periodical literature, the Brethren gave high priority to such traditional devotional practices as Scripture reading, prayer, and singing but also encouraged fasting and spiritual conversations.[14] Yet the Brethren also had several unique practices that contributed to the spiritual development of their members. One was the annual or semi-annual deacons' visit prior to the communion service. James Quinter, in describing this practice, reinforced the spiritual nature of the visit. He encouraged both the visiting deacons and the family being called upon to uphold the intended spiritual character of the visit. Not only were the deacons to ascertain whether families were still in union with the church, but Quinter called upon all the participants to enter into "a season of devotion" through spiritual conversation and prayer. Ultimately, the goal of such visits was the comfort and edification of the members of the church.[15] This practice reminds us that the Brethren stressed the corporate dimensions of spiritual formation as much as its individual dimension.

Another devotional practice that formed the spiritual lives of the Brethren corporately was the love feast. This service, observed annually or semi-annually by the Brethren in the 19th century, consisted of feetwashing, love feast, and bread and cup, and also included the holy kiss or salutation. These acts not only reinforced some of the fundamental commitments of the Brethren faith but also set them apart from most other denominations. First, whereas most Christian groups tend to emphasize only the relationship of the individual Christian before God through the reception of the bread and cup, the Brethren add to this the vital truth that Christ is also committed to forming a community of faith, his body on earth. Each part of the love feast has both an individual and corporate element. Feetwashing reinforces the truths that each of us as individual believers needs to receive ongoing cleansing from sin in our Christian journey and that Christian community can be formed only by loving, humble service toward our brothers and sisters in Christ. The love feast, as well as the salutation, honors the extreme love that Christ has for his people but also calls us to love others with that same love. The bread and cup betoken the sacrificial, redemptive work of Christ that is available to every person but also draws his followers into fellowship with himself and his people.

A second unique feature of Brethren communion is related to the words of institution adopted by the Brethren, drawn from 1 Corinthians 10:16: "The bread which we break is the communion of the body of Christ; the cup which we bless is the communion of the blood of Christ." Very few Christian groups use this passage in reference to the bread and cup, preferring the words of the Synoptic Gospels or those of Paul in 1 Corinthians 11. As I argue in another article,[16] the Brethren, as did the Swiss Brethren, used this passage because it reinforces the idea that the real presence of Christ is found not in the elements but in his gathered body, the church. In this sense the church itself is sacrament; it is the embodiment of our saving Lord. This passage likewise reflects the themes of Christ-mysticism and union with Christ that the Brethren drew from Pietism and Radical Pietism.

I should mention other venues that were spiritually formative for the Brethren. Throughout the 19th century periodical literature, repeated calls were issued for Brethren to give attention to their devotional lives through personal and family devotions as well as through corporate worship. These very reminders are symptomatic of the reality that not all Brethren attended to these devotional practices, but I would venture to guess that they were probably more conscientious about this than we are today. Private devotions were referred to by such terms as "secret" or "closet" devotions, while family devotions were often depicted as the "family altar," the "family circle," or "household worship." Parents especially were admonished to attend to the spiritual formation of their children.[17] Both German and English hymnbooks used by the Brethren also included hymns for private and family devotions; such hymns were identified as morning hymns, evening hymns, table hymns, and parental or family hymns.[18] The hymnal published in 1884 for the newly organized Brethren Church even stated in its title that it was created for use in the home circle as well as other settings.[19]

Corporate worship in the 19th century was not attended by the time consciousness that often characterizes worship patterns among many Brethren groups today. Hymns had more stanzas and were sung much more slowly than would be true of most Brethren groups today, sermons by several elders lasted two or three times longer than our twenty minute messages, and our dash home to watch the football or baseball game or go to our child's soccer match is in stark contrast to the leisurely afternoon fellowship and meals that Brethren families shared with each other in their homes after the meeting. This slower paced, more reflective, community-building approach to worship was deeply formative for 19th century Brethren.

ELEMENTS AND THEMES IN BRETHREN SPIRITUALITY

In the next part of this presentation, I want to focus on the primary elements of Brethren spirituality of the 19th century and then note various changes that were occurring to the more traditional aspects of Brethren devotional life in the latter third of the century. This analysis will draw upon evidence from the periodical literature of the last half of the 19th century as well as the hymnbooks from the 18th and 19th centuries. Note that the rubrics or subject index of the hymnbooks provide a very revealing and accurate representation of the emphases and the relative importance of these emphases within Brethren spirituality in any given period. The rubrics of the most prominent German-language hymnbook of the Brethren, *Das Kleine Davidische Psalterspiel* (1744), and of the first two English-language hymnbooks of the Brethren, *The Christians Duty* (1791) and *A Choice Selection of Hymns* (1830) are especially telling. They provide a theological outline of the hymns in their respective hymnbooks, beginning with the most important themes and generally proceeding to themes of secondary importance. Though the rubrics of all of these hymnbooks generally reflect rubrics found in other contemporary hymnbooks,[20] the subtle changes made by the Brethren editors shed significant light on emphases distinctive to the Brethren. Note also that even though two of these hymnbooks first appeared in the 18th century, they continued to influence Brethren spirituality in the 19th century through continued use and new editions that appeared in that century.

I need to make one preliminary observation about the elements that I include in this section. Brethren spirituality during the 1800s includes elements that could be considered doctrinal or theological. The reason for this is that the Brethren did not distinguish between doctrine and spirituality or between doctrine and practice like we often do today. All of their Christian life, whether it involved the disciplines of the Spirit or the discipline of the mind in studying Scripture or reflecting on doctrine, shared a single purpose: growth in Christlikeness through obedience to his Word and Spirit. This merging of the doctrinal and the spiritual in Brethren practice, which is also characteristic of both Anabaptism and Pietism, is exemplified in Brethren hymnbooks, for they sang their faith and beliefs. Vernard Eller sheds light on this point when he comments that "the Brethren saw doctrine as *correct*, only insofar as it was *edifying*, relevant to one's immediate experience. The test of true doctrine is whether it edifies, not whether it is logically consistent. Just as soon as doctrine wandered toward the abstract and theoretical, . . . the Brethren lost all interest."[21]

Closely related to this point is a key doctrinal conviction that undergirded the worldview of the Brethren up until the 20th century. They were indebted to the Anabaptists for their two-kingdom theology. This theology held that, through baptism, followers of Christ have become citizens of Christ's kingdom. This citizenship either nullifies or supersedes any allegiance to the kingdom of this world. Followers of Christ owe to him their full allegiance and obedience as the Lord and King over their individual and corporate lives. John Cennick, a Moravian evangelist and hymnwriter, penned a hymn that appeared in all of the English hymnbooks of the Brethren prior to 1883. Three of the stanzas of the hymn portray the idea of our ultimate allegiance to Christ quite well:

> Children of the heav'nly King,
> As we journey, sweetly sing;
> Sing your Saviour's worthy praise,
> Glorious in his works and ways.
>
> Ye are traveling home to God,
> In the way the fathers trod:
> They are happy now—and ye
> Soon their happiness shall see.
>
> Lord, obediently we'll go,
> Gladly leaving all below;
> Only thou our leader be,
> And we still will follow thee.[22]

There are several corollaries to this doctrine of the two kingdoms that factored into Brethren spirituality during the 19th century. First, this hymn, though not using the word "pilgrim," conveys strongly the idea that our true home is not to be found in this world. We are on a journey to our true heavenly homeland; to arrive there, we must follow the lead of our spiritual guide, Jesus Christ. This pilgrim imagery is found throughout Brethren literature of the 18th and most of the 19th centuries.[23]

Second, throughout most of the 19th century, Brethren were united in believing that *all of life* falls under the lordship of Christ. James Quinter makes this point abundantly clear in the following declaration:

> ... the claims of Christianity cover our whole life. We are to live not only one day out of seven to the Lord, but we are to live every day to the Lord. ... The terms of the covenant which Christians make with the Lord when they make the good confession does [sic] not only require a specified number of things to be performed at certain times and in certain places for the Lord, while the remainder of our time belongs to ourselves to be used as we may see proper

without any reference to the will of the Lord, but they require all we have, and allow of no excuse. In consideration of a present and future salvation which the Lord promises to Christians, they virtually yield to him the right of all they possess and the control of their whole existence. And whether they are engaged in the exercises of devotion, or in the labors of their calling; whether they be in the church, the shop or the field, they know of no other Master but the Lord. His they are and him they serve.[24]

Brethren of this period did not divide life into sacred and secular spheres with differing customs and allegiances; all of life was to be lived for the Lord and his glory. This point helps to make sense of the rulings of Annual Meeting that served to shape the "order of the Brethren" of the 19th century. Whatever we might think about this attempt in the 1800s to maintain oversight of every aspect of Brethren life, personal and corporate, private and public, through the order of the Brethren, it is reflective of the conviction that life in Christ and life in the Spirit ordered every dimension of life.

Third, the two kingdom theology of the Brethren and Anabaptists is the source for their commitment to the three "nons" reinforced in the baptismal rites of the Brethren: nonconformity to the world, nonswearing, and nonresistance. Throughout most of the 19th century the Brethren exhibited unwavering commitment to these historic convictions.

Brethren spirituality of the 18th and 19th centuries was thoroughly Christocentric. This Christ-centered spirituality drew upon the theme of discipleship found in both the Anabaptist and Pietist traditions. The Catholic and classical Protestant traditions all too often overlooked the life of Christ as having any importance in God's redemptive plan, emphasizing rather the incarnation, crucifixion, and resurrection of Christ, much as does the Apostles' Creed. The Anabaptists, Pietists, and Brethren, however, while still upholding the importance of these other redemptive acts, felt that Christ's teachings and example provided the model for what the Christian life should look like. A fascinating reinforcement of this very point is that, in the first two German-language hymnbooks prepared for the Brethren in Germany and America in 1720 and 1744 respectively, a separate rubric appeared on "following Jesus." In fact, *Das Kleine Davidische Psalterspiel* actually places this rubric in a list of themes that correspond to the Brethren order of salvation.[25]

Later German-language hymnbooks and all of the English-language hymnbooks omit any rubric that corresponds to the concept of discipleship to Christ. Several observations can be made about this point. First, as long as the pietistic heritage of the Brethren remained strong, especially through the first two or three generations of the movement, the theme of following the example and teachings of Christ remained central in Brethren thought. I should also note that the Brethren made use of very few Anabaptist hymns; their German hymnody and much of their German devotional literature was far more dependent upon Pietist influences than Anabaptist. When the shift was made to English as the dominant language and the Brethren had to rely on the English hymnal tradition, the lack of focus on this theme of discipleship in classical Protestant theology and hymnody was reflected in the hymns selected by editors of Brethren hymnbooks. Second, it is true that the theme of discipleship was kept alive by those Brethren with a firm foothold in traditional Brethren thought, notably Peter Nead, Henry Kurtz, James Quinter, Abraham Cassel, and C. H. Balsbaugh.[26] Third, as these Brethren passed from the scene by the latter 1800s and the Brethren relied more heavily on the approach to the devotional life found in American and British evangelicalism, the theme of discipleship to Christ was gradually replaced by current evangelical views of spirituality, including those found in revivalism, and the holiness and Keswick movements.

Abraham Cassel gives a fair representation of the Brethren commitment to following Christ as the model for the Christian life. He states:

> The imitator of Jesus Christ is one, who being interested in him as his propitiation, cannot but choose to follow him as his pattern; for he knows that though it be not the only or principal end why the Son of God was manifested; it is however, a very considerable part of his errand, in visiting these regions of mortality, to give us a fair transcript, and a living copy of all those graces and duties that are pleasing unto God, and that are commanded in the law.[27]

The Brethren looked to the life of Christ for the blueprint for their own Christian life, seeking to emulate the graces, duties, and character of their Lord and Master.

The Brethren understood, however, that the Holy Spirit played the crucial role in guiding and empowering the Christian life, both individual and corporate. In Brethren literature emphasis is placed on several significant roles of the Spirit: in the inspiration of Scripture; in the initial work of salvation, notably, the transformative act of regeneration; in forming the character of believers; and in leading believers individually and corporately into truth. James Quinter illustrates the Spirit's role in forming the character of believers and in leading them to an understanding of truth in the following reflection on the 1863 Annual Meeting (note also the theme of individual and corporate Christlikeness):

> If we diligently cultivate the spirit of christian love, and seek by humble and fervent prayer the hallowed influences of the Holy Spirit, for the subduing of self and prejudice, and for the producing of such a state of mind as will be favorable to the proper reception of truth, we shall be more and more assimilated to Christ; and as we become more like him, we shall become more like unto one another.[28]

Note also this testimony from the obituary of a young woman. The writer observed that her life "gave a perfect illustration of the power of the Gospel of the blessed Saviour, in the formation and symmetrical development of the true Christian character, under the purifying and sanctifying influence of the Holy Spirit."[29] The Brethren were wary of the emotional excesses that were found in the revival and holiness movements, but they did recognize the absolute necessity of the Holy Spirit's inner work of forming the lives of believers to increasingly resemble the character of their Lord.

One of the best means of discovering the qualities that Brethren highlighted in the formation of Christian character is to observe the virtues listed in the rubrics of the various Brethren hymnbooks used in America during the 19th century. The primary German hymnbook of this period, though printed first in 1744, was, as we have noted, *Das Kleine Davidische Psalterspiel*. It listed these virtues as necessary for Christian life and conduct: true spiritual prayer, spiritual watchfulness, spiritual battle and victory, true chastity, denial of the world and self, desire for God and Christ, Christian resignation [to divine providence], true patience and steadfastness, and the heart's complete surrender to God.[30] The first two English hymnbooks of the Brethren, first printed in 1791 and 1830 respectively, mirrored each other in their rubrics. Unlike *Das Kleine Davidische Psalterspiel*, these hymnbooks do not consolidate the Christian virtues in one section; they are scattered throughout the various rubrics. Those rubrics that pertain to Christian formation are: longing after Christ, Christian consolation, the pilgrimage of the saints, the frailty of our life, charity and uncharitableness, penitential hymns, brotherly love, spiritual poverty, and resignation to providence.[31] Though there are some similarities between the lists of virtues found in the *Das Kleine Davidische Psalterspiel* and those found in the first two English hymnbooks, notably, longing for Christ and resignation to providence, the differences are rather glaring. (I should note that the theme of brotherly and universal love does appear in *Das Kleine Davidische Psalterspiel*, but in a section that combines rubrics dealing with the Brethren order of salvation and the ordinances.) The list in *Das Kleine Davidische Psalterspiel* reflects qualities with a strong Pietist, even Radical Pietist, complexion, that we often identify as foundational Brethren virtues. Remember that this piety was literally not translated into the English hymnbooks of the Brethren. The rubrics dealing with Christian character in the English hymnbooks reflect more general British evangelical spirituality; the overwhelming majority of hymns in these hymnbooks were composed by British evangelicals such as Isaac Watts, Charles Wesley, and John Newton. Noticeably missing in the rubrics of these English-language Brethren hymnbooks are spiritual watchfulness, spiritual battle and victory, the denial of the world and self, and the heart's complete surrender to God. These categories of hymns all have to do with living life with a deep sense of our yieldedness to God and to his purposes for our life in this world. Though there are hymns in the English hymnbooks that reflect these themes, the important point is that a conscious ordering of such hymns under more traditional Brethren and Pietist headings is lacking.

Quite in contrast to these more succinct lists of virtues in both the early German and English hymnbooks of the Brethren is the comprehensive list of virtues defining the Christian life in the hymnbook edited by James Quinter, *The Brethren's Hymn Book* (1867). His list includes: adoption, afflictions and trials, aspirations, assurance, backsliding, communion with God, confidence, consistency, consecration, contentment, conversion, courage, the cross, discipline, faith, hope, humility, joy, justification, justice, labor and sympathy, love, obedience, patience, peace, perfection, the Christian pilgrimage, prayer, the race, reproof, safety, self-examination, sincerity, submission, watchfulness, the warfare, wisdom, and zeal. The only virtues with over ten hymns apiece are afflictions and trials (19), aspirations (17), and prayer (20).

Brethren Spirituality

What is interesting about this list is the appearance of an item reflecting knowledge of general Protestant theology, notably justification, and items which reflect interaction with various American religious movements and issues, specifically assurance, backsliding, and perfection. These items suggest Brethren engagement with revivalism and the holiness movement. Samuel Funkhouser reinforces this same point as he analyzes specific hymns in Quinter's collection. Quinter demonstrates an awareness of "the contours of Protestant theology" and reflects emphases found in broader American Protestantism such as revivals, missions, temperance, and even church dedications (the Brethren had always, up to this point in time, called their gathering places "meetinghouses," thereby avoiding the misconception of a building being the church rather than the people of God being the church).[32] In spite of these indicators of Brethren engagement with the religious developments occurring in America, Quinter does include a number of rubrics that mirror earlier Brethren piety: afflictions and trials, communion with God, the cross, humility, patience, submission, watchfulness, and spiritual warfare. Thus, in his depiction of Brethren life and piety, Quinter looks both backward and forward, as will be true of those who will become known as the Conservatives at the time of the division of the 1880s.

In my research for this paper, I happened upon an intriguing statement by Henry Kurtz in 1851 that sheds light on the piety that would be adopted by the other two groups in the division of the 1880s, the Old Order and Progressive Brethren. Kurtz was responding to a query about how best to maintain the principle of nonconformity to the world. Notice his counsel, all of which is one lengthy sentence:

> . . . our old brethren, that have gone before us, did not bind heavy burdens, and grievous to be borne, and lay them on men's shoulders, as the Pharisees of old did . . ., neither did they make a law or rule for others, of what they deemed their own duty in the practice of the principle [of nonconformity to the world], . . . leaving it altogether to the teachings of the Holy Spirit and to the power of the truth and to the free will and option of every individual member, how far they felt themselves called to follow in this practice, and never taking under dealings, as far as we could learn, any member for shortcomings in this practice, unless it was connected with a gross violation of the principle itself; only teaching and exhorting

their fellow-members, to live and act consistent with their professed principles, to which all had given their free and full assent, when received into the communion of the church, and so far from exercising an illiberal spirit in this matter, the obvious difference of appearance in our members generally proves the very contrary to be the fact, and that the danger lays rather on the other side.[33]

Several observations need to be made about this editorial commentary by Kurtz. First, Kurtz indicates that the old brethren, with whose views he was quite familiar, allowed members a fair degree of liberty in the actual expression of nonconformity, as long as it was not "a gross violation of the principle." This liberty was in keeping with the understanding that individual members should be sensitive "to the teachings of the Holy Spirit and to the power of the truth" when discerning issues of nonconformity. Second, he observes that the church does need to exhort its members "to live and act consistent with their professed principles"; members do need to be cognizant of their responsibility to maintain a spirit of nonconformity in all aspects of their life. Third, note that Kurtz sees a danger in being overly prescriptive on matters of nonconformity; in fact he cites the "obvious difference of appearance in our members" at this time as an indication that the practice of allowing individual members to discern the proper application of nonconformity was working.

This citation raises the intriguing question: Why did the Brethren after 1851 begin to move away *from* the liberty given individual members for discerning, through the Spirit and the Word, the proper application of nonconformity to the world **to** reliance on Annual Meeting and the order of the Brethren to prescribe the proper boundaries of the nonconformed life? A warning that appeared a few years later, also written by Henry Kurtz, sheds light on this question. In April 1855 Kurtz reflects on the upcoming Annual Meeting and issues the following admonition:

> Being at all times surrounded by that mixed crowd, THE WORLD, members, who are not constantly on their guard, who forget, that they are *called out from* THE WORLD, and begin to love THE WORLD, will imperceptibly exchange GOSPEL-views and sentiments, for WORLDLY-views and sentiments, . . . and GOSPEL-customs and practice for WORLDLY-customs and fashions, and a spirit of WORLDLINESS will take the place of the holy Spirit of

the GOSPEL. This evil, alas! is felt in all the churches, and what is worse, it is beginning to be felt even at our yearly meetings, not only *outside*, but *within* the sanctuary of our most solemn deliberations. Oh my brethren, if that "mixed multitude" would only cause us some trouble and expense, it would be nothing; but if it has a tendency to rob us of our birth-right, of our spiritual privileges, of our greatest blessings, yea even of the power and spirit of the Gospel, and to draw us down upon a level with the world,-- then indeed it is a GREAT, EXTENSIVE EVIL.[34]

As the cultural distance between the Brethren sub-culture and the surrounding American culture steadily decreased both literally and figuratively from the 1850s on, the concern expressed in the latter quote caused Annual Meeting to attempt to create a fence around the church to maintain the boundaries between the two cultures through rulings of Annual Meeting and the accompanying order of the Brethren. In the process, however, the earlier practice of relying on the Holy Spirit to guide members in the application of Gospel principles established by the church diminished significantly. Especially noteworthy, each of these two approaches for discerning the application of Gospel principles would be championed by one of the two groups that left the main body of the church in the 1880s. The Old Order Brethren would look to Annual Meeting and the order of the Brethren to maintain the boundaries between the church and the world while the Progressives would emphasize the right of individual believers to discern matters of nonconformity through the Spirit's guidance.

Intriguingly, these differing approaches also led to corresponding differences in the form of spirituality esteemed by both groups. The Old Order Brethren valued the spiritual qualities of humility and submission to the decisions of the Annual Meeting while the Progressive Brethren prized individual discernment of and sensitivity to the leading of the Spirit. Unfortunately, the division of the 1880s tended to pull apart two principles that earlier generations of Brethren had held in creative tension: allowance for individual liberty and humble submission to the church. The same can be said for the historic Brethren balance between inner and outer elements of the Christian life and faith; the Progressive Brethren tended to emphasize the inner, spiritual life of the individual before God while the Old Order Brethren felt that maintaining uniformity regarding outward forms and practices would protect the church from an encroaching world and a corrupted Christianity.[35] Speaking as an heir of the Progressive heritage, I have witnessed a desire in the Brethren Church to recapture a greater respect for the consensus of the church and to moderate the strong individualism that has become ingrained in our denominational culture.

Before leaving this section, I want to make an observation about the Brethren reliance on the Word and Spirit in all aspects of their devotional lives. When I am teaching on Brethren thought and practice, I reinforce the point that the Brethren, as a movement, are a Word and Spirit church in contrast to a Word and Sacrament church. The difference between these two perspectives is significant. Word and Sacrament churches, like the Lutheran, Reformed, Anglican, and Methodist churches, are more clergy oriented, generally more traditional, and give more emphasis to ritual and liturgy. Word and Spirit churches, at least in their formative stages, place more emphasis on the role of the laity, are generally more open to change based on new insights from the Word, and often seek to be sensitive to the Spirit's leading in their worship practices. The early Brethren clearly conceived of their church and their piety in the Word and Spirit model.[36]

CHRISTIAN H. BALSBAUGH AS A SPIRITUAL GUIDE FOR THE BRETHREN

The two people during the last half of the 19th century who played the leading roles in shaping the spiritual lives of the Brethren were James Quinter and Christian H. Balsbaugh. You may have noticed how frequently I have already cited the writings of Quinter on various spiritual themes. As the editor of the most prominent Brethren periodicals of the 19th century, he regularly wrote on themes whose purpose was the spiritual edification of the church. But the person who rightly can be ranked along with Alexander Mack Jr. as the most significant spiritual guide for the Brethren prior to the 20th century was Christian Balsbaugh.

Balsbaugh came to this position in the church because of both natural qualities and some tragic occurrences in life. He was born in 1831 and was a fourth generation Brethren. He described himself as "mentally omnivorous" and an "insatiable student." He began teaching school at the age of nineteen, using the income from this work to attend such schools as Harrisburg Academy, Gettysburg Academy, and Freeland Seminary, all in Pennsylvania. He read and studied medicine in Philadelphia and New York during the 1850s. Balsbaugh was always frail of body, but an episode in 1853 seriously jeopardized his health. During his first year of teaching, he had a poorly ventilated schoolroom that caused him to inhale large amounts of coal dust and fumes. As a result, he suffered from ongoing sore throats and an enlarged uvula. In 1853, following the counsel of doctors, he had his uvula excised and was treated with silver nitrate to cauterize the wound. However, continued bleeding led to further cauterizations and silver nitrate treatments over the period of a year. These actions landed him in bed for a year and led to the loss of his voice for seven years. Though his voice returned in 1860, a bout of mental exhaustion again left him speechless from 1871 until 1884. During this period he was confined to bed for three years, even despairing of life on a number of occasions[37]; his sole means of communication was a slate and pencil. In order to write he lay on his back with a board or other support on his knees. Though he had dismissed the idea of miraculous healing much of his life, in 1884 he recovered his voice through the ministry of a Boston faith healer, Charles Cullis. He presumably retained his voice until his death in 1909.[38]

During the second episode in particular, Balsbaugh endured almost constant suffering. In addition, from 1853 on, his infirmities left him incapable of gainful employment. He had to rely on the generosity of others to meet his daily needs. It was within the furnace of affliction that he would learn those qualities that came to mark his ministry of the pen—qualities that he described as "tenderness, sympathy, boundless hope for seemingly hopeless souls, faith in the Infinite Resources of the Godman Savior."[39]

Balsbaugh began his writing for Brethren periodicals in 1860. Hardly a year went by without something from his pen appearing in print in the various Brethren periodicals. From the mid-1870s through the mid-1880s his columns appeared nearly weekly; the total number of his submissions to Brethren periodicals approached one thousand. Not only did Balsbaugh send articles directly to the editors for publication, but recipients of his letters also asked that letters sent to them be published. In fact at one point in 1878 the editors of the *Primitive Christian and Pilgrim* indicated that so many people had sent in such requests that the letters "will likely lay over awhile. As a general rule," the editors noted, "we only put one article from the same author in the paper at a time."[40] As Balsbaugh's spiritual discernment became known, he received a growing number of letters asking for his spiritual counsel. He indicated at one point that he had "a wide correspondence reaching all over America, Canada included, and across the Atlantic, and receive[d] thousands of letters from believers in all denominations."[41] These letters often asked for spiritual guidance, for interpretation of difficult passages in Scripture, and for support and encouragement in the midst of serious trials or after the loss of a loved one.

Balsbaugh testifies that he experienced a radical turning point in his own spiritual journey in the early 1880s. Prior to this time he describes himself as a legalist, emphasizing far too much conformity to the letter of Scripture.[42] Note his own depiction of his writings prior to 1880 and the transforming truth that revolutionized his spiritual life:

> [It is not the case] that they [the earlier writings] are not intrinsically true, but they are legal in spirit while Christian in form. [43] God had to put me in the crucible again and again, and melt me next to nothing, before I could see that all expectation of salvation on the ground of our utmost doing and best morality, is a necessary depreciation of the perfect reconciliation of God and man as accomplished in human nature by Jesus Christ. . . . Since then Christ is my exclusive theme. In the Bible and in Nature I see nothing but Christ. . . . Until we have found the Mediator, and the Eternal Life He has deposited in Human Nature, we have nothing to do with the symbols [the ordinances] expressive of these facts. Jesus is the Name which is above every name, and includes the whole Godhead, end every constituent of humanity in its pristine purity. And this conjunction is not dependent on the observance of any ceremony, but is wholly effected by the Omnipotent Spirit.[44]

As intimated in this extended quotation, Balsbaugh's writing would henceforth revolve around two focal points: the doctrines of Christ and of the Holy Spirit. I need to give brief descriptions of his approach to both of these doctrines. Redemption is wholly linked to the truth that Jesus Christ fully reveals both God and perfected humanity.[45] For Balsbaugh both the incarnation and Jesus' sacrifice on the cross are foundational for salvation, for the incarnation reveals the perfected humanity we are to become while the work of the cross provides complete atonement for human sin.[46] We come to know both the dignity and depravity of humanity through the incarnation and the cross.[47] Balsbaugh gives special prominence to Christ's incarnation, because this act represents the beginning of the restoration of humanity into the image of God.[48] As he indicates, in the incarnation Jesus Christ "realized in Himself as Man for us all that God intended man to be from the beginning. In the Incarnation lies the reason of all that constitutes Christianity in its essence and form."[49]

The work of restoring humanity to its original divine design depends wholly upon the Holy Spirit. Balsbaugh draws an interesting parallel between Christ's incarnation and death and a corresponding incarnation and death that should be true of every believer. The idea that Christ's death calls upon us to die to ourselves and the things of this world is a well recognized concept, derived from Paul's discussion in Romans 6. But Balsbaugh also sees a significant parallel between Christ's incarnation and what should be true of every follower of Christ. Repeatedly he argues that, through the Holy Spirit's indwelling presence and power, we are to be incarnations of the image of God as seen in Jesus Christ. His life is to be our life. As he states in one of his letters:

> Our every possible expression of life rests in the fact that we are incarnations of the Image of God—duplicates of what was in, with and like God from everlasting. We are not our own, and all the nobler and freer and happier because body, soul and spirit are possessed, directed, filled and sanctified by the Holy Ghost, whose office is to work in the Divine essence and peculiarities and lineaments according to our ever-widening capacities.[50]

From this vantage point Balsbaugh has no patience with those who deny or minimize in any way the ability of Christians to live more and more fully what he calls at various times the "Christed" life. He pointedly declares: "Jesus Christ came to show us in His humanity how God lives, and to make it possible for us to live the same life by His immanence through faith. Anything lower than this is not Christianity."[51]

We may legitimately ask whether Balsbaugh reflects Brethren thought in these emphases. He does advocate some concepts regarding Christ's incarnation and the implications of the incarnation for the Christian life that would be unique in Brethren literature. Yet this theme is consistent with the general optimism that Brethren had from the time of Mack and the early Brethren through to his own time about the ability of believers to live a transformed, regenerate life that models the life of Christ through the indwelling power of the Holy Spirit. He likewise reflects the Christ-mysticism that was a recurring theme among the Brethren of the 18th century. Interestingly, Balsbaugh intimates at one point dependency upon the writings of three people: Madame Guyon, a French Quietist who had great influence on the Radical Pietists; Phoebe Palmer, a key advocate of the holiness movement of the second half of the 19th century; and Adolph Saphir, a Jewish Christian from Hungary whose writings influenced the Keswick movement in the latter 19th century. Saphir may also have been the source for Balsbaugh's focus on the implications of Christ's incarnation.[52] These influences on Balsbaugh's thought point both backward to sources that had impacted the early Brethren and forward to sources that were shaping the religious worldview of American evangelicals in the latter 1800s. As we have seen already with James Quinter's editing of *The Brethren's Hymn Book*, there was a trend among the main body of the German Baptist Brethren to draw insights both from their past heritage but also from contemporary American Protestantism. This trend would have a significant impact in the division of the 1880s, as the three groups in the division determined whether they would either hold on to traditional perspectives, move forward into modern American culture, or seek a middle position between honoring the past and engaging the present. For the Progressives and Conservatives of the 1880s, this trend to engaging modern American culture to varying degrees would lead to significant changes in the church during the 20th century.

Changes regarding Brethren Spirituality during the 19th Century

As I conclude this presentation, I want to present in summary statements some of the changes that took place during the 19th century in the Brethren approach to spirituality. I will also venture a tentative description of Brethren spirituality based on the research for this paper. My summary observations are necessarily brief, but I believe they are corroborated by the findings of this paper.

Departures from Traditional Brethren Spirituality

- During this century the Christocentric focus of Brethren spirituality diminished as Brethren began to adopt theological perspectives found within evangelical Protestant thought.[53]

- In a corresponding way, the theme of discipleship to Christ, which was fundamental to Anabaptist, Pietist, and Brethren conceptions of the Christian life, becomes less prominent during the century.
  - It is modified to some degree by conceptions of the Christian life borrowed from revivalism and the holiness and Keswick movements.
- The two kingdom theology of the Brethren/Anabaptist tradition begins to give way to concepts of the relationship between church and culture more reflective of broader American Protestantism.
  - This modification will lead to the appearance of nationalistic hymns in Brethren hymnals of the 20th century, to acceptance of the distinction between sacred and secular, and, for better or worse, engagement with those cultural issues affecting American society in general.
  - The division between sacred and secular allows for the narrowing of spirituality to apply to our sacred lives, leaving our secular lives to be influenced far more by cultural developments in America.
- Consequently, as Brethren engagement with culture increases, there is a tendency for Brethren to give less time and focus to spiritual exercises and disciplines.
- During the 19th century the role and work of the Holy Spirit becomes less of an emphasis as greater stress is placed upon outward means and measures of the spiritual life. Balsbaugh at one point laments that the Brethren did not say enough about "the office of the Holy Ghost."[54]

Returns to Traditional Brethren Spirituality

- The Brethren of the 18th century invariably held that the inward life of the Spirit must precede the outward expressions of the faith. This was a conviction derived from Pietism. Due to the influence of Peter Nead and others during the first half of the 19th century, there was a trend toward emphasizing the outward practices of the church as being the means to the reception of the inward graces. This shift away from the earlier perspective of the Brethren began to be reversed by the end of the 1800s and beginning of the 1900s by writers like Balsbaugh among the German Baptist Brethren and C. F. Yoder and John L. Gillin in the

Brethren Church. They shifted the emphasis to the inner meaning of the ordinances or to the primacy and precedence of the Spirit's work over human actions.55

- ○ Corresponding to this shift was a gradual movement away from the language of "means of grace" that is generally connected with more sacramental views of church rites.

Modifications to Traditional Brethren Spirituality

- Brethren spirituality during the 18th century was significantly informed by their Pietist heritage but increasingly reflected more of an Anabaptist perspective during the 19th century. This change occurred for various reasons. The Pietist spirituality of the early Brethren was maintained by their German hymnody and the devotional literature printed by the Sauer and Ephrata presses. As the German language gradually disappeared among the Brethren in the 1800s, Anabaptist themes, which had been present from the beginning of the Brethren movement, became more pronounced in Brethren devotional literature. Interestingly, this development did not occur because the Brethren were reading Anabaptist and Mennonite literature or devotional sources during the 1800s. Though some Brethren were, most were not. Rather, the Brethren shared with the Anabaptists several key doctrinal convictions that shaped their devotional lives: the two kingdom theology, stress on community, similar views on the theology of baptism and communion, and commitment to the three "nons" of nonconformity, nonswearing, and nonresistance. These shared emphases resulted in a piety that closely resembled that of the Anabaptists/Mennonites during much of the 1800s.

- By the latter part of the 19th century, other influences that were impacting the American religious scene also were beginning to influence Brethren devotional life, notably revivalism and the holiness and Keswick movements.

- One of the unfortunate results of the division of the 1880s was the polarizing effect that it had upon several creative tensions found within Brethren thought of the 18th century, notably the balance between the inner, spiritual aspects of the faith and the outer, formal aspects.

- The other creative tension affected by the division was the balance between individual freedom and submission to the corporate community.
- At their best the Brethren, like the Pietists, sought a middle way between elements of the faith that could be viewed as in opposition without depreciating either side of the balance. The division among the Old Order Brethren, Progressive Brethren, and Conservatives undermined this historic balance with each group tending to emphasize different sides of the dialectic.

All of these changes in the theological, practical, and spiritual aspects of Brethren life left their impact upon the devotional lives of the Brethren.

A Tentative Definition of Brethren Spirituality

I would like to end this paper with a depiction of Brethren spirituality, especially as it was found in the first generations of Brethren life in both Germany and America. This would have been the general conception of the spiritual life among the Brethren at least through the middle part the 19th century.

Brethren spirituality during both the 18th and 19th centuries is grounded in the conviction that God's purpose for his people is that they should fully bear his image and reflect his life in the world. Like the Anabaptists, the Brethren sought to live out this conviction by obediently following the life and teachings of the Son of God, Jesus Christ, as recorded in the Gospels and explicated in the rest of the New Testament. They understood that this Christ-like life must be empowered and animated by the regenerative work of the Holy Spirit and that **all of life**, individually, corporately, and in the world, is to be ordered under Christ's Lordship and rule. Though the individual is responsible for his or her own spiritual development, the family and the church play essential roles in shaping the lives of those entrusted to them. By word and deed, in service and witness, the community of faith joins in God's mission of forming a people for himself who will reflect his life in the world and be his ambassadors of peace, reconciliation, and love.

The 19th century was a critical time of transition and change in the spiritual lives of the Brethren. As we have noted with regard to other factors, their spirituality during this century had elements that looked both backward and forward. Brethren life at the beginning of the century was still thoroughly imbued with a spirituality derived from Pietism and Anabaptism. By the end of the century, Brethren spirituality was increasingly being influenced by modern American religious and secular trends. Unfortunately, those who were most acquainted with the spiritual heritage of the Brethren had generally passed from the scene by the dawn of the 20th century. This new century would hold new challenges for the Brethren in all areas of their identity, including their spiritual lives.

Notes

1 John Driver, *Life Together in the Spirit: A Radical Spirituality for the Twenty-First Century* (Goshen, IN: Institute for the Study of Global Anabaptism, 2011), 1-2, 31.

2 Ibid., 31-33, 60.

3 J(ames). Q(uinter)., "On the Profitable and Intelligent Reading of Scripture," *The Gospel Visitor* 15 (December 1865): 363.

4 Ibid., 363-367.

5 Ibid., 366.

6 Of the nearly 100 titles listed for this period of time in the Brethren bibliography compiled by Donald Durnbaugh and Lawrence Shultz, 55 were various editions of German and English hymn books or devotional literature that contained some hymns. Donald F. Durnbaugh and Lawrence W. Shultz, "A Brethren Bibliography, 1713-1963," *Brethren Life and Thought* 9 (Winter and Spring 1964): 19-34.

7 James Quinter, ed., *A Collection of Psalms, Hymns, and Spiritual Songs; Suited to the various Kinds of Christian Worship; and especially Designed for, and Adapted to, The Fraternity of the Brethren* (Covington, OH: James Quinter, 1867), iii, iv.

8 Theoklitus (pseud.), "Angels. Their Mission," *The Monthly Gospel-Visiter* 6 (March 1856): 62 and Hattie, "Old Hundred," *The Gospel-Visitor* 11 (March 1861): 145.

9 See, for example, James Wirt, "'Christian Employment,'" *Christian Family Companion and Gospel Visitor* 2 (August 10, 1875): 503.

10 "Preface," in *The Christians Duty, Exhibited, in a Series of Hymns: Collected from Various Authors, Designed for the Worship of God, and for the Edification of Christians. Recommended, to the Serious, of All Denominations. By the Fraternity of Baptist's* (Germantown, PA: Peter Leibert, 1791).

11 See S. Z. Sharp, *The Educational History of The Church of the Brethren* (Elgin, IL: Brethren Publishing House, 1923), 41-43.

12 Dale R. Stoffer, *Background and Development of Brethren Doctrines 1650-1987* (Philadelphia, PA: Brethren Encyclopedia, 1989), 90.

13 [Henry Kurtz], "Address to the Reader," *The Monthly Gospel-Visiter* 1 (April 1851): 3.

14 See, for example, Wirt, "'Christian Employment,'" 503; J(ames). Q(uinter)., "Fasting," *The Gospel-Visitor* 11 (January 1861): 8-13; P. M., "Prayer," *The Gospel-Visitor* 12 (August 1862): 229-231; I. G. H., "Prayer a Christian Duty," *The Gospel-Visitor* 13 (November 1863): 331-

335; J(ames). Q(uinter)., "Unceasing Prayer," *The Gospel-Visitor* 13 (November 1863): 335-338; J(ames). Q(uinter)., "Hindrances to Prayer," *The Gospel-Visitor* 13 (December 1863): 354-356; and James Quinter, "Fasting," *The Gospel-Visitor* 17 (April 1867): 115-119.

15 [James Quinter], "Queries," *The Gospel-Visitor* 10 (May 1860): 153-154.

16 Dale R. Stoffer, "Brethren Heritage of the Lord's Supper: Eucharist," in *The Lord's Supper: Believers Church Perspectives*, ed. Dale R. Stoffer (Scottdale, PA: Herald Press, 1997), 187-192.

17 See, for example, C. H., "For the Visiter," *The Monthly Gospel-Visiter* 3 (January 1854): 178; Aristobulus (pseud.), "A Call to the Unconverted," *The Monthly Gospel-Visiter* 5 (March 1855): 51; J(ames). Q(uinter)., "Family Churches," *The Gospel-Visitor* 11 (October 1861): 294-296; and S. B. F., "Family Duties," *The Gospel-Visitor* 14 (June 1864): 184-186.

18 See Hedwig T. Durnbaugh, *The German Hymnody of the Brethren 1720-1903* (Philadelphia, PA: The Brethren Encyclopedia, Inc., 1986), 17, 47, 71, 94, 105, 116 and Samuel S. Funkhouser, "In the Line of *Duty*: A History and Theological Analysis of Early English-Language Brethren Hymn Books and Hymnals, 1791-1884" (M.Div. thesis, Princeton Theological Seminary, 2012), 10, 54, 85, 142, 189.

19 J. C. Ewing, ed. *The Brethren Hymnody with Tunes. For the Sanctuary, Sunday-School, Prayer-Meeting, and Home Circle* (Wilmington, OH: J. C. Ewing, 1884).

20 Hedda Durnbaugh indicates that "the rubrics of *Das Kleine Davidische Psalterspiel* are almost identical with those in the Inspirationist hymnal [*Davidisches Psalter-Spiel*]," though there are also definite similarities with Johann Anastasius Freylinghausen's *Geistreiches Gesang-Buch* as well. Hedwig Durnbaugh, *German Hymnody of the Brethren*, 44. Samuel Funkhouser observes that the first seven rubrics of *The Christians Duty* bear some resemblance to the first nine rubrics of *Das Kleine Davidische Psalterspiel*, but thereafter any further similarity breaks down. He further notes that the rubrics of *The Christians Duty* "largely reflect the emphases and categories of other contemporary English-language evangelical Protestant hymn books, with a few small but significant modifications, additions, and differences in theological accent." The rubrics of *A Choice Selection of Hymns* are basically the same as those found in *The Christians Duty*. Funkhouser, "In the Line of *Duty*," 11, 12, 52.

21 Vernard Eller, *Kierkegaard and Radical Discipleship: A New Perspective* (Princeton, NJ: Princeton University Press, 1968), 137.

22 Quinter, ed., *A Collection of Psalms, Hymns, and Spiritual Songs*, 52-53.

23 Dennis Martin notes that the "chief metaphor for the spiritual life among Brethren from Alexander Mack, Sr., to Jacob Stoll (d. 1822) was the life of a suffering pilgrim in a sinful world." Dennis D. Martin, "Spiritual Life," in *The Brethren Encyclopedia*. This pilgrim imagery would continue to form the Brethren worldview through most of the 19th century as well. It is noteworthy that the first English hymnbook to omit Cennick's hymn cited above is the hymnal published by J. C. Ewing for the Brethren Church in 1884.

24 J(ames). Q(uinter)., "Religion in Secular Business," *The Gospel Visitor* 22 (January 1872): 15.

25 Hedwig Durnbaugh, *German Hymnody of the Brethren*, 17, 46.

26 Nead emphasized the role of Christ as "our exampler [*sic*]" and reinforced the need to obey the teachings of Christ in their totality. Stoffer, *Brethren Doctrines*, 116. See also [Henry Kurtz], "Correspondence," *The Monthly Gospel-Visiter* 1 (June 1851): 42; A[braham] H.

C[assel], "On Imitating Christ," *The Monthly Gospel-Visiter* 3 (July 1853): 27-29; [Henry Kurtz], "A Necessary Explanation," *The Monthly Gospel-Visiter* 5 (April 1855): 80-82; [Selected by the editors, Kurtz and Quinter], "Parental Example," *The Monthly Gospel-Visiter* 6 (December 1856): 342; J(ames). Q(uinter)., "The Obedience of Christ," *The Gospel-Visitor* 12 (June 1862): 162-163; J(ames). Q(uinter)., "How Christians May Sanctify the Lord," *The Gospel-Visitor* 14 (January 1864): 8-11; and J(ames). Q(uinter)., "Christian Usefulness," *The Gospel Visitor* 21 (January 1871): 4-7. As we will see below, the foundation for Balsbaugh's devotional thoughts was the indwelling Christ whose life the believer is to model in her own life.

27 Cassel, "On Imitating Christ," 27.

28 J(ames). Q(uinter)., "Our Annual Meeting of 1863," *The Gospel-Visitor* 13 (July 1863): 219.

29 J. B. Porter, "A Living and Dying Testimony to Christianity," *The Gospel-Visitor* 19 (July 1869): 210.

30 Hedwig Durnbaugh, *German Hymnody of the Brethren*, 47.

31 Funkhouser, "In the Line of *Duty*," 54-55.

32 Ibid., 86, 108-111, 117, 119-120.

33 [Henry Kurtz], "The Fraternity of German Baptists," *The Monthly Gospel-Visiter* 1 (September 1851): 88-89.

34 [Henry Kurtz], "Our Yearly Meetings," *The Monthly Gospel-Visiter* 5 (April 1855): 89.

35 For a fuller discussion of these points, see Stoffer, *Background and Development of Brethren Doctrines*, 142-143.

36 Hedda Durnbaugh has noted that the rubrics that were used in the first two German hymnals of the Brethren, printed in 1720 and 1744 respectively, generally reflected those found in Johann Anastasius Freylinghausen's *Geistreiches Gesang-Buch*, published in two parts in 1704 and 1714. One of the significant modifications that both of these Brethren hymnbooks made to the rubrics in Freylinghausen's list was to replace the rubrics "Of the divine word," "Of holy baptism," and "Of the holy supper" with the rubric "Of the inner and outer word." This change, in which these hymnbooks actually followed the lead of a hymnbook printed for the Radical Pietist group, the Inspirationists, represented an intentional shift away from the Word and Sacrament church model to a Word and Spirit model. The Brethren, unlike the Inspirationists, did include baptism and love feast among their rubrics, but placed these ordinances in sections dealing with exercises and virtues of the Christian life in the 1720 hymnbook and dealing with salvation and its outworking in the 1744 hymnbook. See Hedwig Durnbaugh, *German Hymnody of the Brethren*, 15, 16, 45, 46, 140.

37 C. H. Balsbaugh, "Parting Words," *Christian Family Companion and Gospel Visitor* 2 (April 20, 1875): 241 and C. H. Balsbaugh, "I, Yet not I," *The Primitive Christian* 11 (May 28, 1883): 342.

38 This biographical information is drawn from Christian Hervey Balsbaugh, "Autobiography," in *Glimpses of Jesus: or Letters of C. H. Balsbaugh*, comp. T. T. Myers (Mt. Morris, IL: James M. Neff), xix-xxvii; C. H. Balsbaugh, [Letter to the Editor], *Primitive Christian* 1 (May 30, 1876): 348.; and Balsbaugh, "I, Yet not I," 342.

39 Balsbaugh, "Autobiography," in *Glimpses of Jesus*, xxx.

40 "Editorial Miscellany," *Primitive Christian and Pilgrim* 2 (January 29, 1878): 57.

41 C. H. Balsbaugh, "'Caught up into Paradise,'" in *Glimpses of Jesus*, 413. In another letter he indicated that he needed 500 stamps a week for all the correspondence that he was conducting. C. H. Balsbaugh, "Easy and Difficult," in *Glimpses of Jesus*, 257.

42 See Balsbaugh, "Autobiography," in *Glimpses of Jesus*, xxvi.

43 Because Balsbaugh viewed his writings prior to 1880 having a deficient Christology and Pneumatology, he did not allow any of his articles written prior to this date to appear in the published volume of his letters. Balsbaugh, "Autobiography," in *Glimpses of Jesus*, xxxi.

44 Balsbaugh, "Autobiography," in *Glimpses of Jesus*, xxxi-xxxii.

45 Balsbaugh, "The Divine Discipline of Man," in *Glimpses of Jesus*, 146-147.

46 Ibid.; Balsbaugh, "To a Young Minister," in *Glimpses of Jesus*, 179, 184; and Balsbaugh, "The Great Life," in *Glimpses of Jesus*, 37.

47 Balsbaugh, "The Mystery of Eternal Love," in *Glimpses of Jesus*, 91.

48 Balsbaugh, "The Great Life," in *Glimpses of Jesus*, 37 and Balsbaugh, "The Mystery of Eternal Love," in *Glimpses of Jesus*, 91.

49 Balsbaugh, "The Mystery of Eternal Love," in *Glimpses of Jesus*, 91.

50 Ibid., 92-93.

51 Balsbaugh, "Christ and Anti-Christ," in *Glimpses of Jesus*, 386.

52 Balsbaugh, "Through the Gates of Pearl," in *Glimpses of Jesus*, 414.

53 See Samuel Funkhouser's comments on this point related to Quinter's editing of *The Brethren's Hymn Book*. Funkhouser, "In the Line of *Duty*," 87-88, 118.

54 Balsbaugh, "Easy and Difficult," in *Glimpses of Jesus*, 263. He further observed: "Have we not many among us who conform strictly to sacred ordinances and ecclesiastical usages, whose hearts run over with lust and passion and envy and jealousy and covetousness and levity and whose entire hope of salvation, if they have any, rests altogether on something apart from the Divine immanence?"

55 For Nead's impact on this shift to the outward being the means to the inward, see Stoffer, *Brethren Doctrines*, 108-110, 123-124. For Balsbaugh's position on this issue, see Balsbaugh, "Autobiography," in *Glimpses of Jesus*, xxxii; Balsbaugh, "Fear and Hopes," in *Glimpses of Jesus*, 80; Balsbaugh, "The Holy Spirit," in *Glimpses of Jesus*, 143-144; and Balsbaugh, "The Unsaved," in *Glimpses of Jesus*, 345-346. For the views of Yoder and Gillin, see Stoffer, *Brethren Doctrines*, 174-175.

Brethren Spirituality in the 20th Century[1]

William Kostlevy

My hometown newspaper in Wisconsin often contains job-wanted ads for fabricators or workers capable of fabricating metal. As an historian, I have often been tempted to apply. I too have taken an object or more commonly an historical source and turned it into something new and usable in completely new situations. Of course, I know, as do metal fabricators, that there are limits to one's creative powers. The assignment to write a coherent paper on something called Brethren spirituality even during a relatively short time-period like the twentieth century seems frankly to be beyond my abilities in fabrication. It even begs larger questions? How does one get from Gottfried Arnold to M. R. Zigler or Alva McClain? How does one explain that Dan West, C. C. Ellis, and Anna Mow were members of the same church? Is there a common Brethren spirituality that supported D. W. Kurtz and Louis Bauman in their epic struggles for the soul or perhaps more realistically the cash of Brethren in Southern California? Or should we simply conclude that Kurtz was a liberal and Bauman a fundamentalist, and that both were tied to alien twentieth-century ideologies that bear no relationship to early Brethren experience?

Further, what in the world is spirituality anyway? As Alva McClain once explained with his usual understatement, "No other word in the vocabulary of the doctrine of the Kingdom has been the occasion of more misunderstanding and useless argument."[2] Turning to the *Wikipedia*, I learned (at least on June 13, 2013) that the term lacked a definition but has something to do with the search for the sacred. The *Wikipedia* did hint at something I have always suspected, that this is a word loaded with theological content of a particular Christian tradition, Catholicism. Under Christian spirituality, we have the sub-fields of Catholic spirituality and mystic spirituality. Spirituality is defined as the "practice of living out a personal act of faith." Fortunately as has happened before in my life, I found a Mennonite who was willing to give me direction. In his 2005 book, *Dissident Discipleship: A Spirituality of Self-Surrender, Love of God, and Love of Neighbor*, David Augsburger provided needed clarification and direction. Spirituality, Augsburg notes in a vocabulary drawn from the age of Harold Bender, "invariably boils down to some kind of the practice or apprenticeship in living what we call discipleship." Further, Augsburger notes that "spirituality" has replaced another hard to define word "religion" in common everyday speech. As if to prove Augsburger's claim, I've noticed that thrift stores now tend to place religious books under the category of "spirituality." Most non-Christian spirituality, Augsburger notes, is focused on self-discovery. Most Christian spirituality is focused on self-discovery and the discovery of God as other. This is the emphasis that Augsburger discovers among his students at Fuller Theological Seminary. Augsburger identifies a third form of spirituality as tri-polar. It focuses on self-discovery through self-surrender, love of God, and thirdly love of neighbor. It is, according to Augsburger, fully expressed in the most ridiculous of all acts—the love of one's enemies expressed through the refusal to kill those who may or may not be plotting to kill you.[3]

As I read *Dissident Discipleship*, a familiar vocabulary began to emerge. Terms like self-surrender, phrases like "let go, let come, let be, let God." In fact, Augsburger's ideas, especially his emphasis upon refusing to kill, bear an uncanny resemblance to a message delivered a century earlier in Des Moines, Iowa by A. C. Wieand. In other words, Augsburger has repackaged the essential spirituality of Billy Graham, added an Anabaptist component, and in the process has managed to arrive at the conclusions of an early twentieth century Church of the Brethren leader. Augsburger admits as much, as he indicates this distinctly Amish, Mennonite and Brethren spirituality often is found among Catholics, Protestants and particularly in Charismatic and Pentecostal spirituality. Like Wieand he sees non-violence, the refusal to kill the other, as the deepest expression of self-surrender to the Divine. The spirituality of Wieand (and Augsburger) has a name and a history. Although located in a specific place and time. it has had a global impact that continues to be felt. Its literature continues to be sold and read by millions. The name is "Keswick."[4]

WHAT IS KESWICK?

Keswick refers to a specific teaching on entire sanctification or, as its proponents prefer, "the higher Christian life"; to an annual convention held at Keswick, England; and to related conventions held around the world. Its origins lie in a series of "higher life meetings" held by Quakers turned Presbyterians Robert P. and Hannah W. Smith and an American Presbyterian minister living also in exile in England, W. E. Boardman, in 1873 and 1874. In 1874, the Smiths and Boardman were invited to hold a higher life meeting at the Broadlands, the estate of W. Cowper-Temple, later Lord Mount Temple. This led to similar 1875 meetings at Oxford and Brighton. This resulted in an invitation by the Anglican curate at Keswick, T. D. Herford-Battersby, for the Smiths to hold a similar meeting at Keswick. Just before the meetings, rumors of sexual indiscretion on the part of Robert P. Smith resulted in others assuming the Smiths' roles as leaders of the meetings.

After Smith's so-called "fall," the meetings came under the control of Anglican and Reformed evangelicals who sought to articulate a doctrine of full salvation that was free of American and Methodist perfectionism. In its classic form, Keswick teaching holds that the sinful nature is not extinguished or eradicated, but "counteracted" by a second distinct religious experience following salvation, the Baptism of the Holy Spirit. As with other aspects of Evangelicalism, its genius is best exemplified by the simple slogans it inspired, such as "Let go and let God." Or in the hymns it inspired, such "Trust and Obey." Its most notable American exponent was Charles G. Trumbull, editor of the influential Philadelphia-based *Sunday School Times*. Trumball taught that a simple two-part exercise could lead Christians into a life of victory over the power of sin. First, one surrendered or turned over one's life to Christ, and secondly, one claimed by faith that God will give one victory over sin. This moment by moment victory is dependent on our remaining focused upon Christ.[5]

Introduced into North America by D. L. Moody, who skillfully distanced himself from Methodism's more radical features, Keswick teaching was often wedded to premillennial eschatology and faith healing as well, creating the so-called four-fold gospel of Jesus as savior, sanctifier, healer, and coming king. The merging of these streams was often contested and never complete. Before the early twentieth century, with the exception of a few isolated Reformed critics, Keswick spirituality won broad evangelical acceptance. This, in part, was a result of Keswick's practice of minimizing ecclesiastical differences in the "promotion of practical holiness" even as its inter-denominational attendees affirmed the motto "all one in Christ Jesus."

Beginning in 1895, the four-fold gospel found an important foothold in Philadelphia's First Brethren Church. As Dale Stoffer noted, its pastor J. C. Cassel had close ties to A. B. Simpson's Keswick-oriented Christian Missionary Alliance. Other key figures in introducing Keswick spirituality in the Brethren Church and later the Grace Brethren Church were Philadelphia pastors I. D. Bowman and especially L. S. Bauman (1874-1950). As pastor of the influential Long Beach Brethren Church, 1913-1948, Bauman played a key role in the developing conservative evangelical community in Southern California. His ties to popular Fundamentalist leaders like R. A. Torrey, L. W. Munhall, Robert C. McQuilkin, and Charles E. Fuller placed the thriving Brethren Church and later Grace Brethren Church at the center of popular Keswick piety in one of evangelicalism's most strategic locations.[6]

As expressed by figures like Torrey, McQuilkin, Fuller, and even earlier by evangelists like D. L. Moody, Keswick explicitly rejected much of the optimism of early social gospel proponents. Among Brethren, even figures in the Church of the Brethren, like Juniata president C. C. Ellis, "the character of Christianity" was determined by Calvary, not the personality or even teachings of Jesus. As Ellis saw it, the Kingdom of God was to be actually established by the returning savior "not through the Christianization of our social relationships and spread of the gospel of brotherhood."[7]

Keswick Not Only for Dispensationalists

Ellis was an important national leader in the Keswick movement and wrote a weekly column in the *Sunday School Times*. In truth, Brethren figures such as Ellis, Louis Bauman, and Perry Fitzwater were not merely reacting to Keswick teaching. They were its active creators and promoters. Like our Mennonite neighbors, Brethren were not merely victims of Fundamentalism. Brethren played key roles in the development of Fundamentalism and later Evangelicalism. It should be noted that beliefs similar to Ellis' are frequently presented as the essence of Keswick spirituality. But unlike Ellis, many deeply impacted by Keswick spirituality were not conservative evangelicals. The usual telling of the Keswick story reduces it to a chapter in the history of twentieth-century Fundamentalism. While helpful in explaining the origins of the views of such popular evangelical figures as Billy Graham and Campus Crusade for Christ founder Bill Bright, this narrative greatly reduces the ironies, complexities, and contradictions in what was in fact a fluid and diverse spirituality. Nowhere are the contradictions more evident than in the life of one of its greatest proponents, John A. Wanamaker, the descendent of an early Brethren family in Anwell, NJ. This department-store magnate and one of the principal founders of consumer-driven capitalism was also among Keswick's principal institutional creators. In fact, Wanamaker's first career began in 1858 when he opened Bethany Mission Sunday School in Philadelphia. It was only later that he founded the dry goods store that would evolve into the famous Philadelphia department store that would bear his name.

By the 1890s, Bethany Sunday School was the largest Sunday School in the world and was affiliated with Philadelphia's Bethany Presbyterian Church. Bethany's two pastors, A. T. Pierson and J. Wilbur Chapman, were not only two of the foremost proponents of Keswick spirituality but leading practitioners of the so-called institutional churches. Institutional churches, often considered as part of the social gospel movement, fed the hungry, operated schools for adults, provided job training, offered sports venues, and fought addiction. In effect as one scholar has noted, Wanamaker was a "liberal evangelist" whose non-dogmatic piety emphasized service instead of the old narrowly defined orthodoxy. For Wanamaker, the common Keswick expression "power for service" could be as readily applied to the marketing of commodities in his department store as the evangelization of foreign or even domestic heathen.[8]

If Keswick spirituality served the needs of middle class Christian men active in Kiwanis clubs and other fraternal business organizations, it always contained elements within it that could transcend the cultural needs of the petty bourgeois. Illustrations are legion including Hannah Whitall Smith, author of the most widely read Keswick text, *Christian Secret of a Happy Life*. Not only was Smith forgiven for her theological heresies, such as universalism and restorationism, but she remained active in such political movements as efforts to improve the treatment of Native Americans, the temperance movement, and the fight for women's rights.

It was not uncommon for people to embrace Keswick spirituality without generally frequenting Keswick conventions or embracing all the elements of the four-fold gospel. The case of Church of the Brethren leader Albert Cassell Wieand is especially telling. Wieand, the co-founder and long-time president of Bethany Biblical Seminary, gave the concluding address delivered at the Church of the Brethren 1908 bicentennial celebration. Aptly entitled "The Higher Spiritual Life of the Church," the address squarely located the Church of the Brethren in the broadly-defined evangelical mainstream of North American Protestants. "The consecrated person, the spirit-filled person, the higher spiritual-life person," Wieand insisted, "trusts God for everything." "Just two things in the higher spiritual life,--TRUST and OBEY; surrender and faith, surrender of all," were required of Christians. Interestingly, for a message concluding the denomination's bicentennial, it initially seemed to defend no distinctively Brethren doctrine or practice. Yet as he moved toward his conclusion, the tone changed and the message took on a decidedly Brethren flavor. It was no longer a message that could be delivered at any Protestant revival meeting.[9]

For Wieand, Keswick spirituality was suddenly unhooked from millennialism and refocused on one of the distinctive core Church of the Brethren beliefs, pacifism. "We have," Wieand boldly stated, a "spiritual life of a higher grade." "In the Revolutionary War, in the Civil War…our Brethren have taken a stand…no matter what they must suffer, believing that God would deliver them." Having located non-resistance at the center of the Brethren experience, Wieand now provided a subtle but distinctly Keswick-pointed critique of the emotionalism that often accompanied evangelical revivals. "We do not get excited…but I tell you, the test of the higher spiritual life is how much sacrifice are you willing to make, and how firmly are you willing to stand by the right when it costs something to stand by the right?" Turning away from emotional responses to evangelistic preaching as the hallmark of authentic Christianity, Wieand asserted that faithfulness in opposition to war was a better indicator of spiritual maturity. In effect, he insisted that "the practical demonstration of love and character is what tells whether or not someone is spiritually minded." "Brethren," the Bethany founder concluded, "I believe that our church is the most spiritual church in the world today."[10]

Brethren Spirituality in the 20th Century

Generalization in history often obscures as much as it enlightens. Many Brethren did drink from different wells than Ellis and Wieand. Wieand's partner in founding Bethany Bible School, E. B. Hoff, would spend a lifetime trying to fight the impact of the excesses of evangelical revivalism. In his courses and in the numerous Bible Institutes he conducted across the country, Hoff emphasized that the written Word was often only a husk for the living Word revealed in Christ. It is one of the ironies of the Church of the Brethren experience that it would be an E. B. Hoff disciple, Floyd Mallott, who would most aggressively champion the Brethren roots in Pietism. The continued presence and importance of figures like Hoff, Mallott, and unapologetic liberals like D. W. Kurtz suggest that Keswick piety never held complete sway.

Still among the faithful in the pews, Keswick piety continued to shape the contours of Church of the Brethren devotional life. *Heritage of Devotion*, a 1944 devotional book edited by missionary Lillian Grisso and sponsored by Church of the Brethren women, emphasized the surrendered-life at the same time it attacked contemporary problems such as racial injustice. The sermons of popular Pennsylvania pastor Rufus Bucher bear a remarkable resemblance to those once uttered by none other than D. L. Moody himself. As Brethren moved beyond the mid-twentieth century, writers such as William Beahm and most notably Anna Beahm Mow continued to promote a piety of self-surrender and service to others. Fearful that Brethren were caught up in an emphasis that service was an end in itself, Mow insisted that the purpose of the Christian life, or the "surrendered life," was holiness. Its fruits were fellowship, simplicity and peace. "God's peacemaker," Mow insisted "is neither passive nor a feverish reformer." He is the man completely committed to Christ and his righteousness."[11] At Bethany Biblical Seminary, David Wieand continued to teach courses on prayer and the devotional life into the 1970s, and into the late 1970s Anna Mow was conducting revivals and enriching Grand Rapids publishers. For such figures, the spiritual life remained tied to Bible study, corporate worship, and prayer.

Mow's ideas bear a striking resemblance to those of her friend and fellow missionary to India, legendary Methodist and ecumenist E. Stanley Jones. While slightly more socially radical, Jones emphasized self-surrender, the Kingdom of God as an actual reality, the Sermon on the Mount as an ethical norm, and non-resistance as an expectation for Christians. Fittingly, both

David Augsburger and John Howard Yoder sight Jones as a source for their own Anabaptist convictions. As early as the 1930s, Jones had suggested that Jesus was actually proclaiming a year of Jubilee in Luke 4.

Keswick spirituality played an especially important role among Brethren missionaries. Both Anna Mow and her brother William Beahm, who served as a pioneer Church of the Brethren missionary in Nigeria, remained deeply devoted to the Keswick teaching and experience of full salvation. The simple non-dogmatic Keswick spirituality has played a continuing role in the Church of the Brethren's most significant mission in Nigeria. As early as 1926, pioneer missionary Stover Kulp, in a "covenant" written for new converts, would write: "I believe that Jesus Christ died for my sins and I trust in Him alone to save me from sin and to give me power to live a good life." This Keswick-style spirituality remains a central element in the *Ekklesiyar 'Yan'uwa a Nigeria (EYN)* which continues to use the Keswick-inspired tract by Bill Bright, "The Four Spiritual Laws" in its highly successful evangelistic ministry.[12]

Two other twentieth century movements with direct ties to the Keswick were Pentecostalism and the Moral Rearmament or Oxford Movement of Frank Buchman. Of the two, Pentecostalism with its specific teaching on the Baptism of the Holy Spirit remained more closely tied to classic Keswick spirituality. In the 1970s, the Charismatic or neo-Pentecostal movement would divide Church of the Brethren and Grace Brethren congregations in Northern Indiana. Inspired in part by a Grace Theological Seminary professor, Hobart Freeman, whose Faith Assembly rejected medical treatment, Radical Pentecostalism impacted Brethren congregations and found a receptive audience among students at both Manchester College and Grace College. However, Northern Indiana was also a center for moderate Brethren active in the Holy Spirit Renewal Group that organized Communion Fellowship in Goshen, Indiana. Other Brethren charismatic leaders included Church of the Brethren pastor R. Russell Bixler of Pittsburgh, Pennsylvania, and television personality and Church of the Brethren minister Graham Kerr. Unrelated to these groups was the creation of Christ Assembly, a Dunkard Brethren splinter group that formed as a result of the ministry of Johannes Thalitzer, a product of the 1876 Brethren mission to Denmark which had embraced Pentecostalism by the mid-twentieth century. In truth, it is not much of a leap of faith to move from Keswick understandings of the baptism of the Holy Spirit to Pentecostalism and the neo-charismatic movement's emphasis upon the same experience sealed with experiences such as speaking in unknown languages. Also closely linked to Keswick spirituality and logic was the Moral Rearmament Movement inspired by a failed Pennsylvania Lutheran minister Frank Buchman (1878-1961). Inspired by a sermon at Keswick by popular Keswick leader Jessie Penn-Lewis, Buchman developed his distinctive philosophy of forgiveness and introspection that deeply touched many frequently unaware of its connections with conventional Protestant evangelicalism.[13]

There were of course other competing spiritualities among twentieth century members in the Church of the Brethren. Among young intellectuals, the so-called Christian realism, sometimes called neo-orthodoxy, of Reinhold Niebuhr was often decisive. Others such as C. C. Ellis' own son, C. N. Ellis, turned to the reinvigorated traditionalism and supernaturalism of Karl Barth. Interestingly, Niebuhr and Barth shared a common anti-Pietism, a suspicion of popular evangelism, and essentially discouraged the cultivation of the inner life. Often critical of what he considered to be naïve liberalism, Reinhold Niebuhr found the Keswick inspired social idealism and pacifism of figures like E. Stanley Jones particularly annoying and dangerous. Jones, in turn, would characterize the ethics of Niebuhr as owing more to the Nazis than the man from Nazareth. Among Brethren it was the Keswick-inspired William Beahm who would attack both the followers of Reinhold Niebuhr and the heirs of Dispensational premillennialism for sharing a common tendency to postpone the applications of the teachings of Jesus to a future age.

If neo-orthodoxy failed to deeply impact twentieth century Brethren piety, the older atavistic liberalism, often with a touch of the teachings and ideals of Frank Buchman, remained a constant and powerful undercurrent throughout much of the twentieth century. It played an important role in the Church of the Brethren youth movement, especially in church camps which began flourishing among increasingly affluent Brethren beginning in the late 1920s. Its most important leader was the mystic activist Dan West (1893-1971). Perhaps fittingly for the son of a man who had actually located the site of the Garden of Eden in Adams County, OH, Dan West was impatient with institutions and normal ecclesiastical conventions. His seemingly erratic behavior, sometimes caustic personality, and his not infrequent attacks upon the denomination he served would have led to dismissal in many organizations. Interestingly among Brethren, it only served to cultivate his cult-like status. A product of the early twentieth-century social gospel movement, West's favorite book was a social gospel classic by early twentieth-century Oberlin College professor Henry Churchill King, and he never escaped the hold of William James' classic essay, "The Moral Equivalent of War." Impatient with an emphasis upon religious orthodoxy, he diminished the importance of Christian thought and was frequently misunderstood as promoting the idea that Christian worship was unimportant. "Christ never asks...anybody to worship him," the Heifer Project founder insisted. As he noted in 1966, "Theology and worship patterns are important but not fundamental. Obedience is." The truth was that West deeply cared about appropriate worship. As he witnessed Brethren building costly churches with raised pulpits, choir lofts, split chancels, and crosses, he saw a retreat from gospel simplicity to mainstream respectability. Impatient with self-preoccupation, West was troubled by any excessive emphasis upon subjective religious experience. For West, the purpose of the faith community was not personal affirmation but world-wide service to those in need. In a church increasingly uncomfortable with confrontation, West was often accused of legalism, self-righteousness, and perfectionism. Nevertheless, many young people about to give up on conventional Christianity's doctrinal rigidly and cultural pettiness had their faith reinvigorated by West's broad vision of service. The power and depth of West's personal faith comes to life in a poem he wrote which was published in the *Messenger* in 1967.

> Dear Lord, my cross is heavy. The weight of it
> With other things—is bending down my head
> My knees are weak....My back and arms are sore.
> Do I have to carry it anymore?
> Couldn't I just worship yours instead? [14]

The cultural changes of the 1960s were troubling to West and many others in the Church of the Brethren. As a denomination passionately committed to national prohibition, most Brethren assumed that abstaining from alcohol was a central tenet of the gospel. During the 1950s, the Christian Education Committee of the Church of the Brethren urged youth to sign a three-part pledge. Youth agreed to abstain from the use of alcoholic beverages, tobacco, and thirdly and almost as an afterthought, commit their "life fully to Jesus Christ and His Way of Life." In effect for many, the essence of Christianity was reduced to not drinking and smoking.[15]

The reduction of Christianity to a petty legal code was the life-time concern of Grace Brethren Church leader and Grace Theological Seminary founder Alva McClain. It is hard to image a person more unlike Dan West. While West insisted that Christian doctrine was a decidedly secondary consideration, McClain actually taught a required three-year course on Christian Doctrine at Grace Theological Seminary. While West urged young people to change the world, McClain urged young people to freely accept God's grace and look forward to the truly "blessed hope" of the arrival of the Messiah to set up the just society in their midst. While West's thought was rooted in social gospel idealism and the pragmatism of William James, McClain studied under such prominent national dispensationalist figures as D. L. Moody's successor R. A. Torrey at the Bible Institute of Los Angeles and Philadelphia School of the Bible founder W. A. Pettingill. Still for all his emphasis on grace and the implicit rejection of good works, McClain insisted that the Kingdom of God was a physical and not a spiritual reality and that this Kingdom would be physically established on earth. As McClain insisted, the "liberal-social view" that the ethical and social ideals of the Old Testament prophets could be uncoupled from their eschatological element and used to establish a human society on earth here and now was the naïve hope of those who failed to understand the extent of human sin. McClain, whose thought would resurface in the 1990s among so-called progressive dispensationalists, believed that the teachings of Jesus were for present application and not merely for the millennial kingdom. True for McClain, the attainment of social justice and the abolition of war would be realized only in the kingdom supernaturally established by the coming Messiah.[16]

If McClain's ideas would play a key role in the emergence of so-called progressive dispensationalism, the neo-Anabaptist movement in the Church of the Brethren would decidedly impact evangelical and even liberal expressions of Christianity beginning in the late 1960s and continuing into the twentieth-first century. Two Bethany Theological Seminary professors, Donald Durnbaugh and Dale Brown, led a renewal in the Anabaptist identity among Brethren and in turn played a key role in the Chicago-centered community of evangelical reformers who would found *Sojourners Magazine* and lead to the formation of Evangelicals for Social Action and the evangelical feminist group, Daughters of Sarah. As defined by Durnbaugh, the Believer's Church was committed to the Lordship of Christ, authority of the Scripture, restoration of the New Testament Church, separation from the world, and belief that the Spirit of God could break through denominational barriers. Influenced as well by the 1960s youth culture, the Brethren Action Movement worked to end the US military involvement in Vietnam and against widespread liberal support in the Church of the Brethren for a lessening in denominational identity and possible merger with like-minded Protestants. While gaining wide support, the movement's ties to the counter-culture troubled many in basically conventional Protestant Christian churches. Radicalized Evangelicals who did join Church of the Brethren congregations were surprised to learn that many members in the pews seemed completely indifferent if not hostile to the social causes that had led them to the church in the first place.[17]

In effect twentieth-century Brethren continued to shape and be shaped by powerful religious currents surging across the North American religious landscape. As eighteenth-century Brethren had drawn on Pietist and Anabaptist sources and nineteenth-century Brethren were influenced by Universalism, restorationism, and evangelical currents, twentieth-century Brethren drew on Keswick spirituality and an array of other influences. For many including Wieand, the rejection of war was a central if not the central glue holding together a diverse body of Christians. As this commitment seems to wane, one can only ask what if anything separates Brethren from other well-meaning people called Methodists, Baptists or even Catholics.

Notes

1 This paper needs a disclaimer. It focuses primarily on the Church of the Brethren with some material dealing with the Brethren Church and the Grace Brethren Church. The experience of the Old Order German Baptist Brethren differs. It remains rooted in Brethren tradition and the distinctive understandings of such key nineteenth century figures as Peter Nead and Samuel Kinsey. For an introduction to these religious practices and ideas, see my essay "Theological Writings on Various Subjects: An Introduction," in Peter Nead, *Theological Writings on Various Subjects* (Dunker Springhaus Ministries, 1997). Copies are available from the author of this essay.

2 Alva J. McClain, *The Greatness of the Kingdom: An Inductive Study of the Kingdom of God* (Winona Lake, IN: BMH Books, 1974), 519.

3 David Augsburger, *Dissident Discipleship: a Spirituality of Self-Surrender, Love of God and Love of Neighbor* (Grand Rapids: Brazos Press, 2005), 7.

4 George M. Marsden, *Fundamentalism and American Culture*, 2nd edition (New York: Oxford University Press, 2006), 96. Information of Keswick's primary literature can be located in Charles Edwin Jones, *The Keswick Movement: A Comprehensive Bibliography* (Lanham,

MD: Scarecrow Press, 2007). See also Melvin E. Dieter, *The Holiness Revival of the Nineteenth Century* (Lanham, MD: Scarecrow Press, 1996); William Kostlevy, ed., *The Historical Dictionary of the Holiness Movement* (Lanham, MD: Scarecrow Press, 2009) and the pioneering essay by David B. Bundy, *Keswick; a Bibliographic Introduction* (Wilmore, KY: B. L. Fisher Library, 1975).

5 Douglas Frank, *Less Than Conquerors: How Evangelicals entered the Twentieth Century* (Grand Rapids: William B. Eerdmans, 1986), 116-120. My critique of Frank's insightful, but in my opinion flawed interpretation, is found in William Kostlevy, "Conquerors After All: Keswick—A Misunderstood Tradition," *Reflections: A Publication of the Missionary Church Historical Society* 13-14 (2011-2012), 65-72.

6 On the inroads of Keswick piety in the Brethren Church see Dale R. Stoffer, *Background and development of Brethren Doctrines, 1650-1987* (Philadelphia: Brethren Encyclopedia, 1989), 180-195.

7 Quotations from Stephen L. Longenecker, T*he Brethren during the Age of World War: The Church of the Brethren Encounter with Modernization, 1914-1950: A Source Book* (Elgin, IL: Brethren Press, 2006), 147-149.

8 William Leach, *Land of Desire: Merchants, Power, and the Rise of a New American Culture* (New York: Vintage Books, 1993, 194-202, 116. See especially Leach's discussion of "Holiness or Commercial Hospitality," 115-122.

9 A. C. Wieand, "The Higher Spiritual Life of the Church," in *Two Centuries of the Church of the Brethren, or the Beginning of the Brotherhood: Bicentennial Addresses at the Annual Conference, Held at Des Moines, Iowa, June 3-11, 1908* (Elgin, IL: Brethren Publishing House, 1908), 176.

10 Ibid, 194-195.

11 Anna B. Mow, "The Surrendered Life," *Gospel Messenger*, 10 October 1950, 14.

12 Mary Ann Moyer Kulp, *No Longer Strangers: A Biography of H. Stover Kulp* (Elgin, IL: Brethren Press, 1968), 111.

13 Donald F. Durnbaugh, *Fruit of the Vine: A History of the Brethren, 1708-1995* (Elgin, IL: Brethren Press, 1997), 540-546.

14 Glee Yoder, *Passing on the Gift: The Story of Dan West* (Elgin, IL: Brethren Press, 1978), 16-17, 84-85.

15 *My Pledge*, Christian Education Committee, General Brotherhood Board, nd.

16 McClain, *Greatness of the Kingdom*, 519-526.

17 See William Kostlevy, *Bethany Theological Seminary: A Centennial History* (Richmond, IN: Bethany Theological Seminary, 2005), 144, 146-149.

The Place Of Jesus In Brethren Spirituality

Brian H. Moore

Introduction

My purpose in this paper is to discuss the place of Jesus in Brethren spirituality. I propose to do this through a summary of historical antecedents that helped the founding Brethren formulate their ideas about Jesus, to document the founding Brethren's concepts of Jesus, to briefly follow those concepts in later Brethren life, and then to apply those concepts to some contemporary issues.

Historical Background

Movements do not begin in a vacuum. When Jesus himself apparently burst on the scene, he was preceded by the preaching of John the Baptizer in the wilderness along the River Jordan. When Jesus came, the movement was already moving. When John came, his "program" was preceded by centuries of growing restlessness and anticipation. People in those days were ready for something to happen which would bring hope and restoration to a bewildered generation. Questions raised by the leaders of the populace indicated a hunger and a curiosity, the context for John's movement (John 1:19-22). Movements do not begin in a vacuum; rather, there is continuity, a flow, a transition, sometimes rapid and abrupt, sometimes slow and gradual. But at some point in the transition something identifies that flow as an actual movement, something new. Something announces the end of the status quo. For John the Baptist, it was his baptizing and preaching; for

Jesus, it was his baptism and his preaching which announced the arrival of a change: "The time has come," he said. "The kingdom of God has come near. Repent and believe the good news!" (Mark 1:13, NIV).

Jesus lived and moved, for the most part, within the context of Judaism. He went to synagogues. He sparred with scribes, Pharisees and Sadducees, identifiable groups within Judaism. He often quoted their scriptures, which were his scriptures as well. His life, actions and teaching were perceived as a movement and thus as a threat to the status quo. This threat led the Jewish establishment to press for his execution, supposedly bringing an end to the movement.

The Church was born in the context of Judaism, on Pentecost, a Jewish feast. That movement was readily identifiable as a movement because of the unusual phenomena which accompanied it, i.e., the sounds as of a rushing wind and what seemed to be tongues of fire, a Pentecost such as had never been before and, I might add, has not been since. It was a new movement, but it had a context: within Judaism, within the season of a Jewish feast. The leaders of the movement had been, still were, and to a great extent would be, part of the Jewish system of thought and conduct. It would take some years for the new movement to shed its exclusively Jewish context, a process not without pain–and a few lapses.

When the Brethren movement began in 1708, it was embedded within a larger movement of ideas and directions that were swirling all around a particular geographical area of Europe, especially southern and western Germany and nearby Switzerland. The context of the movement included restlessness, discontentedness, a search prompted by disillusionment with the established churches, and the spiritual hungers that resulted from a "thin" spiritual diet. Ideas were tossed back and forth like beach balls at graduation ceremonies! The Reformation had occurred nearly 200 years before and with it, instability in Church and government. Governments seemed to have only one way to try to achieve stability and that was by force, i.e., war. The Thirty Years' War (1618-1648) contributed to the context of the Brethren movement. The Truce of Westphalia (1648) was not a totally successful agreement as struggles for power continued. Invasions of the area by French legions only heightened the sense of instability and fear. The Brethren movement came about during a time of political and ideological unrest. Movements do not begin in a vacuum.

The Place Of Jesus In Brethren Spirituality

We are most interested in the ideological context of the Brethren movement. Ideas were in motion that had a long history and many antecedents. A variety of reactions indicated the presence of the ideological currents that would eventually help shape the Brethren: favor by some; disagreement by some; magisterial opposition by some.

PIETISM

The Pietism of Philip Jacob Spener (1635-1705) and August Hermann Francke (1663-1727) was never the main stream of the Church. It actually was a stream *within* the main stream, an emphasis that sought to restore the main stream in matters of devotion, holiness and good works. However, a rivulet broke away from the stream of Pietism, a movement that came to be called Radical Pietism. Radical Pietism was not primarily seeking to restore or reform the Church in matters of devotion, holiness and good works; it was fired by ideas that suggested the Church was no longer the true Church and the only acceptable response was to separate oneself from it. But even Radical Pietism was an elusive movement with many contributors to it. Overall, it became a kind of web in which some common themes unified the whole:

- the "fall" of the Church
- disassociation from the fallen "Babel"
- emphasis on the new birth, the Holy Spirit and personal holiness
- emphasis on adult response to Jesus

Some proponents of Radical Pietism held a mystical and spiritualist approach, believing that direct revelation was a viable authority in matters pertaining to Christian understanding. Contributors to the Radical Pietist ideology in the Palatinate where the Brethren movement began were Matthias Baumann (ca. 1670-1727) and Johann Georg Rosenbach (1687-1747).[1] Behind the teaching and practice of these leaders stands a figure whose writings helped give substance to them all: Gottfried Arnold (1666-1714). His writings, especially *The First Love of the Community of Jesus Christ, that is: True Portrayal of the First Christians* and *Impartial History of the Church and Heretics*, helped provide a historical method for formulating one's beliefs and practices.

I have ventured into these backgrounds in order to pull out the views that address the topic under consideration. The Radical Pietists and their antecedents believed the following about Jesus:

- *Johann Arndt* (1555-1621): In addition to the standard orthodox beliefs, the Christian must look to "the 'living example' of Jesus."[2]
- *Christian Hoburg* (1607-1675): The Christian is the one who accepts Jesus' teaching and life as the only standard of Christian conduct.[3]
- *Matthias Baumann*: "The leadership of the church is incumbent upon Christ alone, and not on the secular authorities or the office-holders ordained by the churches. . . . Baumann's understanding of discipleship. . . .accentuated concrete obedience to the letter of Scripture."[4]
- *Johann Georg Rosenbach*: "In the center of his views stands the concept of the 'living imitation of Christ'. . . . As far as the proper standard for the imitation is concerned, Rosenbach refers with striking regularity to the Sermon on the Mount."[5]
- *Gottfried Arnold*: "Christians have been given an example of how they are to walk in a holy manner in this world through Christ's words and deeds. Discipleship to Christ is based on having Christ live within and is expressed in a Christ-like life."[6]
- *Ernst Christoph Hochmann von Hochenau* (1670-1721): "For him, Jesus' life was the definitive standard of faith. The life of Jesus, he writes, is placed before the believers 'by God as an example to be imitated *in everything*'." Hochmann also drew upon the views of Menno Simons (1496-1561) in rejecting infant baptism.[7]
- The Radical Pietists "oriented themselves on the life of Jesus and the congregational practice of the first Christians as their model and guiding principle."[8]

As an aside on our subject of the place of Jesus in Brethren spirituality, let me insert that the Brethren disassociated themselves from the Radical Pietists on three of their views in particular: One, that the church was a spiritual organism and required no outward rites or recognition; two, that revelation was attainable through mystical experiences and thus subjective; and three, that the Kingdom of God was utterly imminent and that believers would establish the reign of God upon earth, a kind of postmillennialism before its time.

The Place Of Jesus In Brethren Spirituality

ANABAPTISM/MENNONITES

The specific role of the Anabaptists (by then, Mennonites) in the spiritual formation of the Brethren is not entirely clear, even after the monumental research projects of Dale Stoffer and Marcus Meier devoted to the origins and development of Brethren thought. That there was interaction between the early Brethren and the Mennonites, especially Andreas Boni and Alexander Mack, has been substantiated, but how much influence these contacts had is somewhat cloudy. That there was harmony between their views seems clear, except on the issue of baptism, the Brethren insisting on immersion and the Mennonites comparatively indifferent to mode. The harmony is most evident in the preeminence of Jesus in their thought, "the admonition to follow the example and teachings of Christ and His apostles (being) a constant refrain in Mennonite literature."[9] Surely the Mennonites contributed to Brethren ecclesiology as well as to a Christocentric hermeneutic, i.e., that all Scripture points to Jesus and proper interpretation begins with understanding Jesus as the key to understanding Scripture. Whereas Radical Pietism emphasized personal and individual spirituality, the Mennonites provided an emphasis on an outward and corporate spirituality. The Brethren would seek to wed these two emphases, but always with Jesus as the focus of life and practice. The Brethren would leave Radical Pietism for reasons noted above, but they would not join the Mennonites because they felt that the Mennonites of their day had lost the vision of the first Anabaptists. They would seek to retain the Anabaptist understanding of the Church and the emphasis on community as well as discipleship. The Brethren would overlap both Anabaptist and Radical Pietist thought with their emphases on obedience to Jesus and following him as example in life.

THE BRETHREN

The pioneer Brethren, led by Alexander Mack Sr. (1679-1735), were influenced heavily by Radical Pietism and, in fact, identified themselves with it. Of particular significance for the Brethren was Ernst Christoph Hochmann von Hochenau, whose preaching and teaching set him apart as the foremost Radical Pietist of that time and place. He was a friend of Gottfried Arnold and of Alexander Mack Sr. and had great influence upon Mack's thought. On one of Hochmann's preaching tours, passing through Schriesheim, Germany, Hochmann met Mack who offered the use of a large room in his mill as a meeting place. Alexander Mack was one of "the restless ones," and his conversations with Hochmann helped him formulate his ideas on what constituted the true Church, although he was a committed Radical Pietist before he met Hochmann.

But Radical Pietism was not a well-rounded Christian view according to the mind of Alexander Mack. While emphasizing Jesus as the standard for life and obedience, it did not seek to establish a community in which obedience could be practiced. It was too private. So the Brethren broke with Radical Pietism, citing a kind of "live and let live" attitude among them.[10] The Brethren were ready to create a movement, to begin a new stream, or rather, to find in their thinking, the old stream of the true Church and give it its proper channel once again. In order to understand what the Church was, they consulted Scripture and early church histories, believing that the true Church existed until the "fall," an idea conscripted from Gottfried Arnold, the theologian of Radical Pietism. They believed in radical obedience to Jesus, and this would be initially demonstrated by following the "mighty example" of Jesus in baptism.[11] As Meier states, the Brethren "were of the opinion that the directives of the New Testament, including Jesus' commandment to perform baptism, were to be followed in a literal sense."[12] The Brethren were literalists in their usage of the Scriptures, but that did not make them legalists, as some have suggested. They were strong in their convictions about obedience: "The true believers and lovers of the Lord Jesus have always looked stedfastly [sic] and singlemindedly [sic] to their Lord and Master in all things."[13]

Even a slight perusal of the writings of the early Brethren, as well as those of later years, indicates a high priority given to baptism. One would think that all that mattered to the Brethren then and down through the years was baptism: at what age (believer's baptism); where (flowing stream?); and especially how (mode). Baptism became "front and center" of the Brethren movement, first, because it identified the activity as a bona fide movement, and second, because it was an act of defiance of the state, true civil disobedience. The act of baptism in the Eder River in 1708 was the outward expression of what had been forming within them for a number of years. The outward nature of baptism accounts for the controversies with which they became engaged. Infant baptism represented union with the state, the status quo; adult baptism represented a break with a centuries-old practice, an embedded tradition, with the generally understood idea of what constituted citizenship. Baptism commands such a prominent role among the early Brethren because it, more than anything else, demonstrated one's willingness to follow Jesus. Following Jesus was of first importance, regardless of the cost. The act of baptism demonstrated that they were leaving "Christendom" (that overarching, controlling, tradition-bound institution) in favor of a simple and unvarnished following of Jesus, his example and his words, a simple but hardy obedience.

Basic radical discipleship, then, was the identifying mark of the Brethren, a trait that would mark our existence from that time on. While the Brethren often courted and sometimes adopted a variety of views about issues of the faith, this trait has been the anchor of our persuasion from the beginning. Echoes of the earliest Brethren beliefs can be found in the writings of all generations since then: Alexander Mack Jr., Peter Nead, B. F.Moomaw, J. Allen Miller, Floyd Mallott, Vernard Eller, Richard Allison, Jerry Flora, Dale Stoffer, and Brenda Colijn, to name a few. Newcomers to the scene like Jason Barnhart and Bill Ludwig are following in their steps. They all would concur with the statement of Paul to the Corinthians which was the life-verse of Menno Simons: "For no one can lay any foundation other than the one already laid, which is Jesus Christ" (I Corinthians 3:11, NIV). In late 2012, the (Ashland) Brethren called a small group of leaders together to begin a process of restating the core of the Brethren faith. The early summary is in keeping with the place of Jesus throughout our history. The outline states in part one that we are a "Christ-Centered People: a People of Word and Spirit; a People in Community; Following Jesus Together." The outline further states in part two that we are "A Kingdom People: People of Loving Obedience; People of Pilgrimage; People of Holistic Witness."[14] The conveners intend that selected authors will expand on the points and sub-points of the outline in order to produce a book that will be used in a variety of applications. The stated purpose of "Operation Bull Moose" is "to engage culture with what it means to be Brethren in order to have Kingdom impact on the world."[15] I will use that purpose statement as a segue to the final section of this paper.

Contemporary Considerations

The first consideration is a question: Which Jesus? One contemporary author has composed a list of hybrid-Jesuses that reflects the way many folks tend to perceive him: "the white supremacist Jesus, the Eurocentric

Jesus, the Republican or Democrat Jesus, the capitalist or communist Jesus, the slave-owning Jesus, the nuclear bomb-dropping America-first Jesus, the organ-music stained-glass nostalgic-sentimental Jesus, the anti-science know-nothing simpleton Jesus, the prosperity-gospel get-rich-quick Jesus . . . the Joe-Six-Pack Jesus, the anti-Semitic Nazi Jesus, the anti-Muslim Crusader Jesus, and so on."[16] The point he is trying to make is that we tend to make Jesus into the image of ourselves, hating what we hate and liking what we like. He goes on to state that "the one I believe to be the real Jesus–the Jesus of Matthew, Mark, Luke, and John, the Jesus of Acts, the letters, and Revelation, too . . . cannot be (so easily) understood and must not be trimmed to fit our preferred framework."[17] That there is only one Jesus, we would all agree; but we may not agree on which facet of this multi-faceted person we should emphasize. The earliest Brethren supremely thought of Jesus as Lord, emphasizing his authority and his right to command, and our role as his subjects whose duty is to obey. He is "an all-powerful Monarch and King" whose "statutes and laws" are to be obeyed.[18] I believe this emphasis was required in their context because of the need to defend their position regarding baptism and the beginning of a breakaway movement. What they really sought was to have the mind of Christ, to align themselves with "the disposition of Christ"[19] The Pietist influences in their origins provided a devotional approach, a relational approach to faith. This prevented their being overpowered with a Jesus of law and code. In the Brethren, Anabaptist and Pietist converge, Anabaptism presenting a stout discipleship and Pietism presenting a warm-hearted devotion, both expressions of the same Jesus who, on one hand, bid his followers to take up the cross of death and then, on the other, told them they were his friends and he loved them as the Father loved him. The Brethren sought to know "the Jesus of Matthew, Mark, Luke, and John, the Jesus of Acts, the letters, and Revelation, too" with a simple approach to knowing him and a singular desire to please him. The question, Which Jesus? would have made no sense to them. The Jesus of Scripture was quite accessible to any who sought to do his will, to any who had no other agenda than to listen to his voice and obey that voice. Neither could they have conceived of a Jesus who was actually different from the Jesus of the written record, any Jesus for whom such expressions as virgin birth or whose miracles were only metaphor for something else. To them, it was not a question of finding him; it was a question of following him.[20] That simplicity of approach is to be commended in our day when scholarship may have displaced discipleship in our theological task. In the words of N. T. Wright, "Simply Jesus" is our goal.[21]

A second consideration is the Brethren approach to Jesus in the light of "the new radicalism." A wave of emphasis on the radical nature of Jesus' demands has been rolling across the Church scene in recent years. Messages from such speakers and writers as Francis Chan, Shane Claiborne, David Platt and Kyle Idleman are challenging comfortable and compromised Christianity.[22] They are using new terms to react to what was popularly known as "easy believism" or "cheap grace" a generation or two ago. As Phyllis Tickle has remarked, every now and again the Church needs to clean out its attic and have a rummage sale.[23] The "radicals" have gotten on their "work clothes," brought moving dollies, dumpsters and brooms, and are proceeding to clean out the Church's attic. It is, they believe, filled with "appealing, comfortable, and convenient" Christianity.[24] "These teachers want us to see that following Christ genuinely, truly, really, radically, sacrificially, inconveniently, and uncomfortably will *cost* us."[25] Place that sentence alongside this one: "The true believers and lovers of the Lord Jesus have always looked stedfastly [sic] and singlemindedly [sic] to their Lord and Master in all things."[26] The Brethren in their way and time were trying to "clean out the attic" of the Church, ridding it of its corruption, deception and needless accumulations. To do so, they needed to "count the cost," for "the demand for faithful obedience. . . is the pivotal point of Brethren thought."[27]

So, the "new" radicalism isn't so new after all! In fact, the Anabaptists of the 1520s are referred to as "The Radicals" and their movement "The Radical Reformation." The Brethren have their roots in that movement as well as that of *Radical* Pietism. Both influences were "radical"! They all wanted to return to the root of Christian faith and the root of the true Church, goals similar to that of the "new radicals." If our spirituality in the twenty-first century is true to the zeal of our forefathers in the faith, we will always be "the radicals."

This leads to a third consideration: Brethren witness in a postmodern and now a post-secular age. By post-secular, we are recognizing that, for all the effort at producing an official godlessness in society, spirituality will not go away. Much of the new spirituality is not Christian, but the search provides the Brethren with an opportunity for witness. From Pietistic influences, the Brethren had garnered a mystical aspect to their faith, not that they depended on the Holy Spirit to be their sole or even primary revelator, but that they were unwilling to reduce their faith to cold, hard logic. They were not illogical or irrational, but they saw the Jesus way as a life, not a system of doctrine and especially not a creed. They saw Jesus as a storyteller, but more than that, they saw him as one who was helping to write their story. Theirs was a narrative theology.[28] The life that was emerging among them was more relational than doctrinal. They counted it a privilege to be included in the life of Jesus, a privilege that was expressed through joyful obedience.[29] This seems highly adaptable to our culture where "religion" is taboo and "church" gets blank stares or mild scorn. We witness to this generation, not by highlighting our distinctiveness or making doctrinal statements that make sense only to us, but we witness by living the story, "using words if necessary," according to Francis of Assisi. Then, when appropriate, tell our story. Let it be a narrative witness, remembering that even though it is our story, it's not really about us. Our story ultimately points to Jesus. To expand upon an illustration from a recent conversation, when someone enters the Brethren "house" they may remark upon the inviting smell of a delicious meal being prepared. Only after they have begun to enjoy the meal of Brethren life do they inquire about the recipes and may even request access to those recipes. That's when the witness moves from relational to propositional. There really is a recipe responsible for this attractive meal! To change imagery, there is a solid skeleton, i.e., theology, in this body, but the skeleton does not draw attention to itself and may not be readily visible. But after a warm hug, the other knows there are muscles and bones within this body known as Brethren. Our first witness is to offer the hug or to emit the aroma of Jesus, to be who we say we are.

A fourth consideration in the light of the place of Jesus in Brethren spirituality is the question of pluralism. In our enlightened world where information, both in content and availability, is overwhelming, it seems extremely narrow to believe that Jesus is the only true Savior. In our day of tolerance and respect (for nearly every view *except* the Christian view), it seems extremely bigoted to claim the exclusivity of Jesus. But pluralism is an ancient problem. In the Old Testament, Israel was emphatically told not to court any other religion, for Yahweh was the only true God! Israel's downfall as a nation came about because they failed to honor Yahweh as the only true God. The state churches of the early Brethren's day did not have a problem with pluralism (except the three recognized churches did not tolerate each other!): the state enforced the uniqueness of Jesus (or at least Christendom). The Brethren did not have other-than-Christian on the menu. I am implying that the early Brethren may not help us with this question: Is Jesus the only way to God?

While it may appear to be reductionist and superficial, the question becomes: Is Jesus really who he says he is? If he is "God's only Son,"[30] that surely makes him unique. If he was raised from the dead, that surely makes him unique. On further thought, perhaps the early Brethren do help us with this question. Their single-minded and wholehearted devotion to Jesus would make the pluralistic question seem preposterous. They would not have entertained the question of Jesus being one among many; perhaps the primary reason we would entertain the question at all is because the exclusivist view is constantly challenged and is quite unpopular. Taking a strong position on the exclusive nature and claims of Jesus does not mean that there is nothing to learn from others' faith traditions or that God has not left a witness among them, as well. But it does insist that "in these last days (God) has spoken (aorist tense, indicating finality) to us by his Son" (Hebrews 1:2, NIV). "In the beginning was the Word" and that Word is also God's final Word!

A fifth consideration is what I am calling the Brethren and the National Rifle Association. Of course, I am not addressing the political issues in which our administration and the NRA and many other gun-toting freedom-fighters are involved. I am only indicating the long-standing Brethren emphasis on Jesus' way of peace in the midst of a culture of violence and murder. Amid the polarities reflected in hard-line posters and government pressure to pass gun legislation, amid the political rhetoric propelled by mass murders, stands a Jesus who speaks peace to a troubled society. All the gun-talk is superficial; the issue at root is the condition of the heart. "Don't take your guns to town, son; leave your guns at home, Bill," but don't get into a fist fight, either! The peaceful spirit is primary. Arguments and counter-arguments will continue *ad infinitum,* but the voice of Jesus stands above the noise of these battles and speaks peace as the better way. The Brethren knew that Jesus' Kingdom was not of this world. Earthly kingdoms rise and fall, but the Kingdom of God endures forever. All power was available to Jesus to overthrow Pilate, Rome and all, but "he opened not his mouth." The Kingdom comes "not with swords loud clashing, nor roll of stirring drums" but by "deeds of love and mercy." And thus shall it ever be. Our Brethren forefathers bequeathed this perspective to us because they saw the futility of war, and they saw Jesus as the Prince of Peace.

A sixth consideration is the matter of joyful obedience. The Brethren sought to follow Jesus in the spirit of the psalmist whose "delight (was) in the law of the Lord" (Psalm 1:2, NIV). Theirs was not the spirit of a reluctant obedience to a tyrannical overlord; theirs was the joy of being counted worthy to be his followers and even to suffer in his name. They could even liken it to a delicious repast: "The food of the new creation . . . is true obedience to the Lord Jesus."[31] Their study of Jesus, i.e., Christology, was not an abstract approach, but rather it was Jesus for "edification, enjoyment of salvation, godliness."[32] A modern writer concurs when she said, "So here is where I finish my rough Christology, by reminding myself and us together that Christ is a mystery best approached with humility *and by way of participation and experience,* poetry and song, communion and love-creating, and only secondarily approached with reason and words."[33]

Joyful obedience needs to be the spirit of the Brethren these days. We need to recover the hardiness of discipleship combined with a joyful countenance! Let our eyes and faces tell the world that there is joy in the journey of following Jesus! We are told that the new generation of believers wants to "feel its faith," rather than just "know" it. If so, I believe the Brethren have an opportunity here because we offer both experience and information.

Summary

Drawing from Radical and Anabaptist resources, the Brethren carved their own way through the wilderness of this world and have left us, their descendents, a trail worthy to be followed. The Brethren began as a people focused steadfastly on Jesus. They had no other desire except to please him by faithful obedience. Even what may appear to us as serious deviations from the original vision were derivatives of seeking to be faithful followers of Jesus in the world. Their insistence and lengthy elaborations on the ordinances of the church were expressions of seeking to be faithful to Jesus. The challenges for the Brethren in the twenty-first century are many and difficult, but adherence to the original desire of the Brethren will sustain us through troubled times. That desire will keep us searching the Scriptures together, seeking to know how to bring the life of Jesus among us to bear on the issues around us. If we are true to that vision, even if we must suffer for it, we shall offer our world what people are deeply seeking: a voice of certainty, a people of community, a life of simplicity, and a way of service and peace, even as our Lord and Master taught us.

A BENEDICTION

Finally, Brethren, let us receive a benediction from William Knepper, one of the Brethren who was held captive in the Jülich prison for nearly four years. He had come to America, and on his deathbed (1755), he wrote a testament to his family. It begins like this:

> [May] Jesus Christ, the bright-shining morning star, the root and offspring of David, enlighten and penetrate the foundation of your hearts, that we may be a light in the Lord, and be filled with the spirit. Amen.[34]

Notes

1 For a full discussion of contributors to Radical Pietist thought, see Marcus Meier, *The Origin of the Schwarzenau Brethren*, Dennis L. Slabaugh, trans. (Philadelphia, PA: Brethren Encyclopedia, Inc., 2008), 39-51.

2 Ibid., 104.

3 Ibid.

4 Ibid., 46-47.

5 Ibid., 48-49.

6 Dale Stoffer, *Background and Development of Brethren Doctrines, 1650-1987* (Philadelphia, PA: Brethren Encyclopedia, Inc., 1989), 31. The Brethren garnered much more from Arnold in their belief system, but this quote summarizes the place of Jesus in Arnold's spirituality.

7 Meier, *Schwarzenau Brethren*, 51. Emphasis supplied by Meier.

8 Ibid., 42.

9 Stoffer, *Brethren Doctrines*, 52.

10 William R. Eberly, ed., *The Complete Writings of Alexander Mack* (Winona Lake, IN: BMH Books, 1991), 38.

11 Ibid., 48.

12 Meier, *Schwarzenau Brethren*, 72. The "literal" is in contrast with the "spiritual" baptism of Johann Dippel and Christoph Seebach.

13 Eberly, *Complete Writings*, 62.

14 Notes from what has been dubbed "Operation Bull Moose."

15 Ibid.

16 Brian D. McLaren, *A New Kind of Christianity: Ten Questions That Are Transforming Our Faith* (New York: HarperOne, 2010), 122.

17 Ibid., 126.

18 Eberly, *Complete Writings*, 44-45.

19 Dale W. Brown, *Another Way of Believing: A Brethren Theology* (Elgin, IL: Brethren Press, 2005), 105, 89.

20 See Stuart Murray, *The Naked Anabaptist: The Bare Essentials of a Radical Faith* (Scottdale, PA: Herald Press, 2010), 56-59.

21 N. T. Wright, *Simply Jesus: A New Vision of Who He Was, What He Did, and Why He Matters* (New York, NY: HarperCollins), 2011.

22 Matthew Lee Anderson, "Here Come the Radicals!", *Christianity Today* (March 2013).

23 Phyllis Tickle, *The Great Emergence: How Christianity is Changing and Why* (Grand Rapids, MI: Baker Books, 2008), 19.

24 Anderson, "Here Come the Radicals!", n.p.

25 Ibid., emphasis Anderson's.

26 Eberly, *Complete Writings*, 62.

27 Meier, *Schwarzenau Brethren*, 86.

28 See *www.gotquestions.org/narrative-theology.html* Some of the thought expressed here is quite compatible with Brethren thinking, e.g., the emphasis on the necessity of community. For an extended investigation of how theology is to be lived as well as understood, I also recommend Kevin J. Vanhoozer, *The Drama of Doctrine: A Canonical-Linguistic Approach to Christian Theology* (Louisville, KY: Westminster-John Knox Press, 2005).

29 W. F. Groff, "Christology" in *The Brethren Encyclopedia*.

30 John 1:14, 16; 3:16, NRSV.

31 Eberly, *Complete Writings*, 36.

32 Stoffer, *Brethren Doctrines*, 3.

33 Laura Stone, "A Brief History of Christology," *Brethren Life and Thought* 57 (Fall 2012): 55. Emphasis mine.

34 Donald F. Durnbaugh, ed. *The Brethren in Colonial America* (Elgin, IL: The Brethren Press, 1967), 560. I would also recommend the entirety of the section, "Devotional Writings," 548-596.

Afterword

After months of research and writing on the subject of "The Place of Jesus in Brethren Spirituality," and after presenting my findings at the Brethren World Assembly, I feel as though a kind of disclaimer is in order. I have tried to be faithful to the earliest Brethren, but I realize in hindsight that it may be nearly impossible for someone who is 300 years distant to truly represent their spiritual life under the lordship of Jesus. Such an intimacy occurs in a context so real to them but so unreal to us that we can hardly recreate it. Research can, at best, only discover and relate indicators of their faith, but it cannot recreate it or even express it. Research is like putting the pieces of a jigsaw puzzle together; perhaps all the pieces fit nicely (which is no small achievement!), but the picture itself is not alive. It is still a picture. Such "reporting" as I have done has a large measure of coldness and formality to it, whereas the earliest Brethren had a devotion to Jesus which was passionate and single-minded. The best we can do is reference it. No, the best we can do is live it, just as they did in their time and place. That, after all, is likely the goal of the Fifth Brethren World Assembly.

Word and Spirit in Brethren Spirituality

Brenda B. Colijn

Introduction

Investigating the concept of Word and Spirit in Brethren spirituality is faced at the outset with two tasks—namely, defining Word and Spirit and figuring out what counts as spirituality. The task of definition is deceptively simple: *Word and Spirit* is a way of referring to the Bible and the Holy Spirit, understood in relation to one another. However, the concept of Word and Spirit appears in Brethren writings in several different contexts—as sources of authority for doctrine and practice; as guides for Christian living and decision making; as a model of congregational life; and even as what other traditions would call *means of grace*—that is, agents of God's transforming power in the life of the church and the individual. I should clarify at the outset that when I say *Word and Spirit* I am not referring simply to what Brethren believe about the Bible and what Brethren believe about the Holy Spirit. Instead, I mean a concept in which the Bible and the Spirit are understood to work together to testify to Jesus Christ.

Furthermore, focusing on spirituality is complicated by the holistic character of Brethren faith. Brethren have seldom differentiated between theology and spirituality in their writings, and in any case, they usually would be suspicious of any theology that is not firmly wedded to practice. The Word/Spirit dynamic tends to be more explicit in their theological writings than in their devotional writings, but in the last analysis, for the Brethren, both doctrine and devotion are about following Jesus. So in true Brethren spirit, while I will focus on the spiritual life, I will not be overly careful to separate spirituality from theology—a distinction that is a modern Western innovation in any case.

Put briefly, Word and Spirit shape the spirituality of the Brethren by centering them on Jesus Christ and enabling them to follow him. Brethren spirituality traditionally is a spirituality of discipleship, understood as a process of growth in Christlikeness, both individual and corporate, through obedience to the command and example of Christ and the apostles, as directed by the indwelling Holy Spirit. Scripture provides the content of the spiritual life, while the Holy Spirit provides its motivation and power. The Bible, especially the New Testament, reveals God's character and will. However, the Holy Spirit, who inspired the Bible, brings about the awakening, the new birth, and the illumination without which the Bible would remain a dead letter. The Spirit also communicates to believers the love of God, which gives them both the desire and the strength to obey. Sometimes Brethren hold Word and Spirit in balance, while at other times the balance tips in one direction or the other.

Brethren Inheritances

From the main body of Christian tradition, the early Brethren received their understanding of the person and work of the Holy Spirit, as well as their faith in the Bible as foundational for faith and practice. They also were likely influenced by the Reformed idea that the inner witness of the Spirit confirms the authority of Scripture. From Anabaptism they inherited—oddly, enough, by way of Pietism—a model of religious authority known as the Inner and Outer Words. In this model, Scripture is the Outer Word, the objective, written record of God's revelation. The Holy Spirit is the Inner Word, who indwells believers and gives them experiential knowledge of God. In their relationship to each other, Word and Spirit are interdependent: the Spirit inspired and interprets the Scriptures, while the Scriptures provide concrete examples and controls for following the leading of the Spirit. Inner and Outer Words together enable believers to discern God's will. Most importantly, both the Outer Word and the Inner Word testify to the Living Word, Jesus Christ, who is the supreme revelation of God, and whom believers follow as Lord and Savior:

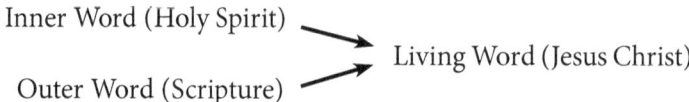

In this model, the inner voice of the Spirit serves as a source of authority in its own right, witnessing to the truth of the gospel and facilitating the believer's relationship with God. In theory, the Inner and Outer Words provide a balanced and consistent witness, because the Spirit who inspired the Scriptures would not later contradict them.

Anabaptist groups were not always successful in maintaining this balance, however, and the excesses of some of the more "Spirit-led" groups caused later Mennonites to place more emphasis on the Word.[1] The Brethren followed a similar trajectory. From an early balance between Word and Spirit, the Brethren moved toward a greater emphasis on the Word to reinforce the boundaries of the community against the threat of acculturation and accommodation to the world. For these later Brethren, the Spirit seems to be ancillary to the Word. Rather than being an independent source of authority, the Spirit serves to direct believers to Scripture, which contains the laws for the Christian to obey:

Holy Spirit ⟶ Scripture ⟶ Laws of Christ ⟶ Jesus Christ

Law language is pervasive in Brethren tradition, but its context seems to undergo some changes in the nineteenth century.

It would be tempting to treat the Brethren's struggle to balance Word and Spirit as an instance of their struggle to integrate their dual heritage in Anabaptism (the Word) and Pietism (the Spirit), but that would be an oversimplification. Pietists as well as Anabaptists had to address the relationship between the inner, more subjective dimension of the faith and its outward expression. For Pietists, the Bible was the sourcebook for ecclesial and personal renewal, while the Spirit was the power of transformation at work in individuals, small groups, and communities. Like the Anabaptists, the Pietists insisted on regeneration by the Holy Spirit as the only basis for a full understanding of Scripture or an authentic Christian life. The Spirit and the Bible together propelled their warm devotional life as well as their commitment to social action. In their understandings of the church, however, Pietists and Anabaptists parted company. Anabaptists opted for the Word in their conviction that they must form a separated fellowship on the model of the New Testament, while the Pietists largely chose to emphasize the fellowship of the Spirit across existing denominational traditions.

Brethren Spirituality

Although the early Brethren followed the Anabaptists in their understanding of the church, their Pietist inheritance heavily influenced their spirituality through their hymnbooks, as Hedda Durnbaugh has pointed out in her study of the German hymnody of the Brethren.[2] The title page of the Brethren's first hymnbook announces its interest in both Word and Spirit by describing itself as the "Spirit-filled hymnbook for all souls who love the truth."[3] The second hymnbook organized the hymns according to a rubric adapted from an Inspirationist hymnbook but changed the category called "Of the Divine Word" to "Of the Inner and Outer Word."[4]

Many of the Brethren's disputes with other groups, as well as their own internal struggles, can be explained as disagreements about how to balance Word and Spirit. They split from Radical Pietism because they wanted to strike a balance between the experience of the Spirit and the commands of Christ. They believed that the Holy Spirit was leading them to form a visible church so that they could carry out God's will as revealed in the New Testament. As they expressed it in the "Open Letter" of 1708, one of them had experienced "a strong agitation of the heart" and others were "moved in their consciences" to "be baptized according to the teachings of Jesus Christ and the apostles."[5]

In most of their disputes the Brethren were reacting to some variety of enthusiasm, so they tended to emphasize the Word over the Spirit. For example, they praised the Quakers' devotion and emphasis on the Spirit but argued that the biblical ordinances of baptism and the Lord's Supper could not be spiritualized away. Similarly, they were attracted to the Ephrata community because of its lively experience of the Spirit, but they were also cautious about the group because of their commitment to test spiritual experiences by the norm of Scripture. (For their part, the Ephrata group claimed that the Brethren were founded on the letter, while they were founded on the Spirit.[6]) Later, the Brethren were suspicious of revivalism because it emphasized instant conversions rather than counting the cost of following Jesus, and it valued emotional spiritual experiences over faithful obedience to the commands of Christ.

The Brethren, however, could also chide other groups for spiritual lethargy. Although he praised the lifestyle of the Mennonites of his day—relative to the lifestyles evident in other groups—Alexander Mack regarded them as "deteriorated Baptists" who not only failed to practice the ordinances according to the New Testament but who also had lost the spiritual zeal of the original Anabaptists.[7] Even the divisions of the Brethren in the later nineteenth century can be attributed to an unresolved tension between Word and Spirit, although in that case those who took their stand on the written Word looked not only to Scripture but also to the minutes of Annual Meeting, while the spirit demonstrated by the more aggressive proponents of reform was not always the Holy Spirit.

THE EARLY BRETHREN

Brethren were confronted with the problem of the balance between Word and Spirit from the outset of their movement. Against the Inspirationist Eberhard Gruber, for example, Alexander Mack had to defend the decision to form a visible church rather than affirming the "new economy . . . of the pure spirit."[8] Against the charge of legalism, he insisted that the Brethren had reestablished outward practices in response to the inner voice, the voice of Christ in the heart, and they had received the inward assurance that their actions were correct.[9] However, he argued that no miraculous manifestations of the Spirit were necessary to justify following the commands of Christ in the New Testament.[10]

Perhaps in reaction to Radical Pietism, Mack's spirituality is very Word-centered. The Holy Spirit, while essential, is very much in the background. The commands and examples contained in the Scriptures are laws established by God, the great king or the good householder, who will punish the slightest disobedience.[11] In practical terms, there is no distinction between the laws and the Law-giver, because "God and His spoken Word are completely one."[12] Similarly, Jesus Christ is the New Covenant ruler or true householder who has recorded his laws in his testament, which he confirmed with his blood.[13] These New Covenant laws must be obeyed even more scrupulously than the old ones were.[14]

The importance of obedience in Mack's spirituality cannot be overstated. Saving faith "must produce works of obedience." Faith in Christ "produces obedience and submission to all of His words and commandments." Obedience is the evidence that one has experienced the new birth.[15] In a statement that would make many Protestants cringe, Mack even asserts that believers "achieve eternal life by obedience."[16] However, this claim is not a defense of works-righteousness but a sober warning that faithlessness to Christ will lead to loss of salvation.

Mack's relentless emphasis on obedience to the written Word is saved from legalism by several factors. First, it comes from a profound conviction of the sovereignty of God and the Lordship of Christ. Obedience is not an attempt to curry favor with God, who needs nothing from human beings, but the only proper response to an Almighty God and loving Father who has acted only for the good of humanity.[17] The metaphor of God or Christ as king also makes a political claim: believers are citizens of Christ's kingdom of righteousness and peace, rather than citizens of the corrupt and violent kingdoms of the world.

Second, the focus of obedience ultimately is not the Outer Word but the Living Word, Jesus himself. The New Testament commands are important because they are the teachings *of Jesus*. The Word that believers follow is "Jesus and that which he taught."[18] Conversion is "enter[ing] the teaching of the Lord Jesus" or even "enter[ing] the state of marriage with Christ in His teachings and ordinances."[19] As disciples, believers must "look singly and alone to their Lord and Master," and they find "the image of Jesus in His teaching and His mighty example."[20]

Third, obedience makes transformation possible. It forms believers in the will of Christ and, as the "food of the new creation," fosters growth in Christ.[21] Fourth, only obedience provides solid grounds for peace of mind and assurance of salvation: "God ordered through His Son that [certain] simple things be done. If man does them in true faith and in obedience holds his reason captive, he will gradually become single-minded and childlike. It is just in this single-mindedness that the soul again finds rest, peace, and security."[22] Finally, obedience is motivated by love, "love for this heavenly King and His holy teaching."[23]

When Mack directly addresses the relationship between Word and Spirit in *Rights and Ordinances*, he describes them as outward and inward witnesses that always agree: "Now the Scriptures are only an outward testimony of those things which were once taught and commanded by the Holy Spirit. . . . Since there is one Spirit and only one, then this holy and unique Spirit cannot will other than that which He willed for salvation many hundred years ago. That which the Holy Spirit ordained for the faithful was written outwardly. All believers are united in it, for the Holy Spirit teaches them inwardly just as the Scriptures teach them outwardly." Mack supports the congruence between inward and outward witnesses by an allusion to the prophecy of the New Covenant in Jeremiah 31: "This law which is inwardly written by the Spirit of God is completely identical with that which is outwardly written in the New Testament."[24]

Word and Spirit are agents of the reign of Christ, who rules over believers "by His Spirit through the commandments which He had left behind in written form." Word and Spirit also empower the Christian life: a believer "reads the Scriptures in faith and hears the inner word of life which gives him strength and power to follow Jesus." Without that Inner Word, the Outer Word remains a "dead letter." But the Spirit will never guide contrary to the commandments of God.[25]

The ordinances demonstrate how the guidance of Word and Spirit works out in practice. The outward form of baptism is meaningless without the inward work of the Holy Spirit. Regeneration requires believers to be born of both water *and* Spirit. The Spirit gives believers the inner motivation to follow the biblical command. But without the outward obedience, the persuasion of the Holy Spirit is in vain.[26] Similarly, the proper administration of the ban depends upon both the process outlined in the New Testament and the counsel of the Holy Spirit through the church.[27]

Mack's hymn "Counting the Cost," which appeared in the 1720 Brethren hymnal, shows the Inner/Outer Word dynamic throughout. Jesus created his church through his Word, which provides the example of Christ for believers to follow (stanzas 1-2). The Holy Spirit fills believers and brings them to maturity in Christ (stanza 4). Word and Spirit together develop in believers the mind of Christ: "Arise, dear soul . . ., the time is now to stem the evil, for Christ himself goes into battle against those who will not listen to him in his outer and inner word. But those who do, have the mind of Christ" (stanza 13). In one instance, however, responding to the Radical Pietist demand for a sign, Mack opts for the Word: "Whoever believes in the word of God will not demand a sign . . ." (stanza 10). Those who demanded that Jesus give them a sign were reprimanded: "Their hearts had to be directed towards faith in God and his word, as the writings of Moses and the prophets directed towards Christ, the light" (stanza 11).[28]

Another Brethren hymn in the same hymnal agrees with Mack that love is the motivation for obedience:

This night we come imploring
Our hearts be set aflame,
That we may grow in love

For Thee, our Lord, more dearly,
Obey Thy Word sincerely,
Directed from above.²⁹

The heavenly direction may imply the ministry of the Holy Spirit. A third hymn similarly casts discipleship in terms of Spirit, obedience, and love:

And now, Lord Jesus, finally
May Thy good Spirit outpoured be,
Thy grace and might displaying;
And thus shall we in this hour start
To live like Thee, with the whole heart
Thy holy love obeying.³⁰

The generation that follows Alexander Mack continues to insist on obedience to the Word but embeds this in a more experiential spirituality, with a correspondingly greater emphasis on the ministry of the Spirit. For example, a tract possibly written by Alexander Mack Jr., *A Humble Gleam of the Despised Little Light of the Truth which is in Christ*, expresses a humble confidence in the Brethren's knowledge of the truth by experience:

[I]t was only our desire to witness in childlike simplicity to that which we are being taught under the guidance of Jesus Christ, the initiator and fulfiller of our faith in the days of our pilgrimage through real experience. Otherwise, although we cannot deny that in regards to the things of which we speak we have been taught by a real experience, we cannot and will not pretend that our experience is higher than it is in itself. We do not wish to call the beginning of the way of Christian teaching the end, because possibly we have not yet reached its end.

Nevertheless, the author believes that their experience has brought them to the truth—that is, "the eternal truth which is Christ himself."³¹

According to the author, the Spirit and the Word testify to Christ and facilitate the believer's relationship with Christ. The Brethren love the New Testament and the commands of Christ because they are "spirit and life." They obey those commands out of love for Christ, whose Spirit recorded them in Scripture. Thus, in a sense, when they obey the command to baptize, they are obeying the Holy Spirit who recorded the command. Furthermore, without the work of the Spirit through the ordinance, water baptism would be meaningless.³² Word and Spirit reinforce each other in the lives of believers, transforming them into living testimonies to Christ: "[A]ll the words of Christ and His Spirit [must] be so read, considered and believed . . . that they shall all gradually change into the reader himself. This is so that the entire New Testament is written into the heart of the reader by the finger of God until the entire life of the reader becomes a living letter of God in which one can read all of the commandments of Jesus Christ."[33]

Like the author of *A Humble Gleam*, Alexander Mack Jr. asserts that the Holy Spirit and the Scriptures can reveal truth because they point to Jesus, who is Truth incarnate.[34] He modifies his father's strong literalism with an emphasis on the Holy Spirit's role in biblical interpretation. Perceptively, he recognizes that giving absolute authority to the letter will create "misery and division" because people will take a stand on one passage while rejecting another that seems to contradict it. The written Word must be read with "spiritual eyes" so that apparent contradictions can be harmonized. Mack trusts that the Holy Spirit, as author of the Bible, can lead believers to perceive its unity. True understanding will be fueled by love: "[A]bove all preserve love, for thus one preserves light. The good God, who is the pure impartial love, can and will supply gradually where insight is lacking here or there."[35]

In a poem on redemption, Mack Jr. describes the spiritual transformation brought about by the Spirit and the Word. The power of God (presumably the Holy Spirit) resounds in the human heart and brings the sinner to conversion through the reconciling blood of Christ. The new believer's faith is strengthened by love, which prompts obedience. The resulting experience produces hope for the eternal life promised in the Word. This hope nourishes the soul as the believer is stirred by the love of God, which presumably is revealed by both Word and Spirit: "The body and the soul rejoice / To hear love's kindly, gracious voice."[36]

William Knepper, an important hymn writer of this period, describes the interdependence of Word and Spirit in his *Testament*. He exhorts his children to pray for the Holy Spirit, who will lead them into truth, both through their inner experience and through the counsel of the church. They should learn the "good counsel" that Jesus brought from heaven so that Jesus will "reveal Himself with His spirit and mind in [their] hearts and entire life."[37] Those who follow Christ's commands "in faith and love, and in an inward fervent obedience" will know from experience that these commands are from God.[38] Spirit and Word facilitate the believer's transformation into Christlikeness. Knepper prays for the Brethren thus: "God grant that we may never cease to hunger after Jesus and His word, until in [the] future we may fully awake in His likeness!"[39]

One of the more mystical of the writers of this period is Michael Franz. In his advice to a congregation, he describes a communal spirituality that he calls inward and outward communion, which amount to love of God and love of neighbor, respectively. The communion of believers is founded on the Word, which unites them in belief and practice, and facilitated by the Spirit, who stimulates their love relationship with God and with one another.[40]

The Word is the seed of the knowledge of God, which is sown by God in the hearts of believers. As it grows, this seed brings believers to be "one heart and one soul with one another" because they "recognize together one evangelical foundation according to the truth." Because they have been born of God, they are "one Spirit with Christ."[41] Having experienced the love of God, believers freely return that love by obeying what God has asked of them, and they stimulate one another to love and obedience.[42]

Nineteenth Century Developments

During the nineteenth century, Brethren continued to express the spiritual life in terms of Word and Spirit, but not always in the same ways as their forebears had done. Both Word and Spirit began to acquire filters that distanced them somewhat from the believer. Brethren tradition became increasingly important as a lens through which to interpret Scripture, and Brethren writers begin to describe the Holy Spirit as working on believers not directly but through "means" such as the Bible and the ordinances.

With increasing acculturation came the need to discern the relationship between gospel and culture. All Brethren remained committed to the gospel, but they began to diverge in their understanding of what the gospel was. For the more conservative wing of the church, the gospel comprehended all the commands (or "laws") of Christ and the apostles, as understood through the practice of earlier Brethren. They charged other Christian groups with obeying only those biblical commands they decided were essential to salvation and discarding the rest.[43] The more progressive wing of the church charged the conservative wing with adding to the gospel the commandments of men in the form of the decisions of Annual Meeting. They took their stand on the "gospel alone."[44]

Word and Spirit in Brethren Spirituality

The confrontation in 1881 between the "Berlin Committee" and Henry Holsinger is expressed in terms of Word and Spirit. In their report, the committee states that Holsinger "refused to have his case investigated by the committee in harmony with the gospel as interpreted by our annual meeting," while in his account, Holsinger says that he asked the committee, "Can you not for once throw by the usages [of the Brethren] and say that you will do 'as seemeth good to us and the Holy Ghost'?"[45] The two perspectives were irreconcilable. Of course, the differences between the parties were more complex than a difference over Word and Spirit, but this dynamic does shed some light on the controversy.

It is difficult to make generalizations about the later nineteenth century from a few examples, but the following three writers seem to be representative of larger trends. These writers place less emphasis on Word and Spirit the further they are from traditional Brethrenism. For Peter Nead, champion of the Old Order, *Word and Spirit* is a constant refrain. In many respects, what he says about Word and Spirit is what Brethren have always said, expressed more carefully and more systematically. The Word and the Spirit testify to Jesus, inviting people to recognize his Lordship so that "he might rule and govern them to the salvation of their souls."[46]

From first to last, salvation is "by and through" the Word and the Spirit.[47] God pursues sinners by the Word and the Spirit, inviting them (but not forcing them) to submit their wills to his, and giving them the ability to do so.[48] In this process, the gospel informs, and the Spirit empowers. The Spirit works with the Word so that the testimony of the gospel will be received.[49] The repentant sinner who trusts in Christ is reborn through the Word and the Spirit, both of which direct the sinner to water baptism, at which time regeneration takes place. The one who has been born of water and the Spirit now has the ability to obey all of the commands of Christ.[50]

After baptism, Word and Spirit testify to believers of their adoption and together provide assurance of salvation: "The believer, by examining the Gospel, finds, that he has proceeded agreeably to the word; and, in examining his heart he perceives that he is operated upon by a Spirit which precisely agrees with the Gospel."[51] Believers are then sanctified by the Word and the Spirit such that they are crucified to the world and the world is crucified to them. Their obedience is motivated by the love of God, which is shed abroad in their hearts by the Holy Spirit "through the knowledge of the doctrine of Jesus Christ."[52] They "walk in the light of the

Gospel" as they are guided by the Holy Spirit. Word and Spirit then enable them to resist temptation as they follow Jesus.[53]

Most of these are traditional Brethren ideas. However, the way Nead relates Word and Spirit actually reveals a shift in Brethren thought. In line with his Lutheran background, Nead declares that God always operates through "means" to effect salvation. To be saved, people must make use of the means that God has ordained.[54] Against revivalism, he argues that revival preachers are using the wrong means to convert sinners—that is, they are using techniques to stir sinners' emotions "in lieu of the word of God," which illuminates the understanding. Word and Spirit are the means appointed by God to enlighten and convict the sinner, so those who are brought to Christ by other means are not really converted.[55] Then faith, repentance, and water baptism are the means of regeneration.[56]

This emphasis on means tends to emphasize the external over the internal. When he thinks about the Spirit as a personal agent, Nead tends to describe the Word as the *means* by which the Spirit works. In fact, he argues not only that the Spirit always agrees with the Word, but that the Spirit never operates independently of it.[57] The Spirit acts *through* the Word and *through* the ordinances established by the Word to bring about salvation. This restricting of the Spirit to the Word is evident in Nead's description of two works of the Spirit—the communication of God's love to the believer, which is attributed not only to the Spirit but to the knowledge of the doctrine of Christ; and the new birth, which cannot take place except in the act of water baptism. Thus while Nead often references the Word and the Spirit, he makes subtle changes in their relationship.

In R. H. Miller's *The Doctrine of the Brethren Defended*, a conservative exposition of Brethren distinctives published in 1876, the concept of Word and Spirit appears infrequently. The Bible and the Holy Spirit continue to play important roles in the spiritual life. The Holy Spirit brings salvation to the individual and makes the spiritual life possible.[58] The Word of God is the standard by which theology and practice should be judged.[59] Miller rejects any spirituality that tries to split heart from life. The inward and outward life will always be consistent, because the heart is the source of one's actions.[60] However, he does not often describe Word and Spirit as working together.

Like some earlier Brethren, Miller describes biblical commands as laws. God as creator and Christ as redeemer establish laws for the governance of nature and the church, respectively.[61] The Bible is a "code of laws," and the gospel of Christ is "a law to the Christian for his government in the church and in the world."[62] It is the duty of the church to ensure that its members obey all of God's commands.[63] But the traditional law language is wedded to Enlightenment-style moralism. For example, the gospel is "the only perfect system by which the Christian can work for the moral and spiritual good of mankind"; it enables Christians "to do the most good possible for the human race."[64]

The Bible appears no longer to be the narrative of salvation and covenant embraced by earlier Brethren but a collection of propositional truths and regulations detached from the relationship between God and God's people. Like other Brethren, Miller affirms the authority of the commands and example of Christ and the apostles.[65] But unlike those earlier Brethren, he treats the New Testament as an inspired *document* rather than a transparent window into the life of Christ and the early church. Miller does say that God is revealed in Jesus Christ, and that the precepts and example of the apostles were "put on record by the Holy Spirit." But he also says that the Bible *is* the revelation of God.[66] He often simply attributes the commands in Scripture directly to the Spirit as author of the document. For example, he says that the holy kiss is "founded on the plain command of the Holy Spirit." He argues for the Brethren version of the ordinances based on "the words used by the Holy Spirit in giving these ordinances." The Holy Spirit provides the "facts," which are "illuminated with the example of Christ."[67] The witness has become the revealer, and what is revealed is information rather than a Person: "[T]he Holy Spirit give[s] to the world a revelation of the great truths of the gospel."[68] Brethren had always contended that the Spirit leads believers into truth, but the references to *facts* and *truths* suggests a propositional view of Scripture that is more characteristic of fundamentalism than earlier Brethrenism.

Nevertheless, Miller still asserts that the Christian's obedience to the "law" of the gospel is motivated by love. The "sacred power of love" moves believers to obey God's commands because they "trust in the God who gave [them]."[69] The goal of obedience is transformation—"a change of mind that changes the man all over, outside and inside, soul, body, and spirit . . . We want all this change of heart wrought by the spirit of God till the man be turned over from the world to the law, the spirit, the image of Christ."[70]

In *A Summary of Religious Faith and Practice or Doctrines and Duties*, published by Progressive J. W. Beer in 1878, the concept of Word and Spirit has disappeared. Although he makes traditional affirmations about the work of the Spirit and the authority of the Bible, he almost never links the two. In the section on the Bible, he does not mention the Holy Spirit's role in inspiration or illumination, although in the section on the Spirit, he notes that the Spirit "moved holy men to speak according to God" and convicts believers of sin "by his word," which may be a reference to the Bible. He nowhere asserts, as so many Brethren had before him, that the Spirit leads believers into truth. The only affirmation in which Word and Spirit clearly work together is divine calling, but even here their connection is diffused by a reference to "providences": "God calls sinners by the Holy Spirit in connection with his word and providences."[71]

THE PROGRESSIVE BRETHREN AND THE BRETHREN CHURCH

For the rest of my survey, I will focus on my own group, the Brethren Church. In their haste to make use of new cultural forms, the Progressives, and later the Brethren Church, borrowed uncritically from other traditions without realizing the impact these borrowings would have on their life as a whole. Under these circumstances, the Word/Spirit dynamic was difficult to maintain. On the one hand, the Pietist emphasis in their devotional lives drew them to the devolved pietism of revivalism, which emphasized easy conversions and emotional highs that undermined simple obedience to the commands in Scripture. On the other hand, their commitment to Scripture led them to make common cause with fundamentalism and later neo-evangelicalism, which tended to de-emphasize the Spirit. Many in the Brethren Church today have an evangelical theology and a revivalistic piety that can undercut the foundation of traditional Brethren commitments such as discipleship, community, and nonresistance.

In general, the Brethren Church has worked with a mixture of Brethren ideas and borrowings from other groups. One example of the Progressives' desire to engage in dialog with other denominations is C. F. Yoder's *God's Means of Grace*, published in 1908. Yoder built upon earlier Brethren discussions of the "means" of salvation by describing numerous Brethren practices as "means of grace," by which he meant that they "minister to the welfare of the race and promote the graces of the Spirit."[72] He particularly emphasizes the teaching function of the ordinances. The dynamic of Word and Spirit plays a significant role in his explanations.

In his discussion of special revelation, Yoder focuses on Jesus Christ, the Holy Spirit, and the Bible as three different means through which God speaks. All three work together. Jesus is "the supreme personal witness of God." The Holy Spirit uses the revelation in Jesus to lead people to God, and the Bible "puts a part of the message of the Spirit in black and white." The Spirit continues to interpret Scripture for believers and uses the Word to guide them into truth. While technical methods of Bible study can be helpful, the guidance of the Holy Spirit is more important, because without the Spirit's help, says Yoder, "we may no more understand the things of God than a cow can receive a college education."[73] The Spirit also uses the Word to bring about the new birth, which Yoder describes in not-very-Brethren terms as "the light of the higher life, and the coming in of that new ideal."[74] The *higher life* language is borrowed from the Keswick movement.

Spirit and Word, like inward belief and outward practices, are mutually reinforcing. The Bible must be read with an attitude of love and a commitment to obedience. As the Spirit then leads the believer into truth, the believer must put that truth into practice. As Yoder puts it, "We cannot expect to be led into more truth until we are willing to obey the truth that we have."[75] Similarly, as believers practice the ordinances taught by the Word and learn the lessons they embody, they grow in inward holiness. Baptism, for example, aids the understanding, enlightens the conscience, and strengthens the will.[76] Yoder criticizes the church for an over-emphasis on the Word and calls for more robust teaching on the Holy Spirit, lamenting that "of recent years there has been little taught in sermon or in song." He even charges that some preachers "have confused the Spirit with the Word, and the church for ages has lacked in power because it has lacked faith in the enduement of the Holy Spirit."[77] Ironically, the revivals of the nascent Pentecostal movement were even then taking place, and twentieth century theology experienced an explosion of interest in the Trinity in general and the Holy Spirit in particular.

J. Allen Miller, president of Ashland College and first dean of Ashland Seminary, is a good representative of the perspective of the Brethren Church in the first half of the twentieth century. Miller writes like a professional scholar, and he shows the influence on the Brethren Church of the rationalism of fundamentalism and neo-evangelicalism, but he also expresses a lively experiential faith. He asserts that the inner witness of the Holy Spirit testifies to the inspiration of Scripture and points out its personal application to the reader.[78] Word and Spirit work together in enlightenment or illumination because "the knowledge of the Word of God must be interpreted to the soul by the Spirit of the living God."[79] Although he expects that baptism will be the *second* act of an obedient faith (after confession, an "ordinance" that entered the church with revivalism), Miller attributes the new birth exclusively to the Holy Spirit, discussing it at length without reference to baptism.[80]

The inner testimony of the Spirit gives assurance of salvation, although believers should be careful not to mistake their own imagination or emotions for the Spirit of God: "The witness of the Holy Spirit and that of our own spirit dare not contravene the spoken word."[81] For Miller, the Spirit and the Word *verify* or *validate* one another. The inner witness of the Holy Spirit verifies one's faith; thus the Spirit is a source of authority other than the Word. However, the Spirit's witness must itself by validated by the written Word.[82] In concept, this perspective is traditionally Brethren, but in terminology, it shows the influence of evangelical rationalism.

Miller describes the Christian life in both rational and experiential terms. He says that growth in the Christian life consists of the Holy Spirit's working in believers to bring them to "the ideal [of] moral and spiritual likeness to God as revealed in Jesus Christ" and set forth in the New Testament.[83] But the Christian also has experiential communion with God, facilitated by the Holy Spirit and involving the divine invitation to share God's "secrets as revealed . . . in his word."[84] In determining God's will, the believer is guided inwardly by the Holy Spirit and outwardly by God's voice "as heard in His Word and as spoken in and through His Church." The believer is "a soul guided, guarded and trained by the Living Word [in this case, probably Scripture] and the abiding Spirit."[85] Thus Miller generally maintains a balance between Word and Spirit, but (in typical Brethren Church fashion) he expresses a bit more confidence in the Word.

In more recent decades, the Brethren Church has been consciously re-appropriating its heritage. Among the recoveries has been the concept of Word and Spirit, sometimes expressed as the Outer and Inner Words. For example, the consensus documents *A Centennial Statement* (1984) and *How Brethren Understand God's Word* (1993) have intentionally held together Word and Spirit as witnesses to Christ. The latter document includes the headings "Jesus Christ, the Living Word," "Scripture, the Outer Word," and "The Holy Spirit, the Inner Word."[86]

Although the Brethren Church has been strongly influenced by evangelicalism, we place a greater emphasis on the Spirit than many evangelicals do. For example, evangelical books on biblical interpretation are full of logical rules but rarely give much attention to the Holy Spirit. Some evangelicals believe that the promises in John 16:13 and 14:26—that the Spirit would lead believers into truth and remind them of what Jesus had said—were intended only to assist the apostles in writing the New Testament. By contrast, most people in the Brethren Church take for granted that these promises are still valid: the Holy Spirit will lead us into truth, whether in biblical interpretation or corporate discernment, and will enable us to find the mind of Christ. We could, however, benefit from a re-emphasis on the early Brethren understanding of these verses—namely, that the Spirit directs us to the commands of Christ not mainly so that we can understand them, but so that we will obey them.

Effective discipleship requires both Word and Spirit—the Word to provide instruction and examples, and the Spirit to bring about transformation. We in the Brethren Church could also benefit from a renewed experience of the Spirit to empower our initiatives in church planting and church renewal. The global growth of Pentecostalism shows that people are hungry for the presence and power of the Spirit. We Brethren could have something to offer them, but first we must experience it ourselves. Word and Spirit together define a spirituality that embraces both the inward and the outward life, both freedom and obedience, both individual and community, all governed by love. As Brethren history demonstrates, however, either Word or Spirit can become an end in itself. We must remember that, as witnesses, both have been given us to lead us to Christ, to help us to follow him, and to shape us, together, into his likeness.

Notes

1 See the discussions of "Inner and Outer" and "Spirit and Letter" in C. Arnold Snyder, *Anabaptist History and Theology: An Introduction* (Kitchener, Ont.: Pandora Press, 1995), passim.

2 Hedwig T. Durnbaugh, *The German Hymnody of the Brethren 1720-1903* (Philadelphia: Brethren Encyclopedia, 1986), 35, 56, 132, 136.

3 Durnbaugh, *German Hymnody*, 12.

4 Durnbaugh, *German Hymnody*, 15, 45.

5 Alexander Mack (?), "An Open Letter," in *The Complete Writings of Alexander Mack*, edited by William R. Eberly, 9-10.

6 Lamech and Agrippa (pseud.), *Chronicon Ephratense*, 50; cited in Dale R. Stoffer, *Background and Development of Brethren Doctrines 1650-1987* (Philadelphia: Brethren Encyclopedia, 1989), 88.

7 Mack, *Basic Questions*, in *Complete Writings*, 37, 40.

8 Mack, *Basic Questions*, 24.

9 Mack, *Basic Questions*, 32, 23, 26, 39.

10 Mack, *Basic Questions*, 25.

11 Mack, *Rights and Ordinances*, in *Complete Works*, 44, 52-53.

12 Mack, *Rights and Ordinances*, 82.

13 Mack, *Rights and Ordinances*, 45, 66, 25.

14 Mack, *Rights and Ordinances*, 102.

15 Mack, *Basic Questions*, 32, 27, 35.

16 Mack, *Rights and Ordinances*, 51.

17 Mack, *Rights and Ordinances*, 53.

18 Mack, *Rights and Ordinances*, 72, 89.

19 Mack, *Rights and Ordinances*, 77, 80.

20 Mack, *Rights and Ordinances*, 60.

21 Mack, *Rights and Ordinances*, 62; and *Basic Questions*, 36.

22 Mack, *Rights and Ordinances*, 53.

23 Mack, *Rights and Ordinances*, 63, 96.

24 Mack, *Rights and Ordinances*, 83.

25 Mack, *Rights and Ordinances*, 84, 100.

26 Mack, *Basic Questions*, 32; and *Rights and Ordinances*, 51.

27 Mack, *Rights and Ordinances*, 66-68.

28 Prose translation provided by Durnbaugh, *German Hymnody*, 21.

29 "Love Feast Hymn," in *European Origins of the* Brethren, compiled and translated by Donald F. Durnbaugh (Elgin, IL: Brethren Press, 1958), 415. The translation is by Ora Garber.

30 "A Hymn of Feet-Washing," in *European Origins*, 418.

31 Alexander Mack Jr.(?), *A Humble Gleam of the Despised Little Light of the Truth which is in Christ*, in *The Brethren in Colonial America*, edited by Donald F. Durnbaugh (Elgin, IL: Brethren Press, 1967), 444-445.

32 *A Humble Gleam*, 431, 436, 445-446.

33 *A Humble Gleam*, 431.

34 Alexander Mack Jr., "Preface to *Rights and Ordinances*," in *Colonial America*, 418.

35 Alexander Mack Jr., "A Letter Concerning Feetwashing," in *Colonial America*, 468-469.

36 Alexander Mack Jr., "*(Redemption)*," in *Colonial America*, 578.

37 William Knepper, *Testament*, in *Colonial America*, 563-564.

38 Knepper, *Testament*, 567.

39 Knepper, *Testament*, 562 (brackets in original).

40 Michael Frantz, *Doctrinal Treatise*, in *Colonial America*, 449, 457.

41 Frantz, *Doctrinal Treatise*, 450-451.

42 Frantz, *Doctrinal Treatise*, 449, 452.

43 Peter Nead, *Theological Writings on Various Subjects* (Dayton, OH: n.p;, 1866; rpt. Youngstown, OH: Dunker Springhaus Ministries, 1997), 39, 50, 437; R. H. Miller, *The Doctrine of the Brethren Defended* (Elgin, IL: Brethren Press, 1915), 230-231. On the commands of Christ as laws, see Nead, *Theological Writings*, 113, 246, 440; Miller, *Doctrine*, 261.

44 "Declaration of Principles, adopted by the Progressive Convention, of the Tunker Church," in H. R. Holsinger, *History of the Tunkers and The Brethren Church* (Lathrop, CA: Pacific Press Publishing, 1901), 534-535.

45 Holsinger, *History*, 502, 506.

46 Nead, *Theological Writings*, 33.

47 Nead, *Theological Writings*, 455, cf. 464.

48 Nead, *Theological Writings*, 43, 410-412.

49 Nead, *Theological Writings*, 466, 310.

50 Nead, *Theological Writings*, 36, 59-60, 103.

51 Nead, *Theological Writings*, 92; cf. 91.

52 Nead, *Theological Writings*, 109, 453.

53 Nead, *Theological Writings*, 199, 456.

54 Nead, *Theological Writings*, 95, 197.

55 Nead, *Theological Writings*, 43.

56 Nead, *Theological Writings*, 45, 60, 90-91.

57 Nead, *Theological Writings*, 35, 49, 311.

58 R. H. Miller, *Doctrine of the Brethren*, 41.

59 R. H. Miller, *Doctrine of the Brethren*, iii.

60 R. H. Miller, *Doctrine of the Brethren*, 239-240.

61 R. H. Miller, *Doctrine of the Brethren*, 220-221.

62 R. H. Miller, *Doctrine of the Brethren*, 261-262.

63 R. H. Miller, *Doctrine of the Brethren*, 238.

64 R. H. Miller, *Doctrine of the Brethren*, 289, 261.

65 R. H. Miller, *Doctrine of the Brethren*, 178, 289.

66 R. H. Miller, *Doctrine of the Brethren*, 3-4, 228.

67 R. H. Miller, *Doctrine of the Brethren*, 220, 196.

68 R. H. Miller, *Doctrine of the Brethren*, 38.

69 R. H. Miller, *Doctrine of the Brethren*, 225-227.

70 R. H. Miller, *Doctrine of the Brethren*, 252-253.

71 J. W. Beer, *A Summary of Religious Faith and Practice or Doctrines and Duties*, in *The Brethren in Industrial America*, compiled and edited by Roger E. Sappington (Elgin, IL: Brethren Press, 1985), 286, 288-289.

72 C. F. Yoder, *God's Means of Grace* (Elgin, IL: Brethren Publishing House, 1908; rpt. Winona Lake, IN: BMH Books, 1979), 13.

73 Yoder, *Means of Grace*, 54-56, 76.

74 Yoder, *Means of Grace*, 67.

75 Yoder, *Means of Grace*, 74-75, 271.

76 Yoder, *Means of Grace*, 35-36, 133.

77 Yoder, *Means of Grace*, 419.

78 J. Allen Miller, *Christian Doctrine—Lectures and Sermons* (Ashland, OH: Brethren Publishing Company, 1946), 121, 138.

79 J. A. Miller, *Christian Doctrine*, 51-52.

80 J. A. Miller, *Christian Doctrine*, 66, 68-69.

81 J. A. Miller, *Christian Doctrine*, 98-99.

82 J. A. Miller, *Christian Doctrine*, 246.

83 J. A. Miller, *Christian Doctrine*, 85, 88.

84 J. A. Miller, *Christian Doctrine*, 96-97.

85 J. A. Miller, *Christian Doctrine*, 321-322.

86 *A Centennial Statement*, in *Brethren Beliefs*, 3-13 (Ashland, OH: Brethren Publishing Co., 1984); *How Brethren Understand God's Word*, in *Brethren Beliefs*, 14-23. For the three headings, see pages 16-17.

Community, Family, and Individual in Brethren Spirituality

Jared S. Burkholder

Community is of course immensely important to Brethren and is tied directly to their early Anabaptist and Pietist heritage. Historically, Pietists and Anabaptists thought of themselves not in terms of *Kirche*, the German word for church, but as a *Gemeinde*, the German word for community or congregation. It signifies an intentional contrast with the institutional churches that surrounded them, and especially it signified the close-knit, voluntary, transcendent nature of the gathered body of believers. For Anabaptists, according to Harold Bender, the *Gemeinde* is a "voluntary and exclusive fellowship of the truly converted believers in Christ, committed to follow [Jesus] in full obedience as Lord; it is a brotherhood, not an institution.[1] This notion included strong themes of discipleship (*Nachfolge*), which took place hand in hand with *Gemeinshaft*, the atmosphere of community, and it involved voluntary yieldedness (*Gelassenheit*) to the authority and discipline of the body of believers. In other words, among eighteenth century Pietists, community was not casual or haphazard; it was intentional. This was perhaps most true of Radical Pietists, who sought intentional community to such a degree that they forsook ordinary patterns of life and assembly. Consider the semi-monasticism of the Ephrata community, the choir system of the Moravians, or even the Schwarzenau Pietists.

This ideal of community, or *Gemeinschaft*, was not reserved for congregational functions. Rather, it was lived out in the context of the family as well. Like other Pietists and Anabaptists, the Brethren encouraged family devotions and sought the formation of their children's spiritual identity. Social and religious gatherings, often on Sunday, took place within the context of family units and around family mealtimes. The family, then, has often served as a smaller subunit of the larger congregation, and children were integrated into the life of the community through ritual practices, such as the ordinances and corporate worship. This ideal of community had ramifications for individual members as well. However, it was not without significant tension. What was the relationship between the corporate body and the individual? Was their room for individuality, for private communion with God? The ideal, of course, is that the community, as the vehicle for sanctification, takes precedence over individual aspirations.

In a nutshell, this is the general framework for how community, family, and individuals are intertwined. But on a more specific level, these issues are a bit more complex, for as Jeff Bach reminded us in his address, spirituality is rooted in particularity–that is, what spirituality looks like is tied directly to the particular historical context one has in mind. The same is true for community. It goes without saying that as diverse and eclectic a tradition as is true of the Brethren, there are multiple contexts represented, and thus, when considering the notion of community, it is probably more accurate to speak of communities in the plural, rather than a singular community, since our particularities are diverse.

So I want to focus on three individuals as a means to highlight examples of this particularity. These historical figures are representative of very different experiences even though they all were part of this eclectic tradition. The people I have in mind are Peter Nead, the nineteenth century theologian that many of us are familiar with; Estella Myers, a pioneer missionary during the first half of the twentieth century who may be less familiar; and Herman Hoyt, the second president of Grace College and Theological Seminary who died in 2000, and who some of you no doubt knew personally.

In looking at these three individuals, I have decided to focus on their sense of historical situation–in other words, how they saw themselves fitting into the sacred narrative. Why this approach? Essentially, I've chosen this approach because a sense of spiritual identity is more often than not defined, in part, by a community's collective interpretation of history. Historical understanding, or what historians call "memory," serves to place one's community within the flow of sacred time, thus providing credibility and legitimacy. The notion that one's community is validated by its place in history is then extended to families, as the building blocks of the larger community, as well as the individual, who receives legitimacy based on his or her membership in the group.

After describing how these individuals likely saw themselves within the scope of redemptive history–how they "fit" within it–I will conclude with some reflections, which I hope will highlight some of the tensions that have come about in a tradition with multiple, and even competing, notions of what it means to live in community. Let me start with some introductions.

INTRODUCTIONS

None of these three individuals were historians in the formal sense. Nevertheless, they all demonstrated an understanding of history and how their lives, and the particular Brethren communities they represented, fit within the flow of Brethren spirituality.

Peter Nead

Nead was the leading nineteenth century spokesperson for the German Baptist Brethren prior to the Civil War. Though elected to the Brethren ministry at the Linville Creek congregation in Rockingham County, Virginia, in 1827, he moved in 1848 to the vicinity of Dayton, Ohio, where he served the Lower Stillwater congregation. He died in 1877, the same year a political compromise settled the election of 1876 and marked the end of the era of Reconstruction. Nead was a respected minister, author, and leader at multiple Annual Meetings. Although not a sophisticated thinker, his theological writings, collected and published together in 1850, represents one of the most cogent articulations of traditional Brethren prior to the fragmentation of the 1880s.[2] If we examine these writings, we get a strong sense of Nead's own understanding of how his Old Order community fit within God's spiritual history.

His sense of identity was consistent with traditional notions within what Donald Durnbaugh and others refer to as the "Believers' Church," that is, those Christian movements, among them various Anabaptist and Pietist groups, that have rejected the institutionalism of mainstream Protestants and Catholics.[3] The true church is comprised only of those who personally believe and therefore follow the radical path of Jesus.[4] For those in the Believers' Church sphere, the history of the church is the story of outsiders. As the church declined, and continues to decline into corruption, small groups of true believers have kept the pure faith alive, albeit under the radar. So the real history of the church is not the history of institutions, or majority positions, or official documents and decrees. It is rather, a narrative that traces "hidden" streams or the thread of the marginalized remnant–outsiders who have preserved Apostolic Christianity and who remain on the fringes of Christendom either voluntarily or by the suppression of political authorities.

We see this in the late seventeenth and early eighteenth centuries with the writings of Gottfried Arnold, whose account of church history pays special attention to Pietists in an effort to bring them more legitimacy. In its most striking form, such as among eighteenth century Moravians, or even among some twentieth century evangelicals, it is an inverting of the normal telling of history. Rather than the orthodox, it is the heretics who represent purity of faith. To be rejected as unorthodox is a badge of honor, because it means you must be on the right track. There is something corrupting about institutions, about large and pervasive movements. If they are popular, they are less authentically Christian–popularity equals worldly innovation. Therefore, to remain true is, by definition, to carefully nurture and preserve outsider status. Admittedly, Nead does not provide a fully developed narrative, but there is the implied sense of his own community as inheriting this thread of authentic spirituality when others around him, including the Lutheran and Methodist traditions he left behind, had succumbed to worldliness. Nead is explicit that only his own community is embodying the "primitive" church. Nead describes the churches around him as "pitiable" for their divisions and denominations; they have "all the pomp and grandeur that Lucifer is capable of inventing" and the leaders of these churches "excel in all the vanities of this life."[5]

Historians categorize this way of thinking as "primitivism." A primitive outlook is one that places ultimate value on the earliest expressions of Christianity, often trying hard to reclaim the mythic purity of the Apostolic era. We also see this as a strong impulse in the Puritans, restorationists among the followers of Alexander Campbell, and in The Church of Jesus Christ of Latter Day Saints. Thus, Nead's writings, including his notions of community, are more than simply explanations of theology, beliefs, and practices. They are an apologetic–an argument for a traditional Brethren interpretation of scripture and the requirements of Christian practice. To use Nead's words, "primitive Christianity" reflects the "simplicity of the gospel."[6] This understanding of Christian history, and his own place within it, frames a traditionalist, literal, and strict application of Brethren discipleship.

Estella Myers

The experience of Estella Myers (1884-1956) was literally a world away from Peter Nead's. Born amid the splits of the 1880s, Myers's family was part of the progressive stream of Brethren in rural Iowa–the Brethren Church. She was one of the first missionaries to be accepted into the newly formed Brethren Missionary Society, an organization in which Louis S. Bauman would become instrumental. In 1918, Myers left for Africa, joining James Gribble, the true pioneer, for ministry in what is today the Central African Republic–one of the shining jewels and early successes of Brethren Missions.

This summer (2013), a student and I have worked to organize and catalogue some of Myers' letters and personal papers for the FGBC archives. Included among these records is a rough and unpublished history, written by Myers, of what she called the "waiting days" or "waiting years"–the time between her arrival in Africa in 1919 and when she and her colleagues finally received permission in 1921 to proceed into the interior.[7]

Where Nead's writing is essentially a defense of traditionalism, Myers writes to chronicle the march of Christian progress into heathen lands. Not surprisingly, given the perils, hardships, frequent desperation, sufferings, death, and sickness, and the strange surroundings of missionary work, she interprets her experiences and those of her fellow missionaries in direct biblical and spiritual language. Their experiences are parallel with the Apostle Paul's, the spiritual strongholds they hope to demolish are paralleled to the walls of Jericho. Jesus' teachings are being fulfilled by them and through them. Myers employs military language. She speaks of prayer as "artillery," conversion of the natives as "conquering," and "victory" when things go their way. They interpret all the events around them as a spiritual battle–Africa is the devil's playground and they are doing battle with unseen forces of evil embodied in local shamans and the foreign culture around them. Beginning their presence in one city, Estella writes thus began the "battle for Carnot." Among Brethren writers, Myers language and imagery would serve as a pattern for understanding missionary progress within the larger scope of sacred history. One later historian of the FGBC entitled his narrative "Conquering Frontiers."[8] The irony of such militant language among those in a nonviolent tradition notwithstanding, this sort of triumphalism is all standard fare for mission histories, especially those of a popular nature, not only among the Brethren, but within the pages of missionary periodicals, biographies, and pamphlets from any number of denominational contexts.

For Brethren missionaries such as Estella Myers, it was not enough to preserve and safeguard traditions as embodied in community. The community must be expanded to include those of every tribe and tongue.

Herman Hoyt

While Estella Myers was on the mission field, divisions were boiling over at the Brethren Church's school at Ashland. Eventually, it erupted during the 1930s and brought about Grace Theological Seminary and divided the allegiances of many congregations. Alva J. McClain, the seminary's founding president, was looking to establish a seminary that more fully represented a denominational institution with a Bible College culture than what he believed existed at Ashland. Myers went with the so-called "Grace group"–a group that included McClain's right hand man, Herman Hoyt. Hoyt, like Myers, had humble beginnings in rural Iowa and had become a popular professor while on the faculty at Ashland. Emerging from the controversy playing a significant role, Hoyt served from 1962 to 1976 as president of the new seminary.[9]

Hoyt had a strong Brethren background and identity, and early on he contributed to the Grace group's attempts to synthesize the Brethren tradition with evangelical and fundamentalist trends. Within the subculture that Hoyt helped to create at Grace Seminary, the specter of liberalism was never far from people's minds. Although Ashland was probably not exactly the bastion of liberalism, Hoyt and others believed it to be. Their identity and sense of purpose was wrapped up in the continued rejection of any hint of liberalism they might find. The pages of *Grace Theological Journal*, for example, which began under Hoyt's tenure and served as the publishing outlet of the seminary, often contained a hard-edge style of apologetic writing that reflected the belief that Grace was standing as a bulwark against theological threats, liberalizing trends, cults, communism, as well as the so-called "new" evangelicals.

As I have written elsewhere,[10]

Prior to 1960, Hoyt's publishing was a mixture of pastoral articles and defenses of Brethren positions, including several books on Brethren ordinances and non-resistance. After 1960, however, Hoyt's writing increasingly took on the flavor of right wing evangelicalism.[11] According to Hoyt, modernity and the march of "progress" were to blame for much of the unrest of the 1960s. Development and progress, Hoyt believed, "have projected a whole host of new things into civilization … as a result, new dangers followed swiftly in the wake of these developments." Innovations in communication and travel were removing the "natural barriers of land and sea." Two world wars had "decimated the earth" and Hoyt predicted a third world war "is now in the making." What is more, increasing space travel and industrial automation were increasing the peril and struggle for survival. Intertwined with these rapid changes were "new doctrines" that more than anything else lay "at the root of the perils that threaten society." Through an "explosion of knowledge that is sweeping the world," Hoyt declared, "the facts of astronomy, geology, and anthropology are outrunning the facts of theology. As a result, men are suffering from a lowering intellectual skyline and a diminishing horizon. Within these narrowing limits and on this lower level of visibility, they are not able to come to a full and rational comprehension of the facts at hand. Unwilling to wait for more light, they rush to faulty conclusions, the first of which is to reject the teaching of the Bible, and the second of which is to construct a new theology."[12] Like others who resented the victories of social progressives, Hoyt believed one need only to observe the social tumult that plagued the nation to see the fruit of America's downward spiral and the results of godlessness. The "insurrection" of student protests on college campuses, the "unbridled excess" of riots "in the name of freedom," and the "gross sensualism into which the human race is now plunging with utter abandon" were all signs of the final days. "The climax of this so-called new morality is yet ahead," Hoyt warned. "This means that the trend is down. It means that the source of this declension is men who are rotten at heart. It means that the course of this declension is progressive through deterrents to lower depths of degradation. It means that the force of this declension grows out of the ever-enlarging moral and spiritual deception."[13] In short, this entire spiritual decline was part of a general increase of paganism, new manifestations of pantheism, and the growing influence of "evil men and seducers." The godlessness perceived in all directions seemed to validate the urgency the administration at Grace felt to construct an institution that would stand strong against the flood of moral decay and theological corruption within society and among their fellow "evangelicals."[14]

It is apparent that Hoyt's sense of his place in Brethren history resembles, at least in tone, that of Nead. Like Nead, Hoyt was pessimistic about the world around him. However, where Nead framed his apologetic approach in the language of traditional Pietism and Anabaptism, Hoyt, along with other Grace faculty such as Old Testament professor and young earth enthusiast, John Whitcomb, increasingly framed their posture of separation in the language of American fundamentalism and the growing Religious Right.[15] Such pessimism was rooted in dispensationalism and an accompanying premillennial eschatology. Eschatological zeal was not foreign to Pietism as a whole. Indeed, watching for the return of Christ was a pervasive motivation for the setting up of Pietist settlements. Neither was it foreign to Brethren specifically. We find eschatological ruminations in Alexander Mack Jr. and in Peter Nead, for example. Yet, within dispensationalism, eschatology was given a place of prominence and laid out with a degree of precision that was innovative among Brethren individuals who adopted it. The founding members of Grace Theological Seminary dogmatically adopted dispensationalism, and eschatology quickly became a favorite topic on which to write. Members of the "Grace group" believed they were living in the end times and the dispensationalist formulations were being fulfilled. Thus, Hoyt's sense of place within history was as a participant in the final era of human history in which apostasy would inevitably grow all around the true community of believers and from which the rapture would signal the start of a precise chain of end-times events. With these introductions behind us, let me move to some reflections.

Reflections on Community, Family, Individual

To be part of any Brethren group is, at least to one degree or another, to give credence to the primitivist understanding of history we find in Nead's writings. We agree with the notion that institutions and established religious movements have often been without warm piety or have been hindered by virtue of being part of main stream society. But this perspective is not without tensions and challenges. Can one be certain of exactly what the early Christian community looked like and exactly what expectations there were for future Christians? How do we explain the fact that many churches and denominations have primitivist New Testament impulses, yet are very different in the way their Apostolic notions are expressed?

There is also what we might call a gnostic flavor to this telling of history. I don't mean the formal heresy, but rather that the true, hidden understanding of history is plain only to those on the inside of the community who have been enlightened. How is it that, even though the majority of so-called Christians down through the ages have missed the boat, my little circle of individuals have been privileged with a higher order of knowledge, and thus I have the true understanding of what God has been doing in history?

With regard to Myers and Hoyt, although their careers were vastly different, their stories prompt us to consider the relationship between Brethren and evangelicals and the tensions that exist therein. By pursuing a more evangelical orientation through going to the mission field, Estella Myers chose to sacrifice her direct participation in her spiritual family, as well as her natural family. She left a dying father, never to see him again, and never married. By sacrificing her own community, however, and in spite of her own racial assumptions, she would help to expand the *Gemeinde*, opening doors that would help bring about the racial and ethnic diversity that was sorely needed. But in so doing, she bent the rules of gender, boldly preaching in Africa even though she would not have been empowered to do this at home in America. Eventually, tensions would surface over membership requirements and discipline. How does one balance traditional community expectations with the diversity that will inevitably come about through outreach and mission? What components of the community (dress, practice, etc.) are essential and must be transferred to a new context, and what components can be modified or let go completely in order to fit a new context? These questions are not insignificant. Indeed, nearly eighty years after Myers first sailed to Africa, the Fellowship of Grace Brethren Churches experienced a schism in part over the question of baptismal requirements for those from different backgrounds, including missionary converts.

Or consider the question of individuality. Before journeying to Africa, Myers recounted an experience of individual "calling," explaining her inward conviction in evangelical fashion. A letter from around 1914 gives us a window into her anxiety over what she should do with her life. She tells of being greatly unsettled and out of sorts. She was "beside herself" and close to a nervous breakdown. But in the end, she says, "We can only do what we feel called to do, and I know then peace and happiness will exist."[16] "I must have peace of mind," she declares,

> and I know I would not feel as strongly as a do to go to the foreign field if I was not called. I have considered it on all sides and can look at in only one way. It may be sacrifice and all that but finally in the end it will be the life worthwhile. I want to do something worthwhile; I am tired of just existing and not accomplishing any good. I have prayed so hard for years to be led to my decided life work and now I believe I have decided on what it is.[17]

Here we see Myers making one of the most important decisions of her life– not in communion with elders, or with ministers or the congregation as a whole, but rather, in individual communion with God. We can assume her church and her family was part of the process, but at the end of the day, she describes this as an individual call, and in fact, at one point, she says that, in deciding to go to the mission field, she was rejecting the influence of others around her. Although there is certainly precedent for individual experience within the Pietist tradition, Myers seems to employ the language of evangelicals as she describes her experiences.

In the case of Herman Hoyt, his brand of fundamentalist/Brethren spirituality was linked more directly with American evangelicals and is arguably a more open departure from traditional Brethren teachings. Take his treatment of nonresistance, for example, which he spelled out in a 1956 publication, *Then Would my Servants Fight*. Although always a staunch defender of nonresistance, his writings on the subject reflected a stronger nationalistic sentiment than more traditional Brethren would be comfortable with. In the super-charged atmosphere of the Cold War era, Hoyt seems to bend over backwards to differentiate between nonresistance as he defines it and other forms of pacifism that were commonly associated with liberalism, communist infiltration, or the socialist left. He also was clear that, unlike Christians, secular nations could and even should engage in war against God's enemies. Although defending the responsibility of the Christian to reject participation in direct combat, Hoyt clearly had a vision of Christian America that was compatible with the Religious Right. In his primary treatment of the subject, one almost gets the feeling that war was a privilege that secular nations could employ as they may, rather than an affront to Jesus' ethical teachings. Thus nonresistance, though essential for the Christian community, was explained in terms that accommodated the sentiments of right-wing conservative evangelicals of the period.[18]

In light of these tensions, some Anabaptist scholars have viewed Anabaptism as a passive victim of evangelical influence. For one writer, evangelicals have even been compared to a virus.[19] For other interpreters, Anabaptist communities may have appropriated elements of evangelicalism, but in so doing they have crafted versions of these traditions that will live on in new and changing contexts. Thus by adapting, the tradition endures. In reality, there is probably a mixture of both interpretations at play.

Conclusion

All three of these individuals exhibit in their work a triumphalistic sense of their own community's place in history. By this we mean that they operate, either explicitly or only implicitly, with a historical narrative in which they and their people are vindicated. For Nead, the counter-cultural ethos of separation from the world demonstrated the superiority of the Old Order ideal of community. Although it would never, indeed it **could** not, literally triumph in the world, he could feel triumphant about the ultimate vindication of the hidden line of authentic Christianity and the way the traditional *Gemeinde*, and the families within it, was being preserved. For Myers, building a church of believers in Africa was the ultimate triumph over the forces of the Devil, demons, and the pagan society of the "dark continent." For Hoyt, the world could fall to pieces all around him, but vindication for the elect would come with the Rapture.

Scholars are accustomed, with good reason, to scoff at triumphalism, for there is reason to be skeptical when history seems to conveniently validate the one who happens to be telling it. Yet, we can be sympathetic because members of various communities, including religious traditions, desperately want what Van Wyck Brooks first referred to in 1918, as a "usable" past–that is, a past that offers something for individuals today.[20] The past, we believe, should provide for us lessons, legitimacy, and a sense of collective identity. So while Nead, Myers, and Hoyt may operate with a measure of triumphalism, we see their historical understandings providing a sense of identity for the communities with which they identify.

Notes

1 Quoted in Stephen C. Ainley, "Mennonite Culture Wars: Power, Authority, and Domination" in Benjamin W. Redekop and Calvin Redekop, eds., *Power, Authority and the Anabaptist Tradition* (Baltimore, MD: The Johns Hopkins University Press, 2001), 137.

2 Peter Nead, *Theological Writings on Various Subjects: Or, A Vindication of Primitive Christianity* (B.F. Ells: Dayton, OH, 1866).

3 Donald Durnbaugh, *The Believers' Church: The History and Character of Radical Protestantism* (Scottdale, PA: Herald Press, 1985).

4 Examples of this language include August Hermann Francke's sermon: "*Die Nachfolge Jesu*" and Johann Arndt's *Wahres Christentum*.

5 Nead, *Theological Writings*, 55.

6 Ibid.

7 Estella Myers, "The Spiritual History of the Mission previous to entering Oubangui Chari," FGBC Archives, 13.1.2.

8 Homer A. Kent, *Conquering Frontiers: A History of the Brethren Church* (Winona Lake: Brethren Missionary Herald Co., 1972).

9 Ronald T. Clutter, "Herman A. Hoyt, a Biographical Sketch" *Grace Theological Journal* 6 (Fall 1985): 180-186.

10 This lengthy quote comes from my forthcoming chapter, "Herman Hoyt, John Whitcomb, and the Fundamentalist response to Neo-Evangelicalism" in *A Cord of Many Strands: Seventy-Five Years of Christian Higher Education at Grace College and Theological Seminary* (Winona Lake: BMH Books, forthcoming).

11 Robert D. Ibach, Jr., "The Writings of Herman Hoyt: A Select Bibliography, 1934-1984" *Grace Theological Journal* 6 (Fall 1985): 187-199.

12 Herman A. Hoyt, "The New Doctrines and the New Dangers" *Grace Journal* 7 (Winter, 1966): 5.

13 Ibid., 4.

14 Ibid., 5-6.

15 This figures largely in Robert Clouse's, "Fellowship of Grace Brethren Churches" in Donald Durnbaugh, ed., *Meet the Brethren* (Elgin: The Brethren Press, 1984), 101-114.

16 Estella Myers to "Dear ones at home," 1913 or 1914. FGBC archives, 13.1.8.

17 Ibid.

18 Herman Hoyt, *Then Would my Servants Fight* (Winona Lake, Brethren Missionary Herald Co., 1956).

19 Bruce Geunther, "Living with the Virus, The Enigma of Evangelicalism among Mennonites in Canada," in George Rawlyk, ed. *Aspects of the Canadian Evangelical Experience* (Montreal: McGill-Queen's University Press, 1997), 223-240.

20 Van Wyck Brooks, "Creating a Usable Past" *Dial* 64 (April 11, 1918).

Brethren Ordinances

Denise D. Kettering-Lane

In 1708, eight women and men stepped into the Eder River in Germany. Each person solemnly testified to their faith and then was dipped into the water three times in the name of the Father, the Son, and the Holy Spirit. When these men and women emerged from the flowing stream, a new Christian group had begun. An ordinance marked the beginning of the Brethren movement and even marked their new name, the *Neu-Täufer* or New Baptists. Throughout the history of the Brethren movement, ordinances have stood at the heart of Brethren spirituality. Baptism, love feast, and anointing have given the Brethren symbolic opportunities to repeat aspects of the New Testament narrative, to connect with Christ, and to demonstrate their unity as a community of faith.

Scholars have long acknowledged that Brethren have focused on orthopraxy rather than orthodoxy. In other words, "right practice" has been central to Brethren life. As former Bethany professor Floyd Mallott used to say, "there was no such thing as a theological heretic among the Brethren, only ethical and practical heretics."[1] Indeed, the Brethren historical record contains numerous accounts of the Brethren trying to get the practice of the ordinances right and changing aspects of practice to match the New Testament accounts of the life of Jesus and the early church as closely as possible. Questions regarding the mode of feetwashing, the type of meat to serve at love feast, the relationship between medicine and anointing, or trine versus single immersion baptism could be, and have been, characterized by some as legalistic. However, such a characterization misses what the Brethren were trying to do. These questions were not simply legalistic details debated among Brethren because they had nothing better to discuss, but they were rather an expression of a deep-seated spirituality rooted in the New Testament.

There has been some difference of opinion about how Brethren have approached ordinances. Donald F. Durnbaugh has stated that the Brethren have adapted the ordinances at various times as needed, being neither too inflexible nor too impulsive in their approach to change.[2] Carl Bowman, on the other hand, has emphasized that Brethren desired to adhere rigidly to the practices and their particular forms, even demanding that other Christians adopt these forms as well.[3] Perhaps there is truth in both of these statements. Certainly the Brethren have adapted their practices over time, as Annual Meeting minutes make clear. On the other hand, it is also evident that in the attempt to recreate the ordinances as practiced in the New Testament, there has been a particular exactness exercised in these practices. These dual impulses stem from the deep spiritual desire for obedience to the commands of Christ. In some cases, this may mean changing aspects of practice, and in other cases it means stridently asserting the rightness of a particular form. Both impulses stem from the same spiritual source.

The purpose of this essay is to consider several elements of Brethren spirituality and how these elements have been evident in the exercise of Brethren ordinances and in Brethren debates around the ordinances. First, we will identify several elements of Brethren spirituality and the nature of Brethren ordinances. Then, we will consider the ordinances of baptism, the love feast, and anointing in order to reflect on how the ordinances exemplify the characteristics of Brethren spirituality. Throughout it will be evident that for many Brethren the practice of ordinances has been central to their spiritual life, particularly as the ordinances have attempted to connect Brethren both to God and neighbor.

Brethren Spirituality

Spirituality is a difficult term to define and by its very nature often remains without a common definition. Within Christianity, the word can refer to a variety of experiences, including mystical visions, receiving communion, walking in a labyrinth, prayer, singing, or any number of other activities. For Brethren, the term spirituality can be particularly elusive because we have instead preferred language around the "spiritual life."[4] Spirituality, generally understood, however, refers to how we know God and recognize God's presence within our life and the life of our community. It not only refers to one's vertical relationship with God but also includes the expression of that relationship in the manner of one's living, and particularly living within community.[5] This tension developed at the origins of the Brethren movement with the healthy relationship between Pietism and Anabaptism. While Brethren tended to reject the extremes of subjective mystical experience in Radical Pietism, they did emphasize aspects of private prayer and devotion. From Anabaptist roots, Brethren tended to stress the shared life of scriptural interpretation and practice.[6] The ordinances blend the spiritual with concrete action, bringing together these two theological streams. Mennonite theologian Thomas Finger has characterized Anabaptist spirituality as a "mysticism of devotion."[7] This form of mysticism has several characteristics that are prevalent in Brethren spirituality, including an orientation to Christ.[8] I will highlight four areas of Brethren spirituality that are prevalent in the ordinances: their Christ-centered nature, obedience and discipleship, association with the suffering of Christ, and their role as a memorial of the New Testament church.

As already discussed, Brethren spirituality has been Christ-centered, a fact that is especially evident in the ordinances.[9] While the ordinances draw on Old Testament allusions and practices, the forms that the Brethren have emphasized arise directly from the life of Jesus Christ and the early church.[10] Even though the ordinances contain references to the other two persons of the Trinity, there is a prevalent emphasis on identifying with and relating to Jesus Christ. Brethren receive a continual invitation into the life of Christ and into relationship with Christ through these actions. Being Christocentric has also led to a strong emphasis on the Bible and particularly the New Testament narratives. The other three characteristics I have identified flow from this Christocentric orientation.

A strong component of Brethren spirituality has been discipleship and obedience. As Donald Durnbaugh observed, the predominant theme in Alexander Mack's writing is obedience.[11] Mack was not alone in this emphasis as it appears frequently in the writings of the eighteenth- and nineteenth-century Brethren and indeed still turns up in Brethren periodicals today. Referring to these acts as "ordinances" rather than using the language of "sacrament," language more common in other Christian traditions, highlights this theme of obedience. Ordinances correspond to imperative statements given by Jesus Christ or the apostles of the first century. Alexander Mack stated, "Faith in Christ produces obedience and submission to all of His words and commandments."[12] Furthermore, discipleship and obedience develop within the community of faith. The ordinances consistently express the unity among the Brethren, emphasizing that the life of discipleship is not an individual pursuit, but rather one that takes place within the context of the gathered community.

Third, the ordinances frequently embody an association with the suffering of Christ. While the Brethren did not experience suffering and persecution in the way that earlier Anabaptist groups of the sixteenth century did, the Brethren attempted to capture this relationship to the suffering Christ through their ordinances. In doing so, Brethren anticipated the potential of future suffering for their faith. This notion tied strongly to the idea of "counting the cost" of discipleship and anticipated an eschatological event that would lead to the suffering of true believers prior to a final reunion with Christ.

For Brethren, there is a strong sense of imitating Christ within the community.[13] Therefore, it is natural that Brethren spirituality centered on recreating the acts that Jesus performed with his disciples as communicated in the Gospel narratives. This memorialism allowed Brethren regularly to repeat these acts. In doing so, they served a didactic function, teaching the Brethren about the faith, as well as memorializing key moments in the life of Christ. Indeed some of the debates around the ordinances stemmed from this desire to reenact accurately New Testament events. These aspects create an interrelated web of themes that are prevalent in the different ordinances. We are now faced with the question: which actions are in fact ordinances instituted and prescribed by Jesus Christ.

What are Ordinances?

Brethren chose the word "ordinance" to refer to actions from the New Testament that present-day Christians are commanded by Christ to do. While the Brethren have favored a symbolic understanding, there is still a sense that these actions demonstrate God's grace and Christ's presence in a special way.[14] These rituals performed by Jesus and the apostolic church became a model for the Brethren, and Brethren have scoured the New Testament for ways to best recreate the original New Testament forms. Changes in practice throughout the centuries have frequently corresponded to this desire to recreate the New Testament church as closely as possible.[15]

The exercise of Brethren ordinances stem from the Brethren understanding of the primitive church. As Carl Bowman has observed, the Brethren placed "unique emphasis upon the outward form of the Christian ordinances: baptism, communion, feetwashing, anointing, and the holy kiss should be practiced *exactly* as originally instituted by Christ and his apostles."[16] Unlike other Radical Pietists, who objected to outward expressions such as baptism and feetwashing, Brethren found these expressions to be the perfect blending of the inner grace of God and adherence to the Gospel texts.[17] In other words, the ordinances provided a significant point of difference between the Brethren and other Pietists.

One of the difficulties for Brethren over time has been identifying what exactly constitutes an ordinance. The number of ordinances has varied at different times, and Brethren have generally resisted developing any sort of formalized list out of a concern that it might be too creedal. While baptism as well as love feast and communion have generally been recognized as ordinances by all the Brethren bodies, the other ordinances have varied over time and included a long list of possibilities including anointing, preaching services, the laying on of hands, kneeling, the annual visit, the holy kiss, plain dress, council meeting, discipline and avoidance, public confession, and annual meeting.[18] None of these practices was specifically unique to the Brethren, as many other Christian groups performed one or more of these activities. The use of so many of these actions together, however, was relatively unique.[19] Brethren attempted to complete all of the rituals commanded in the New Testament.[20]

Given the extensive list of potential Brethren ordinances, we could look at a variety of different activities, but we will here focus on the three most prominent ordinances that most Brethren groups have continued to practice and identify as ordinances: baptism, the love feast and communion, and anointing.

BAPTISM

Baptism remains the central ordinance for all Brethren groups because it initiates the believer into the life of Christ and community. Throughout the 18th and 19th centuries, the topic that was most debated between Brethren and other Christians was the topic of baptism. At baptism, new Brethren renounce sin, the devil, and the will in their effort to follow Christ. Elders and pastors still frequently urge these new members to "count the cost" of the commitment they are about to make. For some people, the level of commitment demanded by the church has been too much, and they have been unable to take this step.[21]

Baptism, in other words, has served as an initiation into the life of obedience and discipleship. For Brethren, conversion involves repentance, turning away from sin. Baptism thus initiates the process of sanctification and growth in faith. It also symbolizes the new believer's promise to follow Christ and leave the sinful world behind. Furthermore, the baptized enters into a covenant with the body of Christ. Obedience is not only to Christ, but is part of what unifies the body of believers and therefore baptism brings the believer fully into the Christian community. This connection between baptism and church membership stresses that the *member* becomes a part of the *Body of Christ*, part of the church. Baptism also demonstrates that the new believer separates from the worldly community in order to participate in the Christian community (some degree of antithesis between these communities is assumed). This ordinance shows the willingness of an individual believer to submit to something larger than himself or herself, namely to Christ and the community of believers. The newly baptized also receives ordination into the priesthood of all believers, as Brethren believe that all church members have a role to play in ministry, not just elders, pastors, or deacons. As such, the believer enters into this life of ministry and discipleship through the act of baptism.[22]

There is also an element of suffering with Christ displayed in baptismal practice. While many Brethren today often have indoor baptisteries or hold baptisms in the summer months, there is a sense in which the traditional Brethren practice of holding baptisms outdoors, even in inclement weather, prepared Brethren for the sacrifice that might be ahead. Again, as Bowman writes, "the physical discomfort and exposure often associated with baptism reflected the cost that primitive Christians could expect to suffer as true followers of Christ."[23] The story of the first Brethren baptism in America on Christmas Day in 1723 at the Wissahickon Creek captures this sacrifice, as the ice reportedly had to be broken before the group could hold the baptisms. Brethren believed that people could not catch a cold by being baptized, even in severe weather conditions. They also believed that "outdoor midwinter baptisms in ice-covered water demonstrated the sincerity of the person being baptized."[24] Furthermore, the kneeling position assumed by the person being baptized emulated the position of Jesus on the cross, where Scripture explicitly spoke of Jesus' head being bowed forward.[25] According to Peter Nead, this position also was the position in which to approach God: "We can read no where in the bible, or Testament, of any of the institutions or appointments of God being observed by presenting themselves before God upon their backs....therefore, kneeling and falling upon the face will be observed in the administration of this sacred ordinance."[26] Alexander Mack's hymn, "Count Well the Cost," emphasizes this theme in the second verse, "Into Christ's death you're buried now/ Through baptism's joyous union./ No claim of self dare you allow/ If you desire communion/ With Christ's true church, His willing bride,/ Which, through His Word, He has supplied."[27] Thus, baptism demonstrated a spiritual identification with Christ's suffering as well as emphasized the suffering of the believers in this life.

The initial baptism of the Brethren in the Eder River set the tone for Brethren spirituality. It was an act of civil disobedience, emphasizing religious freedom and obedience to Christ's commands over and above obedience to civil authority. It was also an act that implied a voluntary acceptance of the Christian faith.[28] The first written document from the original eight Brethren espoused a Christocentric and biblically-oriented spirituality related to the topic of baptism and defended the group's anticipated action. The open letter explains that the Brethren came to the realization that they must be baptized as described in the Gospels, namely as adult believers aware of the potential consequences and commitments required by their action. Furthermore, the letter claimed that it is clear in the book of Acts that believers should receive baptism.[29] Here we see the emphasis on obedience to the Scriptures as part of Brethren spirituality and particularly an attempt to be faithful to the Gospel narratives.

Alexander Mack's written work focuses predominantly on the ordinance of baptism. For Mack, baptism was the primary ordinance for Christians. The outward act of baptism separated the Brethren from other Radical Pietists, and the mode of baptism separated Brethren from other Anabaptists. Therefore, Mack defended believers' baptism and trine immersion extensively, even blaming wars and a desire to kill people on infant baptism. Despite the emphasis on baptism, however, Mack did not say that salvation came through baptism but rather emphasized that faith brought about salvation. Baptism served as the first act of obedience to Christ. Brethren have continued to understand baptism as an outward sign or symbol of an inward faith.[30] Mack also combated the notion that Brethren engaged in works righteousness that emphasized too strongly the act of baptism. Instead, he stressed that the act did not create righteousness, but rather that the state of grace urged the individual on to obedience, an obedience that entailed water baptism.[31]

Mack's *Answer to Gruber's Basic Questions* ardently defends the ordinance of baptism, emphasizing that baptism is an act of obedience, but it is also related to spiritual rebirth. "The spiritual rebirth is nothing else than true and genuine obedience toward God and all of His commandments… we can, therefore, answer that the desire for obedience toward water baptism is inseparable from the true rebirth."[32] Mack draws a clear relationship between the spiritual life, relationship with God, and the act of baptism. Inner birth cannot be separated from the act of baptism. Baptism helps to initiate a new spirituality, a spirituality born of obedience. Here we see the offer of a counter-spirituality to that of the Radical Pietists, who tended to emphasize spiritualism, or the idea that outward signs were no longer a necessary expression. Rather than the Radical Pietist notion of an inner baptism, Mack emphasizes that baptism is a spiritual expression, but an active spirituality that demands action and a public testimony on the part of the believer.[33] Mack reiterated this position in his *Rights and Ordinances*. In the section on "water baptism," Mack speaks repeatedly about baptism being an action that believers undertake out of obedience to God and to God's Word. This obedience clearly stems from faith: "Yes, that has always been the true faith and the true love of all saints and believers. They have done what God has commanded them to do, and have bowed all of their reason and will before the will of their God."[34] Thus, water baptism is an expression of faith and love for God, an action performed in obedience but motivated by a deep spirituality rather than rote action.

A significant aspect of the Brethren practice of baptism was the emphasis on trine immersion, a unique practice even among Anabaptists. According to Alexander Mack Jr., the early Brethren found in "trustworthy histories" the details of trine immersion as the model from the early church.[35] Brethren spent a great deal of time defending the practice of trine immersion. For them, it was not simply a matter of difference from other

Christians, but it was an attempt to be as faithful as possible to the biblical narrative and the model of the early church.[36] In this way, the practice of trine immersion represented the desire to symbolize and memorialize the baptism of Jesus himself as well as the baptisms recorded in the book of Acts. Multiple books defended the Brethren practice of baptism in comparison to infant baptism, sprinkling, etc.: *Testimony on Baptism as Practiced by the Primitive Christians from the Time of the Apostles...* by Peter Bowman, *Defense of Baptism* and *Further Defense of Baptism* by John Kline, *One Baptism* by J.H. Moore, *A Vindication of Trine Immersion as the Apostolic Form of Christian Baptism* by James Quinter, and *Doctrine of the Brethren Defended* by R.H. Miller.[37] Most of these were nineteenth-century attempts to defend the practice of trine immersion as the true apostolic practice.

Peter Nead, the most significant Brethren theologian of the nineteenth century, also defended the practice, as he identified three basic elements as part of salvation: faith, repentance, and baptism. According to Nead, "To be baptized was to bow obediently before God's commands, and 'if there was ever a time when persons should bow themselves, I do believe it should be done in Baptism.'"[38] Nead claimed that the Brethren baptismal practice represented the true mode described in the New Testament.

In 1848, the Brethren Annual Meeting unanimously approved an order of worship for the Brethren mode of baptism that they proposed should be accepted by all congregations. First, two or more brethren were supposed to examine the applicant for baptism and if approved, the church council would then hear the applicant "declare his agreement with us, in regard to the principles of being defenseless, not swearing, and not conforming to the world."[39] Then Matthew 18:10-22 would be read, followed by questioning of the candidate. There were three questions: "Dost thou believe that Jesus Christ is the Son of God, and that he has brought from heaven a saving gospel?; Dost thou willingly renounce Satan, with all his pernicious ways, and all the sinful pleasures of the world?; Dost thou covenant with God, in Christ Jesus, to be faithful until death?"[40] Upon answering in the affirmative to each of these questions, the person would be baptized in the name of the Father, Son, and Holy Ghost. After baptism, the elder would lay on hands, pray to God, and then the person would be received with the right hand of fellowship and the holy kiss.[41] If there was an objection in the local community to the candidate, they would try to reach reconciliation or postpone the baptism until they could reach a unanimous decision. If a person would not submit to the Brethren principles, then the congregation would not go forward with the process.[42] Again, we see in the questions the inner spirituality requiring faith and the call to discipleship tied to the outward act of baptism, the expression of relationship with God in action.

The matter of converts from other Christian churches highlights the central role baptism played in Brethren spirituality and life: rebaptism was required. By the 1830s, a person joining the Brethren would have been asked to be rebaptized unless he or she had already been immersed three times forward. Thus, if a person received baptism in another Christian group by trine immersion, the baptism was considered legitimate and acceptable. Over time, however, the Brethren began to enforce stricter boundaries. In the 1850s, trine immersion itself was not enough; the person would have to be rebaptized unless he or she had been baptized by a Dunker minister.[43] This remains an area of debate in different Brethren groups today, as some require rebaptism for membership, while others will accept baptism from other Christian groups.

One significant difference among Brethren groups today regards age of baptism. Among the Grace Brethren, Church of the Brethren, and Brethren Church, it is not unusual for baptism to occur somewhere between the age of 12 and 16, whereas in Old Order groups, baptism is more likely to occur between the ages of 16 and 22.[44] The younger ages in the Grace Brethren, Church of the Brethren, and Brethren Church may represent a shift from the more traditional association between baptism and discipleship towards a stronger association between baptism and salvation.[45]

Baptism has been understood as the ordinance that initiates life in the community and draws the new member into unity with the other Brethren and the life of discipleship. The way to reaffirm the promises made in baptism for many Brethren has been to participate in the love feast.

LOVE FEAST

As in baptism, we also see many Christocentric themes in the love feast. The love feast celebrates purity and unity as well as the regeneration of the saints. It expresses the love felt by the members of the community for each other as well as the love they have for God.[46] The elements of the love feast reinforce church unity: sharing sop from a common bowl and wine from a common cup represent the shared unity among the believers; eating together helps to cement relationships. The kiss of peace, shared among the gathered sisters and brothers, reinforces that they are in relationship with one another.[47]

The love feast has traditionally contained four parts, each exemplifying spiritual themes. First, there is a period of examination or preparation. During this section of the service, participants sing hymns and the seriousness of the love feast is emphasized. Then, feetwashing occurs according to the John 13 model. The meal follows and is traditionally composed of sop, but in some groups it now consists of a variety of different foods. Finally, the Brethren have the bread and cup of communion.[48] This order of service highlights negotiated change within the tradition. As Alexander Mack Jr. writes, originally the Brethren ate the meal first, but through further study determined that they should begin instead with feetwashing.[49]

Feetwashing symbolizes a variety of different spiritual themes. For example, in feetwashing, many Brethren understand the action as obedience in servanthood and humility, that is, Jesus engaged in an act that was typically reserved for slaves. The humbling that takes place is for both the individual who is washing feet as well as the one who is having his or her feet washed.[50] Feetwashing also exemplifies the purification of the body of believers and cleansing in preparation for judgment.[51] Washing feet symbolizes washing of the whole individual and particularly the washing away of sins. The believer also receives a reminder of his or her baptism in the feetwashing service. Feetwashing further serves as a preparation for the meal and communion by cleansing and purifying the believer.[52] An early Brethren hymn written for the feetwashing service stresses multiple spiritual themes within the service, including servanthood, the memorialization of Jesus' act of feetwashing, humility, entering into the suffering of Christ, and the unity of the believers.[53] Perhaps most striking is verse 7: "He who engages in this rite/ Must note how Christ did it that night/ In deep humiliation,/ And also see that being whole/ Requires the cleansing of the soul/ Through Christ's outpoured salvation."[54] This verse highlights the clear connection between an imitation of Christ in the act of feetwashing and salvation, a spiritual connection with Christ that is lived out in the concrete action of kneeling to wash another's feet. Later Brethren hymns, such as "When Our Great Sov'reign from on High" found in *The Christian's Duty*, also speak about this memorial aspect of feetwashing with lines such as "Arise then, and with due Respect, With humble Shame and Willingness, Do what our Saviour doth direct, Endowed with Disciple's Grace!"[55] Thus, Brethren hymns reinforced the relationship between the act of feetwashing, the community, and the spiritual life.

The agape meal points to the church's unity. As mentioned above, sharing a meal together exemplifies being in right relationship with one another. The love shared among the brothers and sisters sets this meal apart from other meals. Another theme found in the love feast meal itself is the eschatological image of the marriage feast of the lamb when there will be union between the believers and Christ. This meaning appears from the very beginning of the Brethren movement. In *Rights and Ordinances,* Alexander Mack states, "By such a supper they portray that they are members and house companions of the Lord Jesus. They will one day observe the Great Supper with the Lord Jesus at the close of the world and enjoy eternal happiness."[56] Mack's words point to the great eschatological feast that will occur with Christ himself, a theme prevalent throughout the nineteenth century. Brethren printer and writer, James Quinter, for example, wrote:

> this feast of love may be regarded as a representation of the great Marriage Supper of the Lamb, which is to take place when the Savior comes, and his people shall gather themselves together...and sit down in the kingdom of God. O my friends, do not believe that anything commanded by the Lord is a mere formality....because we believe [the Lord's Supper to be] commanded by the Lord, and because we have practically seen and felt its beneficial effects,--we contend for its observance in accordance with the custom of the apostolic church. I believe that in all things the more closely we adhere to the practices of the apostolic church the better. And if that is to be our model, then we must have a feast of charity; we must have something else that we can eat together besides the sacred emblems of the Communion.[57]

Thus, the love feast both looked backward, commemorating the actions of Christ, and looked forward to the future union between Christ and the Church. The love feast foreshadows the life of brotherhood that will occur in the world to come for many Brethren.

The meal also emphasizes the memorial aspect of the supper, as congregations attempted to recreate the meal served in the Gospel narratives as closely as possible, while they simultaneously emphasized the needs of their own communities. It was not always easy to hold these two in tension. The debate around what type of meat to serve during the love feast meal highlights this concern. As early as 1827, a query came to Annual Meeting questioning whether beef or lamb should be used at the meal, recognizing that the original meal was related to the Passover. The Annual Meeting that year declared that mutton was preferable in accordance with the meat served at Passover.[58] Yet by 1853, when a query again came forward about which meat to use, Annual Meeting determined that while lamb is better, "inasmuch as Christ has made us free from the ceremonial law, and as there is no command in the New Testament that it must be so, we should bear with each other in love in such matters."[59] Once again this issue arose in 1855 with a similar result, but beginning in 1858 there was a shift in urging the use of beef instead of lamb. By 1863, a reversal had occurred: beef had become the preferred meat, as Annual Meeting that year began to favor the interpretation of freedom from the law over the interpretation of the Passover meal.[60] Further study of the relevant Gospel passages also suggested that the meal was not actually the Passover and that instead the Passover was yet to come, a still anticipated event. As such, there was an attempt to move away from the meal as a recreation of the Passover feast.[61] This instance could demonstrate a form of legalism, but it should instead perhaps be seen as an attempt by the Brethren to hold the love feast meal in a way that was obedient to Scripture and which corresponded to the Brethren way of life in the nineteenth century. This concern was not simply an argument about meat. It was a discussion about how the material and spiritual life come together in concrete action and lived experience.

While the holy kiss or kiss of charity has sometimes been considered an ordinance alongside practices like the love feast and baptism, it has also been embedded within these practices as a unique expression of Brethren unity and the love between the community members. Traditionally, Brethren have only exchanged the holy kiss with other Brethren as a way to signify their relationships as brothers and sisters in the faith. Members exchange the kiss with members of the same sex on the lips and typically accompany the action with a handshake. The Brethren stressed that all members should exchange the kiss, not only those that might have a close familial or friend relationship. Yet, the kiss should not become a mere formality, but rather be an expression of genuine love and concern shared among believers.[62] In this way, the holy kiss, like the other Brethren ordinances stressed the unity within the body of Christ. The kiss exemplified this characteristic so well that it became part of the other ordinances. The individual would first receive the holy kiss when they came out of the baptismal waters as a way of demonstrating his or her new place within the community of believers. At the love feast, the brothers and sisters exchanged the holy kiss as a way to demonstrate their unity in community prior to receiving communion. It was an act that fundamentally distinguished Brethren from non-Brethren.[63]

So why did this act that carried so many of the key characteristics of Brethren spirituality and belief pass out of use in some Brethren groups? It is clear that those Brethren groups who blurred the lines of separation with the world slowly let go of the practice for a variety of reasons. New hygienic standards at the end of the nineteenth century caused some to question the practice. In the Church of the Brethren, for example, the 1888 Annual Meeting asked that men clip their upper lips to be "decent and orderly" for the exchange of the kiss and complained about the disgusting nature of exchanging the kiss with some Brethren.[64] There were concerns about rotting teeth, tobacco use, and frozen facial hair that caused some to question whether or not the holy kiss was really such a necessary greeting.[65] New converts were made uncomfortable by the kiss and evangelistic fervor made some want to dismiss the kiss. Thus, as an expression of Brethren unity, the kiss has passed out of use among some Brethren and has instead been replaced by a hug or handshake.

Recreating the suffering of Christ occurs throughout the love feast service, but it is most prevalent within the act of communion itself. It serves as a memorial of Christ's death and passion. It remembers the suffering of Christ and reminds the believers that they are partaking in the life that Christ gives. Sharing in this life of Christ is part of the mystery of the Christian faith.[66] Brethren have stressed these sacrificial and memorial themes of communion.[67] The Old German Baptist Brethren begin love feast with the description of the suffering servant in the book of Isaiah, "…he was bruised for our iniquities…and with his stripes we are healed."[68] This reminder of Christ's suffering sets the tone for the service as a memorial of Christ's sacrifice on behalf of the gathered community.

Spiritual leadership has also been an important part of carrying out the love feast, and in most congregations deacons have held a particularly important role in the preparation for the love feast. Their main tasks involve preparing or arranging for the meal, having the table set, ensuring there are towels and basins for feetwashing, and arranging for communion bread.[69] Traditionally deacons are also responsible for the annual visit. Historically, three questions have been asked:

1. Are you still in the faith as declared at your baptism?
2. Are you, as far as you know, in peace and union with the church?
3. Will you still labor with the Brethren for an increase of holiness, within yourself and others?

The 1867 Annual Meeting standardized this wording. In these questions, we again see the emphasis the Brethren placed on obedience, unity, and the ongoing process of sanctification in the life of the believer. If a brother or sister could not respond affirmatively to each of these questions, the deacons would determine if the individual needed to be set back from the love feast or whether the whole of the event might need to be delayed due to a larger problem within the community.[70] However, this process is no longer present in all Brethren groups today. The Old German Baptist Brethren still have the annual visit, inquiring about the state of faith, relationships with others, and whether the member is "willing to receive and give counsel and instruction."[71] Then the members are asked if they will make a financial contribution to the love feast.[72] Here again we see the blending of the spiritual and the material in the celebration of the love feast. Within the context of the ordinances, the Brethren tie their spirituality to concrete acts of giving, certainly, as well as concrete ways of relating to God and neighbor.

Despite the fact that love feast is not quite as popular now among all Brethren groups as it once was, many Brethren express that love feast is a high point in their spiritual life as well as a repeated reminder of their love for Christ and for their fellow believers. Church of the Brethren scholar William Beahm captured this with poignant clarity when he wrote:

> The meaning of the love feast as a whole is in this interrelationship between our religious experience and our social relations, between the power of God and our human needs. It symbolizes our faith with its vertical dimension toward God and its horizontal dimension toward men. Any attempt to curtail the evening's ceremony so as to speed it up, or any attempt to streamline

it so as to reduce wind resistance among the sophisticated, is to jeopardize its richer significance.[73]

For Brethren, the love feast has served as a touchstone event in their spiritual life that connects them strongly to the suffering Christ, the returning Christ, and their fellow believers.

Anointing

While baptism and love feast are ordinances in which all Brethren are generally expected to participate as part of their membership, anointing is not always expected because it is generally reserved for special circumstances. However, anointing carries with it some of these key aspects of Brethren spirituality. Brethren have understood anointing as a practice rooted in both the Old and New Testaments, again emphasizing that the ordinances draw directly from the scriptural account. In the Old Testament, kings and other leaders received anointing as a sign of God's presence with their leadership.[74] Special vessels used in worship were anointed and there was a special oil to be used for that purpose.[75] Spiritual leaders, like the high priest Aaron, also received anointing as part of their leadership.[76] While Jesus did not anoint anyone with oil, he did perform multiple healings; there are 26 healing narratives in Luke's Gospel. When Jesus sent out the 12, he gave the command to heal and when he sent out the 70, he also urged them to engage in healing.[77] In Mark 6:12-13, the disciples are described as healing by anointing with oil. Yet it is the record in the New Testament book of James where we find the most direct reference to anointing with oil. Physical healing and a restored relationship with God stand at the heart of the anointing service; the act of anointing is intended to forgive sins as well as provide physical healing.[78] In this way, we see the identification of the practice of anointing with the suffering motif. When the individual is suffering, he or she should call on the gathered community and the elders so that they can share their suffering and together pray for relief from their ailment and intervention from God.

While there is no direct evidence about when the Brethren started anointing, it is generally assumed that they began anointing with oil sometime in the early 18th century. In 1770 Morgan Edwards produced an account of all Baptist groups in the American colonies and there he mentions that the Brethren in Pennsylvania practiced anointing. The first record from a Brethren source of the practice of anointing is in the 1797 Annual Meeting minutes, which essentially affirms the practice of anointing without much description or elaboration. In 1812, there was a query about the relationship between medical help and anointing. The Annual Meeting determined that after being anointed, a person should not seek further medical attention. This decision was later reversed in 1860, allowing a person to seek medical attention after they had received anointing. Also in 1812, there was a question about whether a person could be anointed a second time if they fell ill again. Annual Meeting affirmed that it was possible to be anointed for a second illness.[79] These debates again point to the tension Brethren felt between the material and the spiritual. They were not simply considering legalistic concerns, but rather weighed the biblical evidence regarding healing in the New Testament against the potential for healing provided by medical doctors. In this way, Brethren adjusted their practice to allow more opportunities for anointing in order to provide spiritual benefit and allow for the possibility of physical benefit as well.

The first outline of a service for anointing was in the 1827 Annual Meeting minutes. The service included the singing of a few hymn verses, a prayer, the actual anointing with oil performed by two elders, the reading of the relevant passage from James 5, the laying on of hands, and a prayer for the sick person. A more detailed service appeared in 1860.[80] These services remain largely unchanged among most Brethren today. The form of the service remains very close to the biblical instructions in James, again demonstrating the obedience theme. However, we also see an emphasis on unity as the brother or sister receiving anointing calls on the help of the community and even more so in later versions of the service has an opportunity to confess sins that may be standing between the individual and God and make restitution with other members of the community.

There were two important questions in the nineteenth century regarding anointing. First, who in the church should preside over an anointing service? Second, who could receive anointing? Annual Meeting repeatedly said that an elder should preside over an anointing, except in cases where an elder could not be obtained. It was also clear that only baptized members should receive anointing.[81] The debate around the question of who could preside over anointing frequently raised the issue of whether the word "elder" in the James passage required an ordained elder or not. Again, we see the attempt the Brethren made to recreate the ordinance in the present day, including a correlation between contemporary leadership and apostolic leadership.

For Brethren, anointing and healing have gone hand-in-hand. For the most part, anointing has been for physical illness and spiritual uplift. It can also serve as a sort of spiritual blessing for the dying.[82] Healing was intended to bring the individual into better relationship with God so that he or she could then go forth from that healing with a renewed spiritual relationship. The healing was a commissioning from God into greater work for the kingdom of God.[83] Anointing symbolizes that the person is placing all of his or her life in God's hands and is willing to submit to the will of God.[84]

Brethren theological writers have not much debated the subject of anointing. Peter Nead stressed that anointing was a way for the sick person to accept the will of God, whether that meant restored health or death. L. W. Teeter wrote that the primary mission of anointing was physical restoration of the body with a secondary goal of three blessings: salvation, that the person might be raised up in prayer, and sins be forgiven.[85] Warren Groff, a Church of the Brethren scholar, has stressed that anointing is a way of entering into the life, death, and resurrection of Jesus, claiming that we anoint in the hope of God's healing, but it is usually in the face of tremendous personal or familial pain.[86] Anyone who is sick can request the service, although it is generally reserved for serious sickness rather than for minor illnesses. It is preferable that the person is fully conscious during the anointing and also that he or she understands the anointing service before receiving it. They also should be prepared to confess their sins and be restored to right relationship.[87]

Anointing remains an important practice in Brethren groups and fits the general quality of the ordinances. In it we see the Brethren attempt to adhere to the scriptural precedents, to demonstrate the unity of the community in common prayer for the sick individual, and to combine the spiritual needs of the community with a concrete action. While anointing may not be practiced in community the same way as love feast or baptism, it remains an important demonstration of love for each other and faith in God within Brethren communities.

Concluding Thoughts

The ordinances have provided a unique expression of Brethren spirituality. They all exhibit the Brethren attempt, from the eighteenth century to today, to recreate the apostolic church. The debates around the ordinances have frequently stemmed from Brethren concerns about what mode or model is closest to the biblical narrative. In this way, the Brethren emphasis on obedience to Christ as a spiritual discipline is evident. We also see in the ordinances the ways that the Brethren have reinforced bonds of community, whether it be through the questions asked at baptism or the kiss of peace exchanged during love feast. In the ordinances we see the Brethren attempt to balance the spiritual life and the needs of the community with concrete action.

Perhaps, however, the ordinances have stood and continue to stand at the heart of Brethren spirituality because they exemplify the nature of the Brethren faith. In these moments and rituals, we see a profound connection to God and particularly to Jesus Christ by memorializing the actions of Jesus and symbolically recreating moments in the life of Christ and the early church. Yet, in them we also see an emphasis on the relationships among the body of believers. In this way, the ordinances remain a key expression of Brethren spirituality across Brethren groups. They are a shared thread.

Notes

1 Quoted in Carl F. Bowman, *Brethren Society: The Cultural Transformation of a "Peculiar People"* (Baltimore, Md.: Johns Hopkins University Press, 1995), 319.

2 Donald F. Durnbaugh, *The Believers' Church: The History and Character of Radical Protestantism*. 2nd ed. (Scottdale, Pa.: Herald Press, 1985), 33.

3 Bowman, *Brethren Society*, 29.

4 Nancy Rosenberger Faus, "Spirituality and Worship in the Church of the Brethren," *Brethren Life and Thought* 39:4 (Fall 1994): 241-242.

5 Faus, "Spirituality and Worship in the Church of the Brethren," 241.

6 Faus, "Spirituality and Worship in the Church of the Brethren," 243.

7 Thomas N. Finger, "Sources for Contemporary Spirituality: Anabaptist and Pietist Contributions," *Brethren Life and Thought* 51:1-2 (Winter-Spring 2006): 5.

8 Finger, "Sources for Contemporary Spirituality," 5.

9 Bowman, *Brethren Society*, 29.

10 For more on the ordinances and the Old Testament, see Denise D. Kettering, "Old Testament Festivals and Brethren Rituals," in *The Witness of the Hebrew Bible for a New Testament Church*, ed. Christina Bucher, et al., (Elgin, Ill.: Brethren Press, 2010), 289-308.

11 Donald F. Durnbaugh, "The Genius of the Early Brethren," *Brethren Life & Thought* 50:3-4 (Summer & Fall 2005): 17.

12 From "Answer to Gruber's Basic Questions." Donald F. Durnbaugh, *European Origins of the Brethren* (Elgin, Ill.: Brethren Press, 1958), 331.

13 Faus, "Spirituality and Worship in the Church of the Brethren," 243.

14 Dale W. Brown, *Another Way of Believing: A Brethren Theology* (Elgin, Ill.: Brethren Press, 2005), 110.

15 Bowman, *Brethren Society*, 76.

16 Bowman, *Brethren Society*, 26.

17 Bowman, *Brethren Society)*, 36.

18 Bowman, *Brethren Society*, 72-73.

19 Bowman, *Brethren Society*, 74.

20 Bowman, *Brethren Society*, 319.

21 Bowman, *Brethren Society*, 32, 53.

22 Brown, *Another Way of Believing*, 121-122; Bowman, *Brethren Society*, 318.

23 Bowman, *Brethren Society*, 58.

24 Bowman, *Brethren Society*, 170.

25 Brown, *Another Way of Believing*, 123.

26 Peter Nead, *Primitive Christianity, or A Vindication of the Word of God* (Staunton, Va.: Kenton Harper, printer, 1834), 75-76.

27 Durnbaugh, *European Origins of the Brethren*, 408.

28 Brown, *Another Way of Believing*, 120.

29 Durnbaugh, *European Origins of the Brethren*, 116-117.

30 Bowman, *Brethren Society*, 53-54; Allen T. Hansell, "Believers Baptism: Walking in newness of life," in *A Dunker Guide to Brethren Beliefs* (Elgin, Ill.: Brethren Press, 2012), 69.

31 Brown, *Another Way of Believing*, 121.

32 Durnbaugh, *European Origins of the Brethren*, 338. For more on Eberhard Gruber's questions in *Basic Questions*, see Hans Schneider, "'Basic Questions on Water Baptism': An Early Anti-Brethren Pamphlet" *Brethren Life and Thought* 43:3-4 (Summer and Fall 1997): 31-63 and Marcus Meier, "Eberhard Ludwig Gruber's 'Basic Questions': Report of a Discovery," *Brethren Life and Thought* 43:3-4 (Summer and Fall 1997): 64-67.

33 For more on this topic, see Marcus Meier, *The Origin of the Schwarzenau Brethren*, trans. Dennis L. Slabaugh (Philadelphia, Pa.: The Brethren Encyclopedia, Inc., 2008), 124-125.

34 Durnbaugh, *European Origins of the Brethren*, 355.

35 Durnbaugh, *European Origins of the Brethren*, 121.

36 Durnbaugh, "The Genius of the Early Brethren," 27.

37 Bowman, *Brethren Society*, 55.

38 Quoted in Bowman, *Brethren Society*, 54.

39 Quoted in Bowman, *Brethren Society*, 56.

40 Quoted in Bowman, *Brethren Society*, 56.

41 Bowman, *Brethren Society*, 56.

42 Bowman, *Brethren Society*, 57.

43 Bowman, *Brethren Society*, 212.

44 Donald B. Kraybill and C. Nelson Hostetter, *Anabaptist World USA*. (Scottdale, Pa.: Herald Press, 2001), 44.

45 Brown, *Another Way of Believing*, 126.

46 Bowman, *Brethren Society*, 59.

47 Bowman, *Brethren Society*, 318-319; William M. Beahm, *The Brethren Love Feast* (Elgin, Ill.: Brethren Press, 1942),7-9.

48 Bowman, *Brethren Society*, 59-60.

49 For a further discussion of this change, according to Alexander Mack Jr., see Denise Kettering-Lane, "Ordering the Love feast: Alexander Mack Jr.'s Liturgical Theology," *Brethren Life & Thought*, 58:1 (Spring 2013): 85-94.

50 Beahm, *The Brethren Love Feast*, 4; Brown, *Another Way of Believing*, 129.

51 Bowman, *Brethren Society*, 369.

52 Beahm, *The Brethren Love Feast*, 4.

53 Durnbaugh, *European Origins of the Brethren*, 415-418.

54 Durnbaugh, *European Origins of the Brethren*, 417.

55 Donald R. Hinks, *Brethren Hymn Books and Hymnals 1720-1884* (Gettysburg, Pa.: Brethren Heritage Press, 1986), 43.

56 Durnbaugh, *European Origins of the Brethren*, 364.

57 Quoted in D.L. Miller, *The Lord's Supper* (Brethren Publishing House, 1892), 8.

58 *Minutes of the Annual Meeting of the Church of the Brethren: Containing All Available Minutes from 1778-1909* (Elgin, Ill.: Brethren Publishing House, 1909), 51.

59 *Minutes,* 137.

60 *Minutes,* 151, 174, 217, 219.

61 Harold S. Martin, *New Testament Beliefs and Practices: A Brethren Understanding* (Elgin, Ill.: Brethren Press, 1989), 50.

62 Bowman, *Brethren Society*, 67-68.

63 Non-Brethren persons only received a handshake in greeting. Bowman, *Brethren Society*, 69.

64 Bowman, *Brethren Society*, 167.

65 Bowman, *Brethren Society*, 167-168.

66 Beahm, *The Brethren Love Feast*, 10-12.

67 Brown, *Another Way of Believing*, 115.

68 Fred W. Benedict, "A Brief Account of the Origin and a Description of The Brethren Love feast," (1967), 1.

69 Association of Brethren Caregivers. *Deacon Manual for Caring Ministries* (Elgin, Ill.: Association of Brethren Caregivers, 1999), 218.

70 Bowman, *Brethren Society*, 62.

71 Benedict, "A Brief Account of the Origin and a Description of The Brethren Love feast," 6.

72 Benedict, "A Brief Account of the Origin and a Description of The Brethren Love feast," 6.

73 Beahm, *The Brethren Love feast*, 14.

74 1 Sam. 10:1-9, 16:10-13; 2 Sam. 2:4

75 Exodus 30:22-34.

76 Exodus 29: 1-18.

77 Luke 9: 1-6; Luke 10:1-12.

78 Dean M. Miller, *Anointing: The Congregation's Use of Anointing for Healing and Reconciliation* (Elgin, Ill.: Brethren Press, 1987), 12.

79 Graydon Snyder and Kenneth M. Shaffer Jr. "On Anointing for Healing," *Texts in Transit II.* (Elgin, Ill.: Brethren Press, 1991), 230-231.

80 Snyder and Shaffer, "On Anointing for Healing,", 230-231.

81 Snyder and. Shaffer "On Anointing for Healing," 231.

82 Warren Bowman, "Anointing for Healing," *Brethren Life and Thought* (Summer 1959): 56.

83 Miller, *Anointing*, 19.

84 Harold Martin. "The Anointing Service." *BRF Witness.org* (Sept./Oct. 2000). http://www.brfwitness.org/?p=1209 (Accessed 8/30/2012).

85 Snyder and. Shaffer "On Anointing for Healing," 231.

86 Warren Groff, "Anointing for Healing," *Brethren Life and Thought* 56:1 (Spring 2011): 50.

87 Bowman, "Anointing for Healing," 57.

The Brethren Heritage Center on Wolf Creek Street in Brookville, Ohio, provided the excellent host facilities for the plenary sessions, breakout panels, and other main activities of the Fifth Brethren World Assembly. (© *Church of the Brethren, photo by Cheryl Brumbaugh-Cayford*)

Evening sessions were held at local church buildings of participating Brethren bodies. Pastor Rick Hartley welcomed the Thursday evening attenders to the Brookville Grace Brethren Church. *(Terry White photo)*

(left) Brother Robert Lehigh of the Dunkard Brethren Church welcomed attenders at the initial session. Lehigh is president of the board of Brethren Encyclopedia Inc, which sponsors the Brethren World Assemblies. *(Dale Ulrich photo)*

(right) Robert E. Alley, immediate past moderator of the Church of the Brethren, chaired the planning team for the 2013 assembly and added his welcome to representatives of all the Brethren bodies gathered for the four-day event. *(Dale Ulrich photo)*

Morning plenary sessions were held in the spacious lower-level gathering room of the Brethren Heritage Center. Here Dr. Dale Stoffer of Ashland Theological Seminary and vice president of the Brethren Encyclopedia Board addressed attenders. *(Dale Ulrich photo)*

The several hundred present represented all seven Brethren bodies descended from Alexander Mack and his original followers in Germany. Participating groups included Church of the Brethren, The Brethren Church, Dunkard Brethren Church, Fellowship of Grace Brethren Churches, Conservative Grace Brethren Churches International, Old German Baptist Brethren Church, New Conference and Old German Baptist Brethren Church. *(© Church of the Brethren, photo by Cheryl Brumbaugh-Cayford)*

Bus tours to sites of Brethren historic interest were conducted each afternoon. Lower Miami Church of the Brethren on Germantown Pike in Dayton, Ohio, founded in October of 1805 by elder Jacob Miller, is the oldest Church of the Brethren west of the Great Miami River and the second oldest in Ohio. Lower Miami is known in the Southern Ohio District as the "Mother Church," because 11 congregations can trace their roots back to her. *(© Church of the Brethren, photo by Cheryl Brumbaugh-Cayford)*

One very special international guest was Bernd Julius (center) of Schwarzenau, Germany, shown here with some of the Nigerian Brethren. Julius at the time was serving as the president of the Schwarzenau Heritage Society (Heimatverein). *(Dale Ulrich photo)*

Gale Honeyman, co-chair of the Brethren Heritage Center Board of Directors and a member of the Church of the Brethren, appeared in period clothing to help with historical interpretation at the Lower Miami church. *(Terry White photo)*

Dr. Marcus Miller (left) and Elder Glen Landes (right), both members of the Old German Baptist Brethren, New Conference, gave a tour of the Abraham Landis farm and the barn where the Old German Baptist Brethren group was formed on November 25, 1881. *(Dale Ulrich photo)*

Dr. Christy Hill of the Grace Theological Seminary faculty was one of the many scholars and academics who presented the results of their research. *(Terry White photo)*

A sweet time of individual and corporate prayer followed the opening session on Sunday evening. *(Terry White photo)*

An excellent panel of young Brethren, assembled and led by Michael Miller of Brookville, Ohio, discussed their perspective on the future of the various Brethren groups. *(Terry White photo)*

This traveling team of young people representing the Conservative Grace Brethren Churches International provided music and testimony in an evening session. *(Terry White photo)*

One of the host churches, Salem Church of the Brethren, treated everyone to an ice cream social and fellowship time following the evening plenary session. *(© Church of the Brethren, photo by Cheryl Brumbaugh-Cayford)*

Pastor Fred Miller from The Brethren Church spoke on "Missions and Evangelism as Brethren Spirituality." (© *Church of the Brethren, photo by Cheryl Brumbaugh-Cayford*)

Dr. Dale Stoffer of Ashland Theological Seminary moderated a stimulating panel on Brethren ordinances. (© *Church of the Brethren, photo by Cheryl Brumbaugh-Cayford*)

Seminars

The Spiritual Writings of Alexander Mack, Jr.

Aaron Jerviss

Introduction

Last year, at the Young Center for Anabaptist and Pietist Studies at Elizabethtown College in Pennsylvania, a three-day conference was held on the life and influence of Alexander Mack Jr., a man sometimes known as "Sander Mack." Those looking to gain a deeper understanding of the man and his legacy are strongly encouraged to pick up the Spring 2013 issue of *Brethren Life and Thought*, which contains all the papers presented at that conference by all the "heavy hitters" of Brethren scholarship. There are articles examining Mack from a theological perspective, a sociological perspective, articles examining the aesthetic qualities of his poetry, and so much more. I read that issue of *Brethren Life and Thought* from cover-to-cover and am indebted to all the Young Center conference contributors, but after I finished reading the issue, my first thought was "Wow, that subject's been picked clean." My goal here this afternoon, then, is to offer something to both those with a considerable body of knowledge of Alexander Mack Jr. and those who know little or nothing about the man. We'll start off with some biographical details about Mack Jr., move into some of the key themes present in his spiritual writings, and then attempt to place Mack within "the big picture" of American religious history by ending with some observations on the influence of the American environment on Mack and its applications for us today. I should also mention that I will be focusing today on Mack's religious poetry. Mack Jr. was a prolific writer who composed both doctrinal works and a significant body of written correspondence, but because of time restraints, we'll look at Mack's poetry only.

Alexander Mack, Jr. Timeline

Alexander Mack Jr. was born in January 1712 in Schwarzenau, Germany, the third child of Alexander and Anna Mack. At the time of Sander's birth, the Brethren movement was less than four years old, 1708 being the year of the Schwarzenau baptisms bringing the Brethren movement into being. In 1720, the Macks moved from Germany to the province of Friesland in the Netherlands, and in that year, when young Alexander was eight years old, Anna Mack died. Two younger sisters died as well around this timeframe. In 1728, Mack Jr. received baptism and entered into full membership of the church. The following year, Sander Mack, his father, and his two older brothers left Europe for good, setting sail for America, where they settled in Germantown, Pennsylvania.

In 1735, Alexander Mack Sr. died, and it appears that this triggered a crisis for both Mack Jr. personally and the Germantown congregation as a whole. Three years later, Mack Jr. and three other young Brethren moved to the Ephrata community, a cloister located in present-day Lancaster County, Pennsylvania. This community was founded in 1732 by Conrad Beissel, a highly charismatic individual who had once led the Brethren congregation at Conestoga. Ephrata's distinct practices included observing the Sabbath on Saturday, Old Testament dietary restrictions, celebrating the virtue of celibacy, and monastic practices including the wearing of a habit, a white monastic robe. Around 1745, personal disputes with Beissel led Mack Jr. and two brothers, Israel and Samuel Eckerlin, to leave Ephrata (to be exact, the Eckerlins were expelled, and Mack Jr. joined them). Along with others, the three attempted to replicate the Ephrata experience on the western frontier of Virginia, but in 1748, Mack Jr. returned to Germantown and returned to the Brethren fellowship. In 1753, Sander Mack was ordained as a Brethren elder and over the next half-century, he devoted much time and service to advancing the Brethren cause. As mentioned earlier, he took pen to paper to defend Brethren faith and practices such as feetwashing and adult believer's baptism. His counsel on spiritual matters was sought out at Annual Meeting as well as at Germantown. Outside the church, Mack worked hard as both a weaver and a father. Mack's wife Elizabeth, whom he married in 1749, gave birth to eight children, although sadly only three of the eight would outlive their parents. Mack Jr. died in April 1803, and thus ended a lengthy and remarkable life, both for what he experienced personally and witnessed historically.[1]

THEMES IN MACK JR.'S POETRY

Early in the twentieth century, Samuel Heckman, a graduate of the University of Pennsylvania, translated Mack's poetry from German into English and placed Mack's poems into two categories: first, hymns and occasional poems; and second, longer poems contributed to Christopher Sauer's religious magazine, a periodical published at irregular intervals between 1763 and 1772. Mack's writings lacked artistic polish, according to Heckman, yet the translator found these same poems "deeply religious, contemplative, and frequently didactic in character, but… not melancholy nor morbid," the product of "a man of great power of thought and keen insight into human nature" and "a man whose heart overflowed with the love of God."[2]

So, what are some of the recurrent themes in these "deeply religious, contemplative" poems? First, Mack places "the world" in opposition to the Christian faith and message. Frequently, Mack makes mention of the "vanities" and "fleeting things" offered by the world. Wealth is described as one of the primary enticements of Satan. In one of his hymns, Mack writes, "It makes Satan rave so madly if one does not love and honor beauteous bubbles as if gods. Oh, depart, tumultuous world, for my beloved is in heaven. He is worthy of all love and honor." Engaged in an endless pursuit of riches, the world scoffs at the Christian notion of simplicity: "It is true, the world says, Christ's teachings are not to be understood; that one is under obligation to follow him in all things in poverty particularly. This would be too unreasonable." If the world is a place of the fleeting and the transitory, it is also an oppressive place. In a piece written for Christopher Sauer's religious magazine sometime in the 1760s, Mack shows awareness of Enlightenment-era intellectual currents as he warns readers of the dangers of "free thought." According to Mack, the freethinker "…is but serving the false image which has taken possession of his soul…the atheist thinks that he is free when he believes that there is no God. He does not know that in mockery of himself he must serve a false god whose aim it is by day and night to enslave the soul." For Mack, then, the freedom of the truth of Christ stands in marked contrast to the slavery of the yoke of Satan found in the world.[3]

If the world is a site of opposition towards Christ and Christ's followers, it follows that the notion of pilgrimage, being a stranger in a strange land, should figure prominently in Mack's poetry. The pilgrim motif was around in Christian circles long before Alexander Mack Jr., but the historian in me can't help but wonder if this imagery resonated with Mack because of his experience as an immigrant. As a Schwarzenau-born Brethren, did Mack perhaps feel a double sense of "alienness," an outsider in both the spiritual and geographical senses? Starting on his 60th birthday in 1772, Mack Jr., with a few exceptions, wrote a brief poem into his diary every birthday, every January 28 up until his death in 1803. The idea of pilgrimage occurs repeatedly in these birthday poems. Two brief examples of this: from 1779, "Once again a year is gone/O thou rock, eternity!/ All my ardent longing goes far beyond this life/towards this true fatherland/for I'm a stranger here below." The next year, in 1780, Mack continues thinking of himself as a spiritual foreigner: "I can no more consider what happens in this world/ For on these pilgrims' roads there shines for me a different light…What brings me pain but helps me on, what brings me joy but holds me back/My true rest I find up yonder when my brief pilgrimage is done." On his final birthday entry written in January 1802, Mack refers to himself as "the poor pilgrim whom the mercy of God has sustained until he is ninety years old."[4]

The experience of traveling as a stranger in a hostile world required some source of hope, and Mack Jr. found his hope in the risen Jesus Christ. A hymn written by Mack first published in 1788 begins, "Jesus Christ the son of God/May praise and honor be given to thee/Who sittest upon the throne round which thousands of angels hover." The influence of Pietism manifests itself throughout Mack's poetry as Christ is referred to as the "Lamb of God," "the Bridegroom," and the "Good and Faithful Shepherd" whose teachings are "sweet as sugar" and "sweeter than honey." One of Sander Mack's longer poems chronicles the trial and crucifixion of Jesus. This is a remarkable poem because it both documents the final hours preceding Christ's death as a historical event, yet it also places the author, Mack Jr., at "the scene of the crime," as it were. The poem reinforces the belief of Christ's death as substitutionary, the shed blood of Jesus being the price of humanity's salvation. A few stanzas from this piece of poetry:

Eight o'clock.
Dressed in white, Thou comest now
To Pilate once again,
For nothing 'gainst Thee can be found
Save only my own guilt of sins.

Nine o'clock.
Wicked men are scourging Thee,
But the guilt I must confess
And in justice I should suffer
What the mad heathen do to Thee.

Ten o'clock.
The crown of thorns Jesus must wear,
The purple robe, the jeers and scorn,
All for me unworthy sinner,
And in addition He is beaten….

Three o'clock in the afternoon.
Now that all should be fulfilled
Which the Scriptures have foretold,
And that they might quench His thirst
They have a sponge filled with vinegar.

And the precious Lamb of God
Drinks it on the cross's beam,
Bows His head and suffers death
So that mercy I can receive.[5]

Finally, Mack Jr.'s poetry stresses the authority of Scripture. At the Young Center conference, one of the great topics of discussion appeared to be: How Pietist was Mack Jr.'s poetry? While Mack desired a heartfelt, Spirit-filled inner life, he also believed in the necessity of staying true to the dictates of Scripture. In a poem published in 1770, Sander Mack writes, "Read what Malachi witnesses…and what Isaiah does not fail to mention, yea, Christ himself informs us about that all-important event on that Day of Judgment…take the Bible in your hand and inform yourself as to where you stand." Samuel Heckman, in his translation of Mack's poetry, noted that Mack was "…fond of paraphrasing passages of Scripture." We are not given any insight into why Mack chose the passages he did, but it remains fascinating that one piece of Scripture paraphrased in German by Mack was the 119th Psalm. Over the course of eighty stanzas, Mack repeatedly proclaims the virtues found in the testimonies, laws, statutes, and commandments of God. Here's a taste from Mack Jr.'s paraphrase of Psalm 119:

> With all my heart and all my soul
> I have thee sought, O Lord, my God.
> Oh, let me therefore never stray
> From Thy great and holy laws.
>
> Thy word alone is the possessor
> Of my heart continually,
> It is thus my soul's protector,
> That against Thee I do not sin.
>
> I'll give Thee praise continually
> For the state of Thy great mercy.
> Teach me in temptation's tests
> To be mindful of Thy laws.

It is important here to note that Radical Pietism, for all its influence on the early Brethren, tended to favor direct revelation over Scripture, and this is certainly the case with Conrad Beissel and his leadership at Ephrata. Radical Pietists feared the danger of legalism if too much attention was directed towards Scripture. The poetry of Alexander Mack Jr., however, seems to nicely balance the experiential and the external. Mack believes in a vital, Spirit-awakened relationship that still recognizes the written word of God in Scripture as a beneficial and necessary foundational document. [6]

Alexander Mack Jr. and the American Religious Experience

In the final part of this presentation, I'd like to talk about how the American religious environment may have influenced Alexander Mack Jr. and what insights we can glean from Mack for our own present-day experience. First, it appears to me that, traditionally, Brethren have tried to explain Mack's years at Ephrata as the result of some psychological or spiritual malady. Perhaps, the theory goes, Mack was so distraught over the death of his father that he just wasn't thinking clearly and substituted Beissel as a father figure. Perhaps the rebellious nature of youth caused Sander Mack to "sow his spiritual wild oats" and step outside his father's faith. Mack himself later blamed a "childlike lack of understanding" for driving him from the Brethren fellowship. When I look at these years, my first thought is that Alexander Mack Jr. was acting American, immersing himself into this new foreign environment. What do I mean by acting American? Mack Jr. seemed to possess a longing for revival, a desire to find a more intense spiritual experience than that offered by his current church home. The years between 1738 and 1748, when Mack Junior stood outside the Brethren movement proper, overlap with the First Great Awakening. There is no evidence of any causal connection between the events of the First Awakening and the life of Alexander Mack Junior, but something's "in the water" during this particular moment of colonial American history.

Mack breaks off from the Brethren not long after the Northampton, Massachusetts revivals overseen by Jonathan Edwards during 1734 and 1735, an awakening ignited by young people coming to grips with their own mortality after other youths in the community died. Again, no evidence exists proving that Mack knew about the occurrences in New England, but here we have Mack Junior, after the death of his father, engaging in a more ecstatic religious experience than that offered by the Brethren and, in so doing, challenging the ecclesiastical authority of his youth. Mack, in other words, displayed all the characteristics of one seeking religious awakening. Historians argue about how many Great Awakenings have taken place in American religious history or even whether there is such an event as a Great Awakening, but Mack Junior certainly falls into a category of spiritual seekers appearing throughout the course of American history desiring personal renewal through a more fervent religious experience.[7]

Closely associated was this longing for revival is another ancient and sacred American religious activity: "church shopping." There is something distinctly American about demanding unlimited choices, and this applies to religion as much as anything else. We lose sight of how revolutionary this idea was in the eighteenth century, but the beauty of the American experiment was that, in the absence of a state church, religious bodies had to compete in a religious marketplace in order to attract followers. In a paper he presented at the Young Center conference, Steve Longenecker quite effectively showed how, in colonial Pennsylvania, religious nonconformity represented the rule, not the exception. Place yourself in Alexander Mack Jr's shoes. All your life, you've shopped at one store and one store only to meet all your needs. Then, in your mid-twenties, the outlet mall rolls into town. You would perhaps be curious enough to visit, enticed enough to actively shop around, and perhaps persuaded to make a significant purchase. This is Alexander Mack Jr. taking advantage of what the American religious environment had to offer, shopping in the American religious marketplace, and yet he does eventually return to Germantown and the Brethren fellowship.[8]

Alexander Mack Jr. is thus an early example, perhaps the earliest, of a dilemma confronting Brethren in their American experience up to the present day: the tension of preserving Brethren distinctiveness versus maintaining spiritual relevancy. In the methods and materials used for spiritual formation, discipleship, or worship, what needs to remain Brethren and what perhaps needs to be imported from the outside? What can Brethren learn from other traditions that is spiritually edifying, and how can those ideas and practices be incorporated without making Brethren indistinguishable from other denominations and religious bodies? How do Brethren keep the ecstatic allure of Ephrata while sticking to their Germantown roots?

Secondly, we find an expectation of the end in Mack Jr's poetry. In a lengthy poem published in 1770, Mack Jr. sees the global stage set for the close-approaching return of Christ. Here are two representative stanzas from that poem:

> These must indeed be the latter days,
> For just as in the times of Noah
> There now delights in foolishness,
> The host of unconverted souls.
> The Day of Judgment is lost to mind,
> Tis said "tis still far off."…
> Now this Son of the Most High
> Stands really here before our door
> His day of judgment is close upon us,
> The signs are most emphatic,
> Yea, the beginning of the distress is past
> As his faithful words informed us.

Sander Mack points to the Biblical account of Sodom and Gomorrah, the volcano at Vesuvius, and recent earthquakes in Palermo, Italy, Lima, Peru, and Lisbon, Portugal as both proof of God's judgment and motivation to "attach oneself to the yoke of Christ." Before engaging in date-setting, however, Mack places this profound verse towards the end of the poem:

> But when and where this is to happen
> Is known alone to gracious God;
> As He wishes so must things be.
> May He only grant that we, according to our station,
> From the bottom of our hearts, humbly and purely
> Fear him and be obedient.

Mack Jr. heeds "the signs of the times" without becoming lost in the speculative. Looking ahead to the Second Coming does not distract Mack from the necessity of holy living in the present moment.[9]

The belief that Christians are living in the last days goes all the way back to the Ascension. Yet, looking over the course of American religious history, from the Millerites of the mid-nineteenth century to the Scofield Reference Bible to Hal Lindsey and the Left Behind novels, there has never been a shortage of eschatological excitement in American religious and cultural life. Indeed, if not for end-time literature, many Christian bookstores would be in trouble. Mack Jr. stands as a reminder to us to keep our eyes open for the real and imminent return of Christ, but not to let the specifics of the hereafter overwhelm the importance of the here and now. Mack echoes the words of 2 Peter 3:11 and 12 which ask: "What sort of people ought you to be in holy conduct and godliness, looking for and hastening the coming of the day of God?"[10]

Finally, I would suggest that the American environment helped confirm ultimate authority for Alexander Mack Jr. At the end of Samuel Heckman's translation of Mack's religious poetry, there is a series of ten short poems written explicitly for young people. Each poem defines a Christian virtue such as beauty, love, wisdom, etc. Two of these poems jumped out at me, one written about nobility, the other about power. On the subject of nobility, Mack writes, "Jesus' nobility is alone eternally worthy of all honors; carnal nobility in spite of its appearance is subject to mortality. Christ's nobility I will praise and worship piously for he proves vigorously that he can ennoble us." In regards to power, Mack observed, "Great and mighty must we call the rulers of the world; therefore I shall acknowledge the power of him who maintains the world. The power of men is limited and soon exhausted and is forgotten in its grave, for the dead are of little importance...when kings depart their power is gone, but Jesus travels these ways with increasing glory." Again, this is material published in 1770 for Christopher Sauer's periodical, and I think the context here may be crucial. Though Mack Jr. fails to mention current historical events, we know that he is writing in a time of contested authority. Throughout the Revolutionary period, Brethren would encounter suspicion and undergo occasional persecution for their earthly loyalties. What I hear Mack saying is, during volatile times in the temporal realm, it is helpful and necessary to remember that Christ outlives rulers and empires, and our foremost allegiance is to a heavenly power.[11]

In my dissertation, I looked at how all three historic peace churches remembered their Civil War experience in the fifty years immediately following the war. When doing research for this project, I noticed the distinction made, particularly by the Quakers, between patriotism and nationalism. Patriotism literally means "love of the land," and even though Quakers considered themselves patriots, they would often say, "We don't subscribe to the saying 'my country right or wrong.'" As Brethren, we can still love our country and acknowledge that God has graciously bestowed special blessings on this nation while continuing to ask the tough questions about America, not shying away from the oppressions of the past, challenging the injustices of the present, and calling attention to the concerns of the future. We can take this one step further; in a highly fractured age, it is tempting for Christians on both the left and right to latch onto political candidates, groups, and agendas and become fixated on these concerns. Alexander Mack Jr. calls us to seek divine eternal power first and maintain a primary identity as heavenly citizens during periods of tumultuous political and social change.

So, Alexander Mack Jr. emerges as a strong spiritual voice of the second Brethren generation. There is no way of measuring how many lives Mack touched through his denominational leadership and pastoral care. Today, we still benefit from the riches of Mack's poetry, noticing the extent of his love for Christ and his concern for staying true to the commands of Christ. Alexander Mack Jr.'s life and spirituality, of course, did not exist in a vacuum. Stretching from 1712 to 1803, Mack's life intersected with vital moments of American history. He lived the immigrant experience, witnessed the turbulence of the Revolutionary years and the formation of the Early Republic, and saw two religious Great Awakenings occur. Eighteenth century Pennsylvania bears little resemblance to 2013, and it would be foolish to suggest otherwise. Some of Mack Jr's concerns, however, mirror our own dilemmas, as we attempt to conceive and practice a distinctly Brethren spirituality within an American context.

Notes

1 Two fine historical summaries of Mack Jr.'s life and work can be found in Jeff Bach, "The Life and Influence of Alexander Mack Jr.: Introduction," and Dale R. Stoffer, "Alexander Mack Jr.: The Pilgrim of Love and Light," both in *Brethren Life and Thought* 58 (Spring 2013): 1-7 (Bach) and 8-24 (Stoffer).

2 Samuel B. Heckman, *The Religious Poetry of Alexander Mack Jr.* (Elgin, Illinois: Brethren Publishing House, 1912), 17.

3 Ibid., 41, 37, 131, 135.

4 Ibid., 59-61, 69. For more on Mack Jr.'s birthday poems, see Karen Garrett, "Marking the Passage of Time: A Study of A. Mack Jr's Birthday Poetry, 1772-1802," *Brethren Life and Thought* 58 (Spring 2013): 66-78.

5 Ibid., 35, 43, 39, 101-03.

6 Ibid., 219, 72-75.

7 For more on the Northampton revivals, see George M. Marsden, *Jonathan Edwards: A Life* (New Haven: Yale University Press, 2003), 150-63.

8 Steve L. Longenecker, "Alexander Mack Jr.: Pennsylvania German and American," *Brethren Life and Thought* (Spring 2013) 58: 25-32.

9 Heckman, *Religious Poetry of Alexander Mack Jr.*, 167, 183, 187-91, 199.

10 2 Peter 3:11-12, NASB.

11 Heckman, *Religious Poetry of Alexander Mack Jr.*, 251-53, 259.

Brethren Hymnody

Peter E. Roussakis

Introduction

If you go to an art gallery to view paintings, most likely along the way you will ask yourself some questions. Why did the artist paint as he/she did? What was the thinking and what were the life experiences of the artist and the period of time in which the artist was working (with the prominent philosophy of the age, world events, etc.) which shaped the artist's approach? Why use those colors? Why create that design? What was the artist trying to convey? The same kinds of questions might be raised when you see a building or hear a piece of music that strikes you. What in the world was the architect thinking when the designs were drawn up? Why did the composer write that kind of melody or harmony, or why choose just those particular instruments? What statement was the artist trying to convey?

Emerging [Focus: Devotional Hymn Content]

The early Brethren sang from *Geistreiches Gesang-Buch* (*Spirit-filled Hymn-Book*),[1] a hymnbook produced in two parts (1704, 1714) at Halle by Johann Anastasius Freylinghausen (1670-1739), son-in-law of the Pietist leader August Hermann Francke (1663-1727). This hymnbook became the standard hymnbook of the Pietist movement. One of the favorite hymn-writers of the Brethren was Paul Gerhardt (1607-1676), viewed generally, next to Luther, as the greatest German hymnist. Many of his hymns were published in *Praxis Pietatis Melica* (*Practice of Piety in Song*), a collection of hymn texts and tunes by Johann Crüger (1598-1662), Gerhardt's organist-composer colleague at St. Nicholas Church in Berlin.

Gerhardt wrote with a reverential intimacy of devotion to God, an outpouring of the heart.[2] His "Give to the Winds Your Fears" (*"Befiehl du deine Wege"*) is one of twelve texts by Gerhardt included in editions of the first Brethren hymnbook in America, *Das Kleine Davidisches Psalterspiel der Kinder Zions (The Small Davidic Psaltery of the Children of Zion)*, published originally by Christopher Sauer (1695-1758) in 1744 at Germantown, Pennsylvania. Four of the original twelve stanzas[3] of "Give to the Winds Your Fears," as translated by John Wesley (1703-1791), are given here.

> Give to the winds thy fears;
> Hope, and be undismayed;
> God hears thy sighs and counts thy tears,
> God shall lift up thy head.

> Still heavy is thy heart?
> Still sink thy spirits down?
> Cast off the weight, let fear depart,
> And ev'ry care be gone.

> Who points the clouds their course,
> Whom winds and seas obey,
> He shall direct thy wand'ring feet,
> He shall prepare the way.

> Leave to His sov'reign will
> To choose and to command:
> With wonder filled, thou then shalt own
> How wise, how strong His hand.

The thought of Gottfried Arnold (1666-1714) had a significant influence on the early Brethren. Arnold emphasized strict reliance upon the scriptures and patterning the church's life according to that of the early church.[4] In his view regarding music, singing, praying, and the exposition of the written Word were important expressions of the early church's spirituality. He cautioned, however, that a corresponding inward devotion must accompany each outward exercise.[5] In other words, there must be a balance of singing with the mind as well as the spirit (e.g., Eph. 5:19; 1 Cor. 14:26). Therefore, he advised singing in a *plain* manner, meaning unaccompanied and in unison, a practice which remained among Brethren through much of the 19th century, and among some to the present day.[6] Actually, for the early Brethren this was not an unusual practice, because in the German heritage of congregational singing, which by the time of early Brethren included a vast storehouse of chorale melodies, hymns were sung in unison by congregations and originally without accompaniment.[7]

Later, Colonial Brethren Elder Michael Frantz (1687-1748), a writer of poetry and prose, wrote in one of the prose articles, *Of inner communion with God:* "If the inward communion with God has been truly realized, it will issue in outward communion ... with all kinds of virtues of love ... To love one's neighbor as one's self shows clearly what communion is."[8] Striving to maintain a balance between the inwardness and outwardness of the spiritual life has been important throughout Brethren history. It is a biblical principle, as the Apostle Paul and James explained: "... obedience that accompanies your confession of the gospel of Christ" (2 Cor. 9:13); "... faith by itself, if it is not accompanied by action, is dead" (James 2:17; also vs. 20 & 26).

Being faithful to the teachings of scripture, expressing devotion to Jesus, "practicing" the faith as did the early church, paying attention to both the inner and outer aspects of the spiritual life, and perseverance amidst the challenges in our Christian journey have been some of the prominent themes expressed in hymns and other writings of the Brethren.

It is understandable, especially because of the persecutions and imprisonments endured by the early Brethren, that "the chief metaphor for the spiritual life among Brethren from Alexander Mack Sr. [1679-1735] to [hymn writer] Jakob Stoll [1731-1822] was the life of a suffering pilgrim in a sinful world."[9] Examples include one of the undocumented hymns in the first Brethren hymnbook, *Geistreiches Gesang-Buch* (*Spirit-filled Hymn Book*), published in 1720 by Christopher Konert at Berleburg.[10]

Thou art a pilgrim true and tried,
If self from self thou sever,
And see the mind and will have died
And are subdued forever.[11]

This metaphor was found in one of the three hymns by Alexander Mack Jr. (1712-1803) included in *Die Kleine Harfe*[12] (*The Small Harp*), a 1792 hymnal supplement to editions of the first Brethren hymnbook published in America, *Das Kleine Davidische Psalterspiel der Kinder Zions* (*The Small Davidic Psaltery of the Children of Zion*), originally published in 1744. The hymn had been written on the death in 1784 of Mack's dear friend and fellow Elder, Christopher Sauer Jr. (1721-1784). Samuel Brumbaugh Heckman (1870-1957), in his volume on *The Religious Poetry of Alexander Mack, Jr.*, offered a prose translation of this five stanza hymn, "Now breaks this house of earth in twain" (*Nun bricht der Hütten Haus entzwei*). The approach of the hymn was to have the deceased speak about his earthly pilgrimage. Stanza one reads:

> Now breaks this house of earth in twain,
> Now the body can decay;
> The pilgrimage is now over;
> Now will my spirit recover;
> The soul has now won the fight;
> My Jesus has overcome the enemy.
> To Him alone be the honor.[13]

The second edition of *Die Kleine Harfe*, published by Samuel Sauer in 1797 in Baltimore, included a hymn, perhaps more of a poem than a verse that could be sung, by Peter Becker (1687-1758), described as the most gifted singer in the colonial church.[14] Translated by J. S. Flory (1866-1960), the first of the fourteen stanzas of Becker's hymn reads:

> Thou, poor pilgrim, wander'st here
> In this vale of gloom,
> Seeking, longing ever more
> For that joyous home;
> Yet many friends oppose thee here
> So that now thou weepest sore, - Patience.[15]

Another hymn text which employed the pilgrim imagery was by Jakob Stoll (1731-1822), referred to as the "foremost Brethren poet of his own and preceding times."[16] Stoll's hymns first appeared in a collection of his poetry and other devotional writings, *Geistliches Gewürz-Gärtlein Heilsuchender Seelen*, (*A Small Spiritual Herb-Garden of the Soul Seeking Salvation*) in 1806 at Ephrata, Pennsylvania. Translated by Ora Garber,[17] stanza seven of Hymn 10, "Shepherd, Thou My Soul Art Tending," reads:

Dearest Jesus, life the dearest,
Thou dost fully know my strife.
My encircling foes Thou hearest
As they taunt my pilgrim-life.
They would take my hope away.
Steel my faith to meet that day.[18]

Garber's rendering of stanza five of Hymn 20, Stoll's "Oh How is the Time So Urgent" (O! *wie ist die Zeit so wichtig*), is the following:

How important and momentous
Are the days of life's brief span:
Teach me, Jesus, how portentous
Are these days to mortal man.
All my earthly days respecting,
None but Thee as mine electing
Here upon my pilgrim way,
May I bear the cross someday.[19]

With the deaths of Alexander Mack Jr. in 1803 and of Jakob Stoll in 1822, the two principal hymn-writers of the turn of the century, was marked "the passage of the first group of great men who lent lustre to the early history of the church, and who produced the first important body of our church literature."[20]

Expanding [Focus: Manner of Singing]

Well into the 19th century, the themes of Brethren spirituality of the 18th century continued to be expressed in the writing of hymns and devotional works and the publication of new editions of Brethren hymnbooks in the German language. In 1791 the fifth edition of *Das Kleine Davidische Psalterspiel* was produced. Numerous editions and reprints were made up to 1853. The supplement, *Die Kleine Harfe,* with its 58 hymns, was bound with most editions and reprints of the 1797 *Psalterspiel*. Other German language hymnbooks were published in the 19th century.[21]

By the late 18th century, however, there was a significant enough population of English-speaking Brethren to warrant a hymnbook in English. Appearing also in 1791[22] was the first English-language hymnal for the Brethren, *The Christian's Duty*,[23] published in Germantown by the Brethren elder and former apprentice in the Sauer printing office, Peter Liebert (1727-1812). With this English-language hymnbook began what Hedda Durnbaugh described as the second of two entirely separate tracks of Brethren hymnody in the 19th century: the German language hymnody and the English-language hymnbooks.[24] It would be impossible to overstate the significance that, with the publication of *The Christian's Duty*, the gradual shift to the English language among the Brethren had formally commenced, and with that, as Durnbaugh concludes, the loss of the original spirituality.[25]

The Brethren did not carry over any of their German hymns into their English-language hymnody until many years later. Beginning with *The Christian's Duty*, an entirely new repertoire of hymnody was introduced. The hymns were drawn almost entirely from the new English hymnody of the 18th century. Of the 365 hymns in the 1801 edition, 116 were from the pen of the Isaac Watts (1674-1748) with his psalms metricized and hymns of "human-composure." Charles Wesley (1707-1788) composed 30 of the hymns while 14 were the work of John Newton (1725-1807). These three hymn writers accounted for over 40% of the contents of the hymnbook. Examples of hymns in *The Christian's Duty* which appeared in many denominational and non-denominational hymnbooks of the 19th and 20th centuries include those by Watts: *Alas, and Did My Savior Bleed*; *Am I a Soldier of the Cross*; *O God, Our Help in Ages Past*; and *When I can Read my Title Clear*. Hymns by Charles Wesley included: *Christ the Lord is Risen Today*; *Come, Thou Long-expected Jesus*; and *Jesus, Lover of My Soul*.

While the hymnody of *The Christian's Duty* is a departure from the 18th century German hymnody of the Brethren, often expressed with the suffering pilgrim motif, it should be said that many of the hymns are not entirely unlike the German devotional themes of individuals being admonished to bend the knee of their hearts and to be cautious regarding the influence of the world. The following titles demonstrate this: *Blessed are the Humble Souls That See*; *Blest is the Man Whose Bowels Move* (bowels meaning one's inner spiritual movement!); *Broad is the Road that Leads to Death*; *I'm not Ashamed to Own My Lord*; *Out of the Depths of Long Distress*; and *O for an Overcoming Faith*. The balance of inwardness and outwardness of Brethren spirituality could not have been more wonderfully expressed than in Watts' hymn, given as Hymn CCLXI in *The Christian's Duty*. Stanzas one and three of the four read:

So let our Lips and Lives express,
The holy Gospel we profess;
So let our works and Virtues shine,
To prove the Doctrine all Divine.

Our Flesh and Sense must be deny'd,
Passion and Envy, Lust and Pride,
Whilst Justice, Temp'rance, Truth and love,
Our inward Piety approve.

In the 19th century there was an increase of focus on the outwardness of the spiritual life. In particular, the notion of "separation from the world" led to many official "taboos" spanning 1778 to 1850. Some of them were dressing fashionably (1804), shaving off beards (for elders) (1804), college education (1831), singing schools in meetinghouses (1838), Sunday schools (1838), the tinkling of bells (1840), protracted meetings (revivals) (1842), joining worldly associations (1848), benedictions with uplifted hands (1849), and working as a butcher in a market (1850).[26] Non-conformity with the world, nonresistance, sectarianism, and nonswearing characterized Brethren spirituality during this period.[27]

The outward emphasis of Brethren spiritual life was not translated into the content of Brethren hymn texts, which remained aloof to these debates and continued to express inward devotional themes not unlike those of the 18th century. Rather, the outwardness was expressed in the "manner" in which Brethren were or were not supposed to sing, no matter which language or hymn repertoire was used. Elder Peter Nead (1796-1877) in his theological writings echoed the thoughts of Gottfried Arnold. Nead said that while there is a "great deal of Singing done which I believe is an abomination unto God," nevertheless, "Singing, if performed agreeably to the Word and Spirit of God, is a part of that holy devotion in worshipping the true and living God."[28] His caution, therefore, was to sing hymns "slowly" so the individual would focus on the meaning of the hymn texts.[29]

Annual Meeting maintained their official stance regarding the inappropriateness of using musical instruments to accompany congregational singing. Hymns continued officially to be sung unaccompanied and with melody only. The hymns were "lined," often led by a Deacon serving as song leader. However, four-part singing was evidenced among some Brethren,[30] in spite of the fact that in 1844 a report on congregational singing stated that four-part harmony was not acceptable.[31] Decisions regarding music made from 1852 to 1874 went so far as to prohibit ownership or instruction on musical instruments.[32]

Through the 1860s Brethren hymnbooks continued to be printed without musical notation. According to Annual Meeting decisions in 1825 and 1838, Brethren were prohibited from providing a meeting place for or teaching in "singing schools" (which taught people to read musical notation).[33] The prohibition was "moderated" in later meetings (1862, 1874), most likely due to the fact that some Brethren musicians traveled about as singing school teachers. More changes were on the way.

Excepting [Focus: Hymnbook Compiling & Manner of Singing]

The period of the mid-19th century to the 1880s could be called the Excepting Era, because increasingly during this period many Brethren took exception with other Brethren for not being open to certain "ways" which might be positive for edification, training, and expression. The more conservative Brethren continued to be cautious about "innovation" and took exception with Brethren who, in their view, may have been caving into the ways of the world. The issues of higher education, missions, a paid ministry, Sunday schools, revivals, prayer meetings, private devotional exercises, social gatherings, and the use of instruments in worship all served to polarize the Brethren, so much so that schism resulted in the 1880s of which we are all aware. Although instrumental accompaniment for congregational singing was introduced in the Philadelphia congregation in the 1870s, Annual Meeting took exception and formally disapproved.[34] Some Brethren families owned pianos or reed organs for the use of accompanying singing in their homes.[35]

The year 1867 was especially significant, for it had been decided at Annual Meeting previously to issue an official English-language hymnbook, which came to fruition in 1867, described by Hedda Durnbaugh as the "most significant event of the nineteenth century in respect to Brethren hymnody ..."[36] After eighteen years of discussion and delay, *A Collection of Psalms, Hymns, and Spiritual Songs*[37] was published at Covington, Miami Co., Ohio by James Quinter (1816-1888), Brethren pioneer educator and journalist. He served as the 1867 hymnbook's principal compiler.[38]

The hymn inventory of this words-only, pocket-sized hymnbook of 818 hymns, included many texts by Isaac Watts, Charles Wesley, and many other writers represented in *The Christian's Duty*. Brethren who took "exception" with future hymnals with musical notation continued to use this 1867 collection as late as 1901.[39]

As might be anticipated, however, exception arose by German-speaking Brethren regarding the non-existence of German-language hymns in this officially approved hymnbook. In response, the Annual Meeting of 1868 officially directed a committee, which included Henry Kurtz (1790-1874), noted editor of church publications, to produce a collection of modest length of German-language hymns, not to exceed 200. The result was the publication in 1870 of *Neue Sammlung* (*New Collection*), a text-only, pocket-sized hymnbook. It exceeded the suggested number of hymns, including 303. *Neue Sammlung von Psalmen, Lobgesängen und Geistlichen Liedern* (*New Collection of Psalms, Songs of Praise and Spiritual Songs*) provided a suitable supplement to *A Collection of Psalms, Hymns, and Spiritual Songs*, and in subsequent printings they were bound together with the English portion occurring first. At the 1872 Annual Meeting both hymnbooks were officially approved for use in Brethren churches.

Of subjects and numbers of hymns in the 1867 hymnbook, the greatest number was fifty on the subject of death, such as the following morbid text by Isaac Watts (hymn 580). The first three stanzas read:

> Why should we start, and fear to die?
> What tim'rous worms we mortals are,
> Death is the gate of endless joy,
> And yet we dread to enter there.
>
> The pains, the groans, the dying strife,
> Fright our approaching souls away,
> Still we shrink back again to life,
> Fond of our prison and our clay.
>
> Jesus can make a dying bed
> Feel soft as downy pillows are,
> While on his breast I lean my head,
> And breathe my life out sweetly there.

By way of contrast, the greatest number of hymns in *Neue Sammlung* was under the subject of Christian belief, of which there were forty-four.

In spite of all the rulings and taboos formulated, the spirituality of this period has been described as a growing "revivalist piety," emphasizing personal experience with God and a deep concern for others, cultivated in prayer meetings and revival services with gospel singing.[40] That sounds similar to the early Brethren practices.

ENERGIZING [FOCUS: HYMN TUNE COMPOSITION & PUBLICATIONS]

After the divisions in the 1880s, the long-standing opposition to revivals and many other matters continued to be the position of the Old German Baptist Brethren (also referred to as the Old German Baptist Church). The popularity of the gospel song genre, however, became a major ingredient not only in the hymnic expressions of The Brethren Church, newly formed in 1883, but also in the German Baptist Brethren (Church of the Brethren). The revivalist piety[41] which grew since the mid-century led to a prevalent opinion "that hymns should be of a devotional rather than a doctrinal nature."[42]

While the controversies and divisions were spiritually draining, the 1880s through the early 20th century were also times of energizing. Freedom to move onward must have been sensed by both the German Baptist Brethren and The Brethren Church. Many of the negatives of the past were turned into positives by both fellowships. This aspect is seen in the activity of hymn and tune book production and hymn tune composition.

One of the results of the divisions was the publication of *The Brethren Hymnody with Tunes for the Sanctuary, Sunday School, Prayer Meeting, and Home Circle* for The Brethren Church. This was the first Brethren denominational hymnbook with round note musical notation.

The title says it all, that these Brethren desired to move onward in the ways they worshiped, studied and nurtured their piety. Louis F. Benson's analysis that this modest-sized hymnbook was "a much inferior [hymn] book"[43] is well-taken. Nevertheless, it represented the changes which had taken place and would burst into full bloom in the Church of the Brethren as well. *The Brethren Hymnody with Tunes* symbolizes a significant energizing of the Brethren to move forward, to evangelize, to make disciples, and above all, to "enjoy" being Brethren Christians, focusing less in hymnody on death and dreariness, and more upon resurrection and the hope we profess because of our faith in and followship to Jesus. Many hymns of the Gospel song genre were included.

Directed by the first Brethren Church denominational meeting in Dayton, Ohio, in 1883, John Cook Ewing (1849-1937), the pioneer Brethren musician, music teacher and composer, was called upon to compile the *Hymnody*, which he published in 1884 at Wilmington, Ohio.

Before the formal divisions, J. C. Ewing was the first music instructor at Huntingdon Normal School (later Juniata College) and conducted singing classes in many locations. He had been entrusted with the revision of the unsuccessful 1872 edition of the first hymnal published for the Brethren with musical notation, *The Brethren's Tune and Hymn Book*, utilizing shape-notes. In the much more widely accepted 1879 revision were seventeen original tunes by Ewing, and two by his student and successor at Juniata, William Berry (1852-1956). After the divisions, Ewing aligned himself with the "Progressives" and was employed as the first music instructor at Ashland College.

Ewing contributed seventeen tunes to this hymnbook. One is the tune ASHLAND set to a text, "Almighty Sov'reign of the Skies," of unknown authorship. The significance of this tune lies in the fact that years later for *The Brethren Hymnal* (1951), noted Church of the Brethren music professor at Bridgewater College, Nevin W. Fisher (1900-1984), arranged the tune and wedded it with the lead text of *The Brethren's Tune and Hymn Book* (1879), "Is There a God," the text being altered by Kenneth I. Morse (1913-1999). The much improved tune was renamed by Fisher as PIONEER in honor of J. C. Ewing.

J. C. Ewing's significance cannot be overstated.[44] He paved the way for future hymnic production in Church of the Brethren. One of his main accomplishments certainly was being a suitable teacher and mentor for William Beery, who contributed many years of fruitful music ministry in the Church of the Brethren. A prolific hymn tune composer, Beery composed his last tune at the age of ninety-six.

Gospel hymns had become so popular that there was a desire in the Church of the Brethren for collections of hymns and songs specifically for use in Sunday School and for the advancement of the cause of missions. This led to the publication of *The Brethren's Sunday School Song Book, for use in Sunday Schools, Prayer and Social Meetings* (1894), compiled by William Beery by authority of the Annual Conference. This was one of many gospel song collections during this period. The 185 hymns, set in shape notes, were prefaced by six pages of the Rudiments of Music. The song book contained mostly gospel songs, including six tunes by J. Henry Showalter (1864-1947), six by George B. Holsinger (1857-1908), and twenty-five by William Berry.

Appearing for the first time in this collection was the text "Take My Hand and Lead Me, Father" by Gertrude A. Flory (1862-1930) for which William Beery composed the tune. The hymn was carried over into all future Brethren hymnals. Stanza one, as printed in the 1894 song book, is given here.

> Take my hand and lead me, Father,
> Through life's stormy pilgrimage;
> Let Thy light shine brighter, Father,
> On its dark, mysterious page;
> For I find my feet oft straying
> From the path of truth and right,
> Feel the need of Thy protection,
> And Thy light to shine more bright.

By the turn of the century in a great number of congregations, *The Brethren's Sunday School Song Book* had replaced the 1879 *Brethren's Tune and Hymn Book* as their main collection of hymns and songs used in worship. In addition, at the 1900 Annual Meeting it was reported that leading congregations had adopted non-Brethren hymnbooks.[45] It was decided that a new hymnbook should be produced. A year later, *The Brethren Hymnal: A Collection of Psalms, Hymns and Spiritual Songs* (1901) was the result. A word-only edition and an edition with shape-note musical notation were published. Of the 742 entries, a section was included with seventy-five Sunday School, Prayer Meeting, and Evangelistic hymns. Many of the authors and composers included in this thoroughly Anglo-American hymnal illustrate the desire on the part of the hymnal committee to sing hymns from a wide spectrum of denominational traditions.

Except for the last printing of the last German language hymnbook, *Ein Sammlung* in 1903 and with the publication and use of *The Brethren Hymnal* (1901), there were no longer two tracks of Brethren hymnody as there had been in the 19th century. With that shift completed, Hedda Durnbaugh laments: "... the Brethren have lost their German heritage and, along with it, the type of piety and spirituality that the hymns reflect ..."[46]

One of the other Brethren hymn authors represented in the hymnal was Elder Abraham Cassel Wieand (1871-1954), co-founder and president of Bethany Theological Seminary. Wieand's hymn, "On the Radiant Threshold" (hymn 76) represents the kind of "churchly" hymn text favored increasingly by Brethren hymnal compilers in the twentieth century. Stanza 1 of his hymn for The Lord's Day reads:

On the radiant threshold
  of this dawning day,
In the sacred stillness,
  We will pause and pray.
In the morning, noon, and evening,
  We would seek Thy side;
O do Thou, dear Lord, befriend us,
  O be Thou our guide.

ENDEAVORING [HYMNS REFLECTING MORE FORMAL WORSHIP, MAINLINE-ISM, SOCIAL CONCERNS, CULTURAL RELEVANCE, AND INCLUSIVE-ISM]

Following what we've referred to as the Energizing Era of Brethren hymnody with its revivalist piety and gospel songs, the Church of the Brethren practiced all of the ways which caused so much controversy from the 1850s to the 1880s: instruments in the sanctuary, mission activities, higher education, evangelistic efforts, Sunday schools, Bible studies and prayer meetings. However, family worship, once wide-spread among Brethren, gave way increasingly in the 20th century to private devotional exercises.[47]

"After 1900 change was more difficult to resist. Sometimes pianos and organs were installed or 'set in' meetinghouses for special occasions such as weddings and youth programs."[48] As the 1920s drew to a close, three-fourths of all Brethren congregations had musical instruments, and one-fourth had organized choirs, one purpose of which was to support congregational singing.[49]

It was clear that the Brethren were evolving; that is, they were maturing, progressing, developing, not only in theological debate, but also in their views on worship and hymnic activities. Even in the midst of the controversies in the 1920s over liberalism on the one hand and fundamentalism on the other, the Church of the Brethren managed to produce a hymnal in 1925 which would serve them for the next quarter of a century, and in this writer's view, help to steady the spiritual ship.

The *Hymnal: Church of the Brethren* (1925), compiled by a committee chaired by J. S. Flory, with William Beery serving as the chief music consultant, was the first Brethren hymnal which was produced in two musical editions, one with round notes, and one with shape-note notation. Also for the first time, the 1925 hymnal contained "Musical Responses" for church choirs. There was also a section of "Responsive Readings" of Scripture, printed prayers, choral or spoken offertories and benedictions, "Hymns for Opening" and "Hymns for Closing." All these worship aids indicate a growing trend toward more formal worship services, far different from that of the basic Singing-Praying-Preaching practice of the early Brethren!

Of the 484 hymns, a significant number were authored or composed by Brethren. One we'll mention is of the inward devotional type by Elder John W. Wayland (1872-1962). The quality of his poetry stands out, the theology clear and true, and is in this case a prayer hymn for coming to Christ and growing in him, a hymn of invitation and dedication, a hymn exuding the devotion of the author. Stanzas two and three of "Gracious King, Enthroned Above" read:

> In the merit of Thy Son,
> Lord, I come to Thee;
> Christ for me has favor won,
> Lord, I come to Thee.
> Let me now be reconciled,
> Though a wand'rer from the wild;
> O receive me as a child,
> Lord, I come to Thee.

> With the Spirit for my guide,
> Lord, I come to Thee.
> All myself in Thee to hide,
> Lord, I come to Thee.
> Cares unbidden fill my breast;
> Sorrow has my soul oppressed;
> Give a fainting pilgrim rest,
> Lord, I come to Thee.

An example of a hymn which indicates Church of the Brethren movement toward mainline Protestantism in hymnody is a text by Ray Palmer, American Congregationalist, who for many years ministered at the Congregational Church in Bath, Maine. Stanza three of Hymn 270, "My Faith Looks Up to Thee," reads as follows:

> While life's dark maze I tread,
> And griefs around me spread,
> Be Thou my guide;
> Bid darkness turn to day,
> Wipe sorrow's tears away,
> Nor let me ever stray
> From Thee aside.

Two other examples from the *Hymnal: Church of the Brethren* (1925) reveal other aspects of an evolving Brethren spirituality during this theologically controversial period. The first is a hymn authored by William Pierson Merrill (1867-1954), an American Presbyterian educated at Union Theological Seminary in New York City. He was an author on subjects pertaining to liberalism, in particular, "world brotherhood by the Christian spirit and ideals."[50] Hymn 36, "Rise Up, O Men of God," is included in the section of the hymnal for "World Peace and Brotherhood," certainly in line with the Brethren positions of getting along with others and of nonresistance. The 1911 Annual Meeting had formed a Peace Committee to assist conscientious objectors and to distribute peace literature.[51] Stanza three reads:

> Rise up, O men of God!
> His kingdom tarries long:
> Bring in the day of brotherhood
> And end the night of wrong.

One interpretation of what was meant in this stanza was given by A. E. Bailey. "Two thousand years of theological wrangling and the drive for power have only postponed the kingdom of God [on earth]; the rule of God secured only by cultivating the attitude of brotherhood, for that alone will cure the ills of society."[52] This is the Social Gospel.

The other hymn is "Where Cross the Crowded Ways of Life" by Frank Mason North (1850-1935). He was educated at Wesleyan University in Connecticut, and served pastorates in the Methodist Episcopal Church. From 1916 to 1920, he served as president of the Federal Council of Churches of Christ in America. Stanzas one and four read:

Where cross the crowded ways of life,
Where sound the cries of race and clan,
Above the noise of selfish strife,
We hear Thy voice, O Son of man!

The cup of water given for Thee
Still holds the freshness of Thy grace;
Yet long these multitudes to see
The sweet compassion of Thy face.

Stephen L. Longenecker wrote of North's hymn (Hymn 339): "Written in 1905, North's hymn applied faith to urban problems, a classic Social Gospel approach … "[53]

The Brethren Hymnal (1951), among other things, served to advance more formal worship,[54] congruent with that of many standard mainline Protestant churches.[55] The 1951 hymnal may certainly be included in the remark by Robert Stevenson: "The hymnals of the larger denominations grow more and more 'respectable' musically with each new edition."[56]

A hymn which is a classic example of the standard style of the times, illustrating excellence in both text authorship and tune composition, and which also was a denominational favorite, is hymn 225, "Move in Our Midst," text by Kenneth I. Morse (1913-1999) set to the tune PINE GLEN by Perry L. Huffaker (1902-1982). Stanza one reads:

Move in our midst, Thou Spirit of God;
Go with us down from Thy holy hill;
Walk with us through the storm and the calm;
Spirit of God, go Thou with us still.

Although there was a section of 57 gospel songs in the 1951 hymnal, referred to as "Songs of Salvation," there had been a reluctance on the part of the hymnal committee to include these because, in their view: "They distract from genuine worship and are psychologically disintegrating in their efforts upon groups and individuals."[57]

In the 1940s, the outward spirituality in the Church of the Brethren, which was "formerly expressed in revival meetings, missions education, and the encouragement of daily devotional exercises was transferred to social action, peace testimony, and relief and service ventures."[58] In addition, from the mid-twentieth century onward, hymnic activity endeavored to find ways to express the church's relevance to society amidst significant membership decline. Whereas in the nineteenth century hymnic expressions remained aloof to the squabbles of the period, during the 1960s onward, there was a conscious attempt to author hymn texts and compose hymn tunes which expressed the spiritual concerns of the day. Examples include "Brothers and Sisters of Mine" authored by Kenneth I. Morse (1913-1999), Church of the Brethren elder, journalist, editor, poet and hymn writer. It was wedded with the tune MINE ARE THE HYNGRY by Wilbur E. Brumbaugh (1931-1977). This hymn in *The Brethren Songbook* (1974), a hymnal supplement, is superior in every way, as literature, as message, as music, and as an example of what spiritual themes were important to Brethren at this time. The four stanzas of this hymn of social concern and Christian responsibility are given here.

> Brothers and sisters of mine are the hungry,
> who sigh in their sorrow and weep in their pain.
> Sisters and brothers of mine are the homeless,
> who wait without shelter from wind and from rain.
>
> Strangers and neighbors, they claim my attention.
> they sleep by my door-step, they sit by my bed.
> Neighbors and strangers, their anguish concerns me,
> and I must not feast till the hungry are fed.
>
> People are they, men and women and children,
> and each has a heart keeping time with my own.
> People are they, persons made in God's image,
> so what shall I offer them, bread or a stone?
>
> Lord of all living, we make our confession:
> Too long we have wasted the wealth of our lands.
> Lord of all loving, renew our compassion,
> and open our hearts while we reach out our hands.

Another example is hymn 407, "We are People of God's Peace" by Menno Simons (1496-1561) as translated by Esther C. Bergen (b.1921), in the latest *Hymnal: A Worship Book* (1992),[59] published jointly by the Church of the Brethren, the General Conference Mennonite Church, and the Mennonite Church in North America. Stanza three reads:

> We are servants of God's peace,
> of the new creation.
> Choosing peace, we faithfully
> serve with heart's devotion.
> Jesus Christ, the Prince of Peace,
> confidence will give us.
> Christ the Lord is our defense;
> Christ will never leave us.

One other example from *Hymnal: A Worship Book* is again by Kenneth I. Morse, who wrote "Strangers no More" (Hymn 322). He teamed up with excellent musician and composer, Dianne Huffman Morningstar (b.1944), who composed the hymn tune by the same name [STRANGERS NO MORE]. The hymn begins with the refrain:

> For we are strangers no more, but members of one family,
> Strangers no more, but part of one humanity;
> Strangers no more, we're neighbors to each other now;
> Strangers no more, we're sisters and we're brothers now.

> Stanza two reads:
> Where diff'ring cultures meet we'll serve together.
> Where hatred ranges we will strive for peace.
> Come, take my hand, and we will pray together
> That justice come and strife and warfare cease.

And finally, Kenneth I Gibble (b.1941), author and composer, wrote the text for hymn 1102 in the *Hymnal Supplement Series* (from 2001 onward) which resonates with today's linguistic and theological orientations. Stanza one reads:

> God of creation, show us your glory,
> Splendored in sunshine, shadowed in night,
> Maker and Shaper, tell us the Story,
> Of your great mercy, justice and might.

Conclusion

What have we discovered? The shape of Brethren hymnody as an expression of our spirituality has been influenced by the Bible and the thought of persons such as Gottfried Arnold, Michael Frantz, and Peter Nead; by the concern for a balance between the inner and outward aspects of the spiritual life; by persecutions and other forms of suffering; by the emergence of English-speaking Brethren and the gradual shift from the German language and its expressions to the English language hymnic preferences; by the official rulings of Annual Meeting regarding music restrictions; by the trends in hymnody and hymn singing outside of the Brethren circle; by the "innovations" advanced by the Progressive Brethren, including vocal and instrumental music making; by the popularity of the Gospel hymn genre; by the advent of the Brethren hymn tune composer; by the trend toward more formality in worship; by the theology of the Social Gospel; by the genuine concern for peace and the welfare of others; and by the challenges of the culture from the 1960s onward, including civil rights, the sexual revolution and the concern over inclusive language. All these have served to shape what Brethren sang, what Brethren authors wrote, what hymnal compilers chose to include, what type of hymn tunes composers produced, and in what manner Brethren have sung their hymnic expressions of the spiritual life.

Notes

1 Dale R. Stoffer. *Background and Development of Brethren Doctrines 1650-1987* (Philadelphia, PA: The Brethren Encyclopedia, Inc., 1989), 67.

2 Catherine Winkworth, *Christian Singers of Germany* (New York: MacMillan & Co. Publishers, 1869), 209-210.

3 Hymn 52 in *Das Kleine Davidisches Psalterspiel der Kinder Zions* (1833 Edition). Discussed also in Albert Edward Bailey, *The Gospel in Hymns: Backgrounds and Interpretation* (New York: Charles Scribner's Sons, 1950), 327-328.

4 Stoffer, *Brethren Doctrines*, 32, regarding the thought in Arnold's *Die Erste Liebe Der Gemeinen Jesu Christi, Das ist: Wahre Abbildung Der Ersten Christen (The First Love of the Community of Jesus Christ, That is: True Portrayal [Abbildung] of the First Christians)*, 1696.

5 Stoffer, *Brethren Doctrines*, 33.

6 Discussed in Hedwig T. Durnbaugh's "Music in Worship, 1708-1850," *Brethren Life and Thought* 33 (Autumn 1988): 271.

7 Manfred F. Bukofzer, *Music in the Baroque Era* (New York: W. W. Norton & Company, Inc., 1947), 79. Also, for a fine discussion of the chorale melodies indicated in *Das Kleine Davidische Psalterspiel der Kinder Zions*, see Nevin W. Fisher, *History of Brethren Hymnbooks*. Bridgewater, PA: The Beacon Press, 1950.

8 Cited in Donald F. Durnbaugh, *Fruit of the Vine: A History of the Brethren 1708-1995* (Elgin, IL: Brethren Press, 1997), 138. The full title of Frantz's work is *Einfältige Lehr-Betrachtungen, und Kurtzgefaßtes, Glaubens-Bekäntniß des gottseligen Lehrers, Michael Frant-*

zen (*Simple Doctrinal Considerations and a Concise Confession of Faith of the pious Teacher, Michael Frantz*) published posthumously by Christopher Sauer Jr. in 1770. See also Stoffer, *Brethren Doctrines,* 96-97 for discussion of this subject.

9 Dennis D. Martin, "Spiritual Life," in *The Brethren Encyclopedia*.

10 For a thorough discussion and analysis of the 1720 hymnal and all other German hymnbooks of the Brethren, see Hedwig T. Durnbaugh. *The German Hymnody of the Brethren 1720-1903* (Philadelphia, PA: The Brethren Encyclopedia, Inc., 1986).

11 This hymn text, "The Christian Pilgrim," was translated by Ralph W. Schlosser (1886-1978) and is included in Donald F. Durnbaugh, comp. and ed,, *European Origins of the Brethren* (Elgin, IL: The Brethren Press, 1958), 411-413.

12 *Die Kleine Harfe* (The Small Harp), published by Samuel Sauer (1767-1820), youngest son of Christopher Sauer Jr., at Chestnut Hill, Pennsylvania in 1792, was a hymnal supplement to the first Brethren hymnbook published in America, *Das Kleine Davidische Psalterspiel der Kinder Zions* (*The Small Davidic Psaltery of the Children of Zion*), published by Christopher Sauer (1695-1758) in 1744 in Germantown, Pennsylvania.

13 Samuel B. Heckman, *The Religious Poetry of Alexander Mack, Jr.* (Elgin, IL: Brethren Publishing House, 1912), 43.

14 Martin Grove Brumbaugh, *A History of the German Baptist Brethren in Europe and America* (Mount Morris, IL: Brethren Publishing House, 1899), 208.

15 J. S. Flory, *Literary Activity of the German Baptist Brethren in the Eighteenth Century* (Elgin, IL: Brethren Publishing House, 1908), 206-208.

16 This comment is given in the note which accompanies the translation of four of Stoll's hymns by Ora Garber in *Brethren Life and Thought* 16 (Fall 1971): 227.

17 The Garber translations were included in *Brethren Life and Thought* Vol. XVI (Fall 1971, Number 3): 227-231; in *Brethren Life and Thought* Vol. XVII (Spring 1973, Number 2): 71-76; and in Roger E. Sappington's *The Brethren in the New Nation: A Source Book on the Development of the Church of the Brethren 1785-1865* (Elgin, IL: The Brethren Press, 1976), 445-453.

18 Sappington, *The Brethren in a New Nation*, 448.

19 Ibid., 453.

20 J. S. Flory, *Literary Activity*, ix.

21 Primary 19th century German language hymnbooks included: *Die Kleine Lieder Sammlung* (*The Small Collection of Songs*), 1826; *Die Kleine Perlen-Sammlung* (*The Small Collection of Pearls*), 1858; *Neue Sammlung* (*New Collection*), 1870; *Das Christliche Gesang-Buch* (*The Christian Song Book*), 1874; and *Ein Sammlung von Psalmen, Lobgesängen, und Geistlichen Liedern* (*A Collection of Psalms, Hymns of Praise, and Spiritual Songs*), 1893.

22 Discussion of the significance of these two 1791 hymnbooks is given in Hedwig T. Durnbaugh, "1791: A Watershed Year in Brethren Hymnody," *Brethren Life and Thought* 45 (Summer 2000): 100.

23 The full title of the hymnbook was *The Christian's Duty, exhibited in a series of Hymns: collected from various authors, designed for the worship of God, and for the edification of Christians. Recommended to the serious of all denominations. By the Fraternity of the Baptists.*

24 Hedwig T. Durnbaugh, "Changes in Brethren Hymnody: Trends and Implications," *Brethren in Transition: Twentieth Century Directions and Dilemmas*, Emmert F. Bittlinger, ed. (Camden, ME: Penobscot Press, 1992), 193-203.

25 Ibid., 194.

26 Carl F. Bowman, *Brethren Society: The Cultural Transformation of a "Peculiar People"* (Baltimore, MD: The John Hopkins University Press, 1995), 80-86.

27 See Stoffer, *Brethren Doctrines*, 106-110, for more thorough discussion of "The Devotional Lives of the Brethren" and "Doctrinal Developments," and 112-113 for summary statements regarding Brethren spirituality during the first half of the 19th century.

28 Peter Nead. *Theological Writings on Various Subjects; or a Vindication of Primitive Christianity* (Dayton, O.: New Edition, 1866), 176-177. Reprinted by Dunker Springhaus Ministries, Youngstown, OH, 1997.

29 Ibid., 176.

30 Nevin W. Fisher, "Musical Instruments," *The Brethren Encyclopedia*.

31 Nancy Rosenberger Faus, "Singing," *The Brethren Encyclopedia*.

32 Fisher, "Musical Instruments," *The Brethren Encyclopedia*.

33 Nancy Rosenberger Faus, "Singing Schools," *The Brethren Encyclopedia*.

34 Faus, "Singing," *The Brethren Encyclopedia*.

35 Ibid.

36 H. T. Durnbaugh, "Changes Reflected in Brethren Hymnody," 197.

37 The full title of this hymnbook was *A Collection of Psalms, Hymns, and Spiritual Song; suited to the Various Kinds of Christian worship; and especially designed for, and adapted to, The Fraternity of the Brethren. Compiled by Direction of the Annual Meeting, Upon the Basis of the Hymn Books Formerly used by the Brotherhood.*

38 See Earl C. Kaylor Jr., "Quinter, James" in *The Brethren Encyclopedia* for more on his life and work.

39 See Hedda R. Durnbaugh and Nevin W. Fisher, "Hymnals," *The Brethren Encyclopedia*.

40 Stoffer, *Brethren Doctrines*, 158. See also Dennis D. Martin, "Spiritual Life," *The Brethren Encyclopedia*.

41 A summary of the characteristics of the revivalist piety is given in Stoffer, *Brethren Doctrines*, 158-160.

42 Hedwig T. Durnbaugh, "The Lost Hymns of the Brethren, 1720-1880," *Report of the Proceedings of the Brethren World Assembly (Elizabethtown College, Elizabethtown, Pennsylvania July 15-July 18, 1992* (Ambler, PA: The Brethren Encyclopedia, Inc., 1994), 27.

43 Louis F. Benson, *The English Hymn: Its Development and Use in Worship* (Richmond, VA: John Knox Press, 1962), 366.

44 An account of the life and work of J. C. Ewing and a thorough examination of his hymn tunes is given in *John Cook Ewing (1849-1947): Pioneer Brethren Musician, Teacher and Composer* by William Berry (1852-1956) and Peter E. Roussakis (Kokomo, IN: Meetinghouse Press, 2010). This is the first publication of Berry's heretofore unpublished 1942

manuscript of the life and work of J. C. Ewing, supplemented by musical analysis of Ewing's tunes by Peter E. Roussakis.

45 Bowman, *Brethren Society*, 161.

46 H. T. Durnbaugh, "Changes Reflected in Brethren Hymnody," 200.

47 Dennis D. Martin, "Spiritual Life," *The Brethren Encyclopedia*.

48 Nevin W. Fisher, "Musical Instruments," *The Brethren Encyclopedia*.

49 Bowman, *Brethren Society*, 257.

50 Bailey, *The Gospel in Hymns,* 572.

51 Stephen L. Longenecker, *The Brethren During the Age of World War: The Church of the Brethren Encounter with Modernism,1914-1950* (Brethren Press, 2006), xxxii.

52 Bailey, *The Gospel in Hymns*, 101.

53 Longenecker, *Brethren During the Age of World War,* 285.

54 Ibid., 100-102.

55 Donald F. Durnbaugh, *Fruit of the Vine*, 520.

56 Robert Stevenson, *Protestant Church Music in America* (New York: W. W. Norton, 1966), 126.

57 Donald F. Durnbaugh, *Fruit of the Vine*, 521.

58 Martin, "Spiritual Life," *The Brethren Encyclopedia*.

59 Discussion of this hymnal is found in Nancy Rosenberger Faus, "Hymnal: A Worship Book," *The Brethren Encyclopedia*.

SEPARATION FROM THE WORLD AND ENGAGEMENT WITH THE WORLD

Carl Bowman

PROLOGUE

THIS ESSAY WILL REFLECT FLEETINGLY UPON A TOPIC THAT MERITS GREATER consideration: Brethren understandings of their relationship with the world. This being a conference on spirituality, however, I would be remiss not to begin by remarking upon that topic.

Theologians, historians, and ministers each build their understandings from favored texts and sources. Few, however, have grasped the sociological insight that a full understanding of Brethren spirituality can be developed only by turning to the primary source: survey research — specifically, the 2006 Brethren Member Profile. In that study, which I directed under the auspices of Elizabethtown College's Young Center for Anabaptist and Pietist Studies, we asked a representative sample of members whether they identified themselves religiously as "spiritual." Most do not; only 40 percent do.[1] In fact, when presented with a plethora of possible religious identities — including Dunker, Pentecostal, Mainline, Inclusive, Anabaptist, Evangelical, Fundamentalist, and others — and being told they could select as many as they wanted, just over a quarter chose only one religious identity: "Brethren" and nothing more.

About two-thirds of church members, however, took us up on the offer to describe themselves with multiple labels. Of those who did, only 3 percent called themselves "Pentecostal." Slightly more (6 percent) claimed to be "charismatic," and 7 percent said they were "Pietist." These unpopular identities had the closest direct connection to spirituality; others were much more popular. Eleven percent, for example, claimed the "Dunker" designation, 13 percent said they were "Fundamentalist," 15 percent were "inclusive," 19 percent claimed to be "Mainline," and 21 percent called themselves "Evangelical." Even more said they were "plain living" (26 percent) and "Anabaptist" (29 percent). If you've been reading attentively, you've noticed that contemporary Brethren are four times more likely to call themselves Anabaptist than Pietist, so that scholarly debate is effectively settled by the "genius" of survey research.

Actually, apart from "Brethren," the only religious identity selected by a majority of those who chose more than one was "spiritual" (at 58 percent). The profile of those who call themselves "spiritual," however, defies easy prediction. Religious liberals, for instance, are only slightly less likely than conservatives to claim "spiritual." Brethren who embrace the relativistic belief that "all views of what is good are equally valid" are about as likely to be "spiritual" as those who do not. Brethren who say that "Christians should do all they can to convert non-believers" are just slightly more likely to claim a "spiritual" identity than those who do not. Brethren who say that "Muslims and Christians worship the same God" are about as likely to be "spiritual" as those who think they worship different Gods. And Brethren who say, "the greatest moral virtue is to be honest about your own feelings and desires" are slightly more inclined to claim "spiritual" than those who disagree.[2]

Together, these findings yield a clear picture of what "spiritual" means to members of the Church of the Brethren; it can mean anything at all. All types of Brethren claim it — young and old, liberal and conservative, faithful or not. The worst spin on these findings is that "spiritual" is broadly attractive to Brethren but semantically hollow. The best spin is that "spiritual" is language that unifies Brethren of different faith commitments, because like "mission" and "family," it resonates with so many. Experience teaches me that the Old Order Brethren among us see themselves as "spiritual," as do Grace Brethren, Dunkard Brethren, Nigerian Brethren, evangelical Brethren, progressive Brethren, and New Age Brethren. Even Brethren who have come to think of themselves as agnostic or post-Christian — and there are a few — would more likely embrace the term "spiritual" than "believer" or "religious."

At a Conference such as this, it is important to keep in mind that those in attendance may have very different symbolic practices and meanings in mind when using the same word. As such, the shared language of "spirituality" may foster an appearance of common focus and purpose, but this perception likely exceeds the unity of belief and conviction that underlies it. Sociology teaches us that this is often the case with intangible rhetorics. Like "spirituality," "community," "character," and "values" rhetorics reflect shared human aspirations more than shared practices or beliefs. The Brethren Member Profile found broad support for being "spiritual," but a subsequent probe — What do you *mean* by spiritual? — would have revealed many differences.[3]

These observations may be a digression from my assigned topic of "separation from the world," but being familiar with the survey data, I couldn't resist commenting upon Brethren claims to be spiritual at a conference on Brethren spirituality. Identity, after all, has everything to do with whether we engage or separate ourselves from the world. Those who separate themselves from the surrounding culture always do so out of a sense of their own exceptionalism, their understanding that their way of life, or the life they have been called to, is not only distinct, but distinguished. It has often been said that groups like the Brethren, Mennonites, and Amish saw themselves as "in the world but not of the world." It is less often pointed out that they have also generally seen themselves as above the world, but they have.

On Exceptionalism

In my work at the University of Virginia's *Institute for Advanced Studies in Culture*, the topic of "American exceptionalism" crops up from time to time. Whether America was framed historically as a city on a hill, as having a manifest destiny, or, more recently, as the leader of a new world order (by virtue in large part, of its military might), America has been thought of at different historical junctures, in different ways, as exceptional. The importance of exceptionalism is exemplified by the fact that President Obama is routinely criticized for getting it wrong. Republicans have criticized him for insufficiently recognizing American exceptionalism. But when he does, Russian President Vladimir Putin lectures him in a *New York Times* Op-ed that, "It is extremely dangerous to encourage people to see themselves as exceptional, whatever the motivation."[4]

America's tradition of exceptionalism, however, is spectacularly unexceptional. The Romans, British, Chinese, Germans, and Aztecs have all had their moments in the sun, their eras of exceptionalism. Indigenous peoples throughout human history have cherished the knowledge that it was *they* who were exceptional. Destiny or God, however conceived, had smiled directly at them and set them apart as the chosen people. Indeed, the knowledge that all living creatures ascended from the nearest lake or descended from the closest mountain is more universal than you might think. Many throughout history behave as if Truth with a capital T was proclaimed in the next village. Illinois is the Brethren "heartland" if you're from Chicago, while Pennsylvania is the "heartland" if you're an eastern Dunker. Wisconsin is God's country if you're from upstate Wisconsin; Ohio's Miami Valley is God's country, for those who live here, and Virginia's Shenandoah Valley is God's country if you're from the shadows of the Blue Ridge mountains.

The Brethren have been anything but an exception to this human tendency to see oneself, and one's own, as exceptional. From Mack's book, *Rules and Orders of the House of God as bequested in his last will and Testament* (the New Testament),[5] to the late nineteenth century's *Brethren's Card*,[6] to mid-twentieth century books such as Kermit Eby's *For Brethren Only*, to scholarly debates regarding the "genius of the Brethren," to the Brethren marketing trope — another way of living, Brethren expressed their exceptionalism for nearly three hundred years. Let us review a few highlights.

THE BRETHREN FOUNDING AS AN ACT OF EXCEPTIONALISM

In 1708, the first Brethren tract ever penned — framed as an open letter and assumed to be penned by Alexander Mack himself — testified to Brethren exceptionalism in many ways. Mack wrote, "… we have left all sects because of the misuses concerning infant baptism, communion, and church system, and unanimously profess that these are rather man's statutes and commandments, and therefore do not baptize our children, and testify that we were not really baptized."[7] Here we find that the founding Brethren clearly distinguished "all sects" — meaning the established churches — from their own church creation. The established churches were depicted as following "man's statutes"; the Brethren, meanwhile (according to Mack), followed "simply the teachings of Jesus Christ," leaving behind "man's commandment and teaching established after the statutes of the world."[8] For Brethren to claim openly in a letter directed to outsiders that they had never been baptized, even though they had been physically baptized as infants, was to implicitly inform readers of the letter that *they* remained unbaptized as well, a very strong challenge in church circles.

To be exceptional, by definition, you have to be different. And where there are differences, there are boundaries defining those differences. The boundaries of Brethren exceptionalism were defended through the 18th and 19th centuries and into the 20th century by a method many today would consider harsh, a strong church discipline. In the same 1708 letter, Mack wrote, "There is also an exact relationship and brotherly discipline according to the teachings of Jesus Christ and His apostles. When a person does not better himself, after faithful warning, he must be expelled and cannot be treated any more as a brother."[9] (Elsewhere, Mack wrote that no true church of Christ could exist without excommunication.[10])

With historical hindsight, we might consider it inconsistent, even ironic, that Mack rejected existing church systems as "man's statutes" and claimed that the Brethren followed nothing but the "teachings of Jesus," only to advocate church discipline and the necessity of excommunication a few paragraphs later. This seeming inconsistency was not entirely lost on Mack himself, who appears to have anticipated such objections when he wrote this justification of Brethren excommunication:

> We are truly assured that our Lord Jesus Christ, who at that time was given power and might in heaven and on the earth, is the initiator of our action, and will know how to carry it through wisely, and also provide here the one and the other [church leader] to whom He will entrust wisdom and understanding. The ways of the Lord will then be orderly prepared, without giving offense and annoyance to the God-loving brethren and sisters.[11]

Once again, unlike the human-inspired systems of other churches, the Brethren system of correction and excommunication was exceptional, being the work of Jesus himself. Brethren leaders who oversaw the discipline, meanwhile, were touted as nothing other than Christ's instruments, exercising discipline within His church without giving offense. (Henry R. Holsinger many years later would likely have disputed this point.)

What is more, Mack suggested that "the world" outside the church would find Christ and His disciples to be "a stumbling block and an annoyance," for they took offense at the very Word on which the church was founded. The world, as Brethren understood it, included most of those who lived in their communities. Whether the baptismal metaphor for separating from such neighbors and joining Christ's true church was the Biblical flood or a burial, baptism was considered an act of separation, symbolizing the death of the old person, coming out from the world, and being reborn into a new spiritual order. This order represented not just a spiritual longing for Christ and for discerning Christ in the same way as one's brethren, but a willing submission to the laws of the Kingdom written outwardly in Christ's "last will and testament" (the New Testament). Mack's understanding was that his open letter contained not "one point which is not from the teachings of Christ and His apostles."[12]

So Brethren believed their own church system, unlike Catholic or Calvinist systems, derived directly from Jesus. Their order — and they did speak of an *order* during the early 18th century, though it was different from their institutionalized, late 19th century "order of the Brethren" — was nothing more or less than the New Testament Order of Jesus and the first apostles. They saw themselves as having been born of a new spirit and died to the world, while most so-called Christians still danced with it. They organized, becoming the Schwarzenau Brethren that our contemporary churches descend from, in order to harness their awakened spirituality in a manner consistent with the Outer Word of scripture. They saw little tension between the Inner Ear of the spirit and Outer Ear of scripture; it was all one and the same, the Inner Ear providing the capacity for submitting to the Outer Ear recorded in the New Testament.

Beyond Mack's writings and the many 18th century doctrinal and devotional tracts that have been mentioned at this meeting, recent historical scholarship sheds additional light on early Brethren exceptionalism. The published papers of the 2012 Young Center conference on the life and influence of Alexander Mack Jr. makes for engaging reading along these lines. Jeff Bach's 2003 book, *Voices of the Turtledoves*, offers fascinating context for understanding both the early Brethren historical moment and their movement, whom they connected with and whom they separated themselves from. The Ephrata group that broke away under the leadership of Conrad Beissel had a more mystical bent than those who remained with the Germantown Brethren. Beissel's "direct revelation" from above wasn't something that Brethren of the early eighteenth century were completely unfamiliar with, but they were cautious about such claims, insisting that "new light" be directly tied to the old light of the New Testament. Beissel's direct revelation went too far for the Germantown Brethren, as did his claim to a status too high among the saints to be called simply brother or sister. Still, the Ephrata community's flirtation with the Brethren — first belonging and then not belonging, winning over some important members (including Alexander Mack Jr.) and then losing them again — reveals much about both the strength of spiritual awakening among the earliest Brethren and the constraints and controls placed upon such awakening.[13] Brethren were clearly engaged in a sifting time, attempting to discern what belonged within their faith fellowship and what did not.

Another recent work that teaches much about early Brethren separation from the world is Marcus Meier's *The Origin of the Schwarzenau Brethren*. If in *Brethren Society* I emphasized "separation" from the world, "divorce" better captures some of what I read in Meier's book. To cut to the chase, the mythology of Brethren origins that I learned as a child in church membership class emphasized gathering around the Word, studying it together, and adult baptism, things most of today's Brethren are very comfortable sharing with their spiritual ancestors. Meier's Brethren-origins narrative, in contrast, tells the story of Philadelphian-inspired radicals who quit their jobs and property and left their home communities, believing the second-coming of Christ was nigh and they were about to enter another age.[14] Such a scholarly depiction of our founding Brethren comes closer to the turn-of-the-century "Left Behind" series of Christian novels than to what I was taught about Brethren origins as a child. Meier's account suggests that for the founding Brethren, "leaving the world" wasn't just figurative language for a life of discipleship; it was a literal expectation, central to Hochmann von Hochenau's preaching in the years prior to 1708.

According to Meier, the founding Brethren also separated themselves from the world in these ways, among others:

- Early on, many Brethren rejected personal property and sexual intercourse, believing that they had moved beyond carnal union and should seek only union with Jesus, whom they would soon see face to face.
- They rejected communion with members of the Reformed church, thinking that sharing the Eucharist with those who were not spiritually and morally reborn might bring judgment upon themselves.
- Some of them rejected formal worship services altogether.

BRETHREN SPIRITUALITY

- The best indications are that Brethren may have looked different from those around them, dressing in a simple fashion and likely wearing beards as well. (Our current renderings of Alexander Mack in children's books and historical reenactments have been culturally airbrushed, reflecting the way modern Brethren want to imagine Mack rather than the historical record of the time, sparse though it may be.)
- Brethren rejected the theology of eternal damnation, replacing it with a belief in universal restoration.
- They rejected war and fighting.

Unlike some Radical Pietists who were more free-spirited, Brethren came to share the Anabaptist insistence upon uniting in an ordered faith fellowship, obedient to the rule-book of the Gospel. Yet the Brethren longing for *spiritual* unity — evidenced in sameness of practice — nudged them closer in some ways to the Amish than to Mennonites, some of whom had become more liberal in their church expectations. Brethren, for example, adopted the Amish practice of not just excommunicating, but socially avoiding members who would not heed the united counsel of the church. (Based upon its prominence in Mack's writing, the "Ban" might even be considered one of our founding church ordinances.) Even though social avoidance was quite unusual for a group from Pietist origins, Meier doesn't cast it as reflecting an embrace of Anabaptism and rejection of the more free-spirited approach of Pietism, as some have done, but instead sees it as a Pietist group's way of coming to terms with the fact that the world had not ended. Since Christ's new age had not been established, Mack's Brethren had the choice of returning to their old faith communities or discerning another way forward, a way to tend their spiritual flame while unifying themselves in a manner consistent with the New Testament.

Regarding separation, given their earlier abandonment of jobs, marriage, and personal property in anticipation of Christ's return, *the organization of the Brethren in 1708 should not be seen as a separation from the world of the established churches* — for many of them, that had happened a couple of years earlier — *rather, their organization represented a step back into the practical realities of worldly life* — human marriage, personal property, church organization, teaching and discipline, etc. — practices they resorted to because Jesus had not returned.

19TH CENTURY: SEPARATION ACCUMULATION

In his presentation at this conference, Dale Stoffer referred to the three "nons" of Brethren history: nonresistance, nonswearing, and nonconformity to the world. These markers of nineteenth century Brethren separation can be stated simply, as they were in the 1848 baptismal decision that enshrined them as membership requirements, or they could be spelled out in incredible detail. Permit me to elaborate upon the details by taking us back for a moment to the late nineteenth century...

Imagine for a moment that we are gathered in a simple meetinghouse. The year is 1883. A church Messenger (or Delegate) is about to read the Minutes of the recent Annual Meeting for our consideration, presenting what will be known to future generations as the "Annual Conference report." Unlike those future generations, however, everyone waits in eager anticipation, for all must digest the report as rules for living, which we might be held accountable for. The church Messenger is now ready to begin. If you think he reads too long, then imagine that you have an Old German Baptist sensibility toward time and preserve the capacity to listen attentively indefinitely. He reads:[15]

> It is not considered apostolic and therefore not expedient to number the members of the church to ascertain her numerical strength, inasmuch as the apostles never gave the exact number of believers.
>
> And it is the duty of all members who have no reasonable excuse to faithfully attend public worship, and if they neglect to do so, they should be visited to ascertain the cause, and if no good reason can be given, they should be kindly admonished to heed *Heb 10: 24,25*.
>
> A member should be tried where his membership is, except he commit an offense in his church and changes his membership before it is settled, he shall then go back to the church he left, and there be tried.
>
> The Holy Kiss or Christian salutation should not be neglected. Members should observe it at times of meeting for public worship, at time of feet-washing, and before breaking of bread and all other suitable times and places. And no member can withhold it from any who are not walking worthily, except by action of the church, in dismissing such members or in cases where members are defiled

by the use of tobacco or strong drink, but when meeting in cities, towns or at public gatherings, it is left optional. And no member may extend this Christian salutation to aliens or expelled members.

It is a dangerous and alarming evil for members to conform to this world, in fashionable dressing, building and ornamenting houses in the style of those high in the world, and ought not to be among the humble followers of the lowly Jesus. And to specify more fully what is regarded as fashionable: wearing of gold or jewelry of any kind, female hats, hoops, vain superfluities, ruffled and costly garments, and brethren should not get costly and fine burial cases, and expensive tombstones, carriages and harness of fancy styles, and the use of sleighbells, except circumstances require them, neither should brethren wear a fashionable beard or mustache only, and it is not granted to members to have their likenesses taken, nor to get and use musical instruments, nor to teach instrumental music. Neither should members attend places of amusement, such as State and county fairs, celebrations, shows, mass meetings, and political meetings, etc. And members who will indulge in any of the above named things and thus cause offense, and who will not be admonished to put them away, must be held as disturbing the peace of the church, and be dealt with as not hearing the church, according to Matt. 18. And Brethren are admonished and urged to wear our time-honored round breast coat with standing collar, the hair plainly, not fashionable, or roached [layered, or neatly trimmed], and in case a brother is conscientious in wearing a full beard [meaning beard plus mustache], others should bear with him.

No member can be allowed, according to the gospel, to take any part, either directly or indirectly in military services. And if a brother should be put into the army, and proposes to shed blood, he cannot be held in fellowship with the church, considering all things the great doctrine of peace is so well sustained and so strongly enjoined by the great Prince of peace, and our brotherhood is so well established in these blessed principles, that if any will not conform to them, he is not of us, and therefore his Christian fellowship must be dissolved. No brother is allowed to carry a deadly weapon either for war or to use violence under any circumstance.

Separation from the World and Engagement with the World

It is recommended that members refrain from voting, fearing that we compromise our nonresistant principles, but forbearance is recommended toward those who do vote — not making voting a test of fellowship, hoping that in time they will see with the body of the brethren on this subject. It is not consistent for the brethren to hold and serve in any of the public offices of our government, such as representatives in the legislative, judicial or executive departments, justice of the peace, sheriff, constable, county supervisor, overseer of the poor, or any other office wherein we would be required to compromise our Christian principles, as taking or administering oaths of office, or employing force in the duties of the office, and if brethren do so they will fall under the judgment of the church. And brethren should not serve as jurors, either as grand or petit, if they can avoid it, and especially where a person is tried for life.

No member of the church should buy or sell a note or bond by which a poor person might be oppressed.

Brethren are admonished to be very careful in engaging in all kinds of business, and especially business done by incorporated bodies, such as R.R. and banking companies, as by so doing they may be brought into dangerous associations, with ungodly men.

Members are not advised to have their property insured, neither are they forbidden if done in a mutual way, and brethren are permitted to organize a mutual fire insurance company.

But as to life insurance, members are advised to make use of no such privilege, the confidence we have in each other, in our mutual care for one another, ought to induce members, who have taken out policies in life insurance companies to abandon the organization, and members who refuse to do so shall be held amenable to the church.Funerals should be conducted strictly in accordance with our plain, unassuming and humble Christian principles, avoiding all appearance of conformity to this world, such as superfluity in eating, extravagance in clothing, and not to get fine burial cases, and that a neat white shroud is most becoming in dressing our dead.

It is not right for ministers to solemnize marriages in cases where parties are divorced and second parties yet living. And it is wrong for members to receive ministers of other denominations into their houses to officiate in the marriage of their children. And parents should give their children timely warning against marrying near relatives, such as cousins, etc., that they would not ignorantly do what they might afterwards seriously and conscientiously regret.

Our old brethren have thought it right according to I Cor. 5:9-11 to put members in avoidance, but brethren who do not endorse the doctrine of avoidance, should respect the decision of a church that puts a member in avoidance, and should not speak against the avoidance to the avoided one.

Members should not attend lyceums or debating societies, which indulge in theatrical performances for mere amusement.

There should not be more than two or three different colors in the binding of our hymn-books, and they should be plain, with no ornament or superfluity in the binding, such as gilt or flowering.

To hold lectures on the subject of temperance exclusively is considered not advisable for a brother. And in carrying out these temperance principles it is not admissable for brethren to attach themselves to temperance societies.

And further, it is hereby seen that it is the duty of all the members of our beloved brotherhood to abstain from the use of all intoxicating drinks as a beverage, using them only, if need be, for medical and mechanical purposes.

Members should be urged not to use tobacco in any form except for medical or mechanical purposes, and especially should they abstain from its use at the time and place of public worship, as it is an unbecoming and filthy habit and very offensive to most brethren and sisters who do not use it, and is therefore inconsistent for brethren to raise it.

Brethren shall not preach, publish, or sell books, for or against the doctrine of universal restoration [the doctrine that all people shall eventually be restored to God, that Divine punishment is not eternal].

The Church Messenger then admonishes us to hear all of this as the united counsel of the Brethren under the guidance of the Holy Spirit. Furthermore, he notes, it is the belief of the Brethren that all of it is either directly enjoined by the Gospel or consistent with our Gospel principles. Living by these rules will reflect our spiritual understanding that Jesus guides all aspects of living, that everything we do should testify to the fact that we are more than just nominally Christian. It is available in written form with scriptural citation for those who desire to review it.

Returning to our twenty-first century vantage point, the historical record clearly indicates that this degree of behavioral specification — of practical (not theological) precisionism — accumulated throughout the nineteenth century, accelerating particularly from the 1840s through the 1890s. During the early twentieth century, several progressive Brethren authors looked back to that period with anything but nostalgia, referring to it as the "wilderness period" or "dark ages" of Brethren history, an era that had concealed the fact that Alexander Mack was actually a great, university trained scholar, that early eighteenth century Brethren had founded the first Protestant Sunday School, and that early Brethren had produced and printed important literature at a prodigious rate. These scholars were inspired by Martin Grove Brumbaugh's clarion call to "no force in religion"; they shared a view that the alleged "wilderness period" of heavy behavioral prescription was a shameful retreat from the world.

Whatever our views of nineteenth-century Brethren history, depicting it as a retreat from the larger world could not be farther from the truth. Just as the initial organization of the Brethren represented a turning toward the world, not away from it, so the extensive list of nineteenth century rules just recited represented the same. Every single one of them — from the colors on hymn book bindings to how to relate to railroads — wrestled with the complications of *engaging* the outside world in a way that reflected their spiritual understanding that the gospel, to borrow twentieth-century rhetoric, calls for "another way of living." Like their eighteenth century predecessors, nineteenth century Brethren had not yet embraced the mainstream Protestant notion that each individual would chart their own course, remaining true to their personal convictions rather than to the common understandings of the faith community. Those who published these 1880s minutes still believed that another "way" of living did not, in the aggregate, amount to other "ways" of living. By the late 19th century,

Brethren had long since abandoned the practice of social avoidance, but they still preserved the early eighteenth century conviction (and hope) that the Holy Spirit would guide them toward a common Christian walk.

Had our nineteenth-century ancestors *not* been extending into the world — expanding in size, geography, location, information sources, and size of membership at a pace that differed dramatically from the comparative localism, isolation, and slow expansion of the preceding century, this accumulation of precise rules would not have occurred. The fact that it did reflects a genuine effort to sustain their distinctive witness while engaging the world, not a separation from the world as has sometimes been described. The *Brethren's Tracts and Pamphlets* of the same period, which would strike many of us as strangely sectarian today, were also means of engaging outsiders and introducing the Brethren to new members who were being added by the score. The early *Brethren's Card*, which referred to the Brethren not as a denomination or organization but as a people, in the way that Jewish people or Native Americans peoples are commonly invoked today, and went on to distill distinctive Dunker practices, was produced as a "calling card" of sorts, a way to reach out to neighbors, friends, and acquaintances who might be interested in the church.

And so it has been for centuries. What often looks in retrospect like something sectarian, a sign of separation and withdrawal from the world, has often been a gesture of articulation, of engaging the world with core commitments that the church holds dear. Just as Marcus Meier suggests that Anabaptism and Pietism may be threads of the same cloth, interwoven in a way that is difficult to separate, so what appears as separation and engagement with the world may be part of the same encounter. Both of these impulses — the impulse to separate and to strongly engage — are born of a sense of distinction, of having something to offer and preserve, of possessing a rare or distinct testimony, insight, or window upon Christ's truth. If this is so, it is only logical that the "three nons" of Brethren history were articulated most concisely in an Annual Meeting decision on baptism, a decision laying the grounds for bringing more people in.

Notes

1 These findings are nationally representative of Church of the Brethren members eighteen years of age and older. For a full presentation and discussion of findings, see Carl Desportes Bowman, *Portrait of a People: The Church of the Brethren at 300* (Elgin, Illinois: Brethren Press, 2008).

2 Previously unpublished breakdowns from the Brethren Member Profile data.

3 This follows logically from the fact that members of widely divergent beliefs and opinions embraced the "spiritual" religious identity.

4 Vladimir V Putin, "A Plea for Caution From Russia," <http://www.nytimes.com/2013/09/12/opinion/putin-plea-for-caution-from-russia-on-syria.html>

5 *Rechten und Ordnungen des Haufes Gottes* was commonly known in English as "Rites and Ordinances" during the mid-twentieth century. Donald F. Durnbaugh pointed out that *rechten* was more appropriately translated as rights, meaning laws or statutes in the original German. See Donald F. Durnbaugh, *European Origins of the Brethren* (Elgin, Illinois: Brethren Press, 1958), 323.

6 A photograph of this early version of the Brethren's Card appears in Carl F. Bowman, *Brethren Society: The Cultural Transformation of a "Peculiar People"* (Baltimore: Johns Hopkins University Press, 1995), 187. See Volume 4 of the Brethren Encyclopedia for a description of how the Card's content was modified over time.

7 William R. Eberly, ed., *The Complete Writings of Alexander Mack* (Winona Lake, IN: BMH Books, 1991), 10-11.

8 Ibid., 11.

9 Ibid., 12.

10 More precisely, the answer to Question 22 in Mack's *Basic Questions* is, "The ban is an essential and necessary part of the church of Christ, as long as it remains in combat here in this wicked world among wolves and evil spirits. There can be no church of Christ without the ban." See ibid., 33.

11 Ibid., 12.

12 Ibid., 13.

13 See Jeff Bach, *Voices of the Turtledoves: The Sacred World of Ephrata* (University Park, Pennsylvania: Pennsylvania State University Press, 2003) for more information on the dynamics of separation and relationship between the Ephrata and Germantown Brethren.

14 For an excellent recent examination of the social and theological connections of the early Brethren movement, see Marcus Meier, *The Origin of the Schwarzenau Brethren* (Philadelphia: Brethren Encyclopedia, Inc., 2008).

15 This collection of Minutes is excerpted from what I have called the "Bootleg Annual Meeting Minutes of 1883." In 1882, a year after the Old German Baptist Brethren withdrew from the German Baptists and the same year that progressive leader Henry R. Holsinger was expelled by Annual Meeting, the so-called "mandatory decision" was passed by Annual Meeting and a group of fifteen brethren "chosen from the different sections of the Brotherhood, and representing the views of the Brotherhood in general" was selected to revise the Minutes, omitting all rulings that were obsolete or conflicted with later decisions, or which seemed to conflict with the "express or implied meaning" of Scripture. Members of the committee were B. F. Moomaw, G. D. Bowman, S. A. Fike, D. P. Saylor, C. G. Lint, I. J. Rosenberger, R. H. Miller, Daniel Chambers, Daniel Vaniman, S. S. Mohler, John Forney, David Bechtelheimer, John Zook (Cedar Rapids, Iowa), Daniel Hays, and C. Bucher. Each member was instructed to perform the entire task independently and then submit their work to the entire committee. Their individual efforts would then be folded together into a coherent narrative of Brethren behavioral expectations and presented to

the Annual Meeting for adoption. The compiled and integrated statement was presented to the 1883 Annual Meeting and then published for general distribution as *Minutes of the Annual Meetings of the Brethren, Revised From Former Editions by a Committee Authorized by Annual Meeting of May 30th, 1882. Designed as a Handbook of Reference in Church Work of the General Brotherhood* (Huntingdon, PA and Mount Morris, IL: Brethren Publishing Company Printers, 1883). The purpose of publication and distribution was to enable the churches to study it before submitting the document to the 1884 Annual Meeting for final approval. After all of this effort, however, the 1884 Meeting rejected the work, the primary rationale being that it omitted decisions which, however archaic or obsolete, had reflected the Holy Spirit inspired work of the Brethren in their day. Since the published and distributed work, printed in the same format as other Annual Meeting records of the late nineteenth century, has largely disappeared, my conjecture is that there was a general understanding that extant copies should be destroyed. In conversations with Brethren historians over the years — including Donald Durnbaugh, Dale Stoffer, and Jeff Bach, it became clear to me that they had never seen the published document and were unaware of its existence. In spite of its rejection by Annual Meeting, I consider it to be a unique summary of Brethren normative understandings and behavioral expectations of the early 1880s. The methodical, narrative manner of its composition is historically unique, and the Full Report (stenographic transcript) of the Annual Meeting proceedings reveals that it was not rejected for its substantive content, but rather because Brethren were wary of a distillation of their positions that eliminated rulings of historical import.

I call it the Bootleg Minutes of 1883, "bootleg" reflecting the fact that it should no longer exist, but it does. All of the statements in this excerpt are direct quotes from the work, but the ordering of the quotations is my own, and ellipses have been omitted to improve readability, and thereby enhance our ability to imagine being there. The year after these "Bootleg Minutes" were rejected, a classified "Revised Minutes," organized by topic, was approved by the 1885 Annual Meeting, the condition for its acceptance being that *all* historical Minutes had been included in the work. For our twenty-first century purposes of understanding the past, the fact that obsolete and superseded decisions had been omitted from the rejected "Bootleg Minutes," and that they had been woven together in narrative form, makes the rejected document a better source for understanding mid-1880s German Baptist Brethren than the approved document of 1885.

Brethren Devotional Literature and Poetry

Karen Garrett

THE TOPIC FOR THIS PRESENTATION, *BRETHREN DEVOTIONAL LITERATURE and Poetry*, is a very broad topic. We will barely make a dent in the material we could cover. Brethren have written many poems and much devotional literature since 1708. For a few years, I have been researching Brethren writing, focusing on poetry and hymn texts. My main focus within that broad topic has been Brethren Spirituality in both the eighteenth and nineteenth centuries. I narrow my focus by researching only writing by Brethren. As I agreed to prepare a paper for the World Assembly, I decided to expand my research to include writing from Brethren who lived or live, in the twentieth and twenty-first centuries in addition to the eighteenth and nineteenth centuries.

I am a member of the Church of the Brethren, but my interest is not limited to Church of the Brethren writers. I am interested in Brethren thought from all the Brethren denominations or groups. I have included some variety in this paper, but not as much as I had hoped. There has simply been more written than I can include in a one-hour presentation. This paper discusses some of what I have learned. I suggest you continue learning with your own reading and research projects.

We begin with a prayer/poem by a current poet from a book published in 2012. We will then read and discuss poetry from across the decades. I will read this poem aloud so you can hear Kay Bowman's prayer, "Blessed by Burdens."[1]

Out of pain have come poignant poems;
Out of problems, the sweetest songs;
Out of suffering, the greatest spirits;
Out of tears, the rights from wrongs…

From adversity have come the most blessed lives;
From harsh conditions, the most compassionate souls;
From trouble, those filled with the greatest peace;
From sorrow, those who console…

Therefore, may I find comfort in my suffering Lord,
Find peace in my pain;
For from my trials of deepest testing
Will come rich blessings of greatest gain.

We begin this paper with a brief introduction to share my understanding of Brethren spirituality. I look to poetry and devotional writing to teach us what Brethren understood about spirituality. Nineteenth-century Brethren writer, Samuel Kinsey (1832-1883), wrote of the need to be spiritually minded in his essay, "Spiritual Desires."[2]

> He who makes a profession of religion should be spiritually minded. His desires should be spiritual not carnal…
>
> We read "for to be carnally minded is death, but to be spiritually minded is life and peace," Rom. 8:6. We should desire to see God's people thrive to see the church pure, see the glad tiding of salvation proclaimed, and to see them proclaimed in primitive purity.
>
> We should desire to see sinners converted, and above all to have our own souls saved. Those who are really spiritually minded will do all they can for the accomplishment of the above ends.

Included with the essay is a poem in which Kinsey described his personal spiritual practices. He would not have used the words "spiritual practices," but in the twenty-first century we call them spiritual practices. As you read the poem, take note of themes that relate to spirituality.

> I love to see God's word proclaim'd;
> To ruined sons of earth;
> I'd love to see them all rejoice,
>   At a redeemer's birth.

I love to sit and meditate,
Upon my actions past;
I love to think of all the joys,
That may be mine at last.

I love to see God's people thrive,
And flourish as the rose;
I love to see them all unite,
And banish far their foes.

I love to turn my thoughts within,
And feel my littleness;
I love to give my heart to him,
Who my poor soul will bless.

I love to read God's holy word,
And meditate His law;
I love to know His allwise plan,
Which He through Christ foresaw.

I love to view*[3] th' angelic host,
That throng the heav'ns above;
I love to think of endless joys,
For all who Jesus love.
I love to see th' assembled church,
Swell loud their Maker's praise;
I love to see them all unite,
n sweet and solemn lays.[4]

The first thing I want to note is Kinsey's use of the pronoun "I," which is used fourteen times in the poem. Kinsey's normal practice was to use the word "we" rather than refer to himself. During the nineteenth century, Brethren made it a practice to use the communal words, we and us. Their focus was on community rather than individual goals and personal ideas. Some Brethren continue that practice. In the Church of the Brethren, most people are comfortable saying "I." Kinsey's use of "I" is out of his normal pattern so it may say something significant. Perhaps he used "I" for this poem because being spiritually minded is a response that starts in the heart of an individual that is then encouraged through community.

Several characteristics of spirituality are included in this poem. I will share a few; you may note others. The inwardness of spirituality is described in stanza four. These inward thoughts often put an individual in proper perspective in relationship with God. Kinsey's inward thoughts led him to sense his "littleness" compared to God's greatness. In this stanza, Kinsey expressed an assurance that God will bless his "littleness," expressed as his "poor soul." The humble attitude of Kinsey's heart expressed his spirituality.

Meditation is one of the spiritual disciplines often mentioned in current culture. Meditation is thinking or pondering on things that are sometimes unexplained truths. In stanza two, Kinsey described meditation as having two different paths. Kinsey meditated on his "actions past," and "joys" that will be his "at last," heavenly rewards. Meditating on individual actions, be they successes or failures, in light of God's plan, and joy that one is partaking in God's plan, are integral to spiritual growth. Stanza five points to another aspect of meditating, reading and meditating on "God's holy word." In this stanza, the meditating led Kinsey to "know His [God's] allwise plan" carried out by Christ, referred to as "redeemer" in stanza one, meditating on the plan of salvation. Interestingly, in stanza one, as Kinsey refers to God's word being proclaimed, he uses the word "see," rather than "hear." God's word being proclaimed usually means the word is preached or spoken. Kinsey would have heard the word read and preached. He did not use the word "hear" he used the word "see." One way to "see" God's word is to "see" oneself and other Christians proclaim faith through actions. Seeing the faithful actions of individuals and of the church adds dimension and depth to proclaiming scriptures.

Kinsey continued, in stanza six, describing God's "allwise" plan by pointing to Eternal Life in heaven. He used an asterisk to introduce a footnote. In the footnote, he clarified that he was viewing the angelic host with "an eye of faith." This made clear that for Kinsey, knowledge of heaven is a spiritual knowledge. During our earthly life, we can know of heaven only through faith. This inner knowing is based on God's promises revealed through scripture. The focus of Kinsey's thoughts on heaven brought him "endless joy." Kinsey wrote this hymn during the American Civil War,[5] which for many was a time of fear and rage rather than joy. Spirituality is often evidenced by an ability to have an inward attitude informing one's outward actions that is in contrast to a larger cultural reality or situation.

Kinsey included a corporate aspect of spirituality in the final stanza. While spirituality begins within the individual heart and soul, it can also find expression when worshipping in community. In this stanza, Kinsey reflects on the "assembled church" united to sing and praise God. A thread of the corporateness of spiritual mindedness runs throughout the poem. In stanza one, all are rejoicing; in stanza three, God's people are thriving and united against "their foes." In the final stanza, their praise is "sweet and solemn." A community of believers gathered in worship, study, and fellowship provides mutual encouragement and helps develop each individual's spirituality.

Kinsey's poem gives voice to five markers we can use to discern spirituality in the writing of other poets to see if they agree or if they add something new. All of these markers do not need to be present in a given poem to determine Christian or Brethren spirituality. The markers of spirituality are:

1. The expression of a personal relationship with God and the characteristics of God in that relationship.
2. The use of scripture or allusion to scripture.
3. The mention or evidence of inward reflection or meditation.
4. Expression of faith in an eternal heavenly relationship with God.
5. The desire for unity with other believers.

There could be other markers, but these five markers will be used for our discussion in this paper.

The earliest poem we will consider is "Bind My Soul Well" written by Wilhelm Knepper (1691-ca.1743) in the early eighteenth century.

Bind my soul well,
On Thee, Jesus. In love teach me,
How I should live,
Steadfast, after Thy Spirit's driving power.
Open, Thyself, oh Life's-Source,
Flow into my soul

Jesus, it is known to Thee,
That I was born blind and dumb.
Yes, a dry and wasted land.
Without Thee, I am lost.
In blood and sin's slime,
I lay, Oh, God's lamb!

Jesus, open my sight.
My eyes, they are so dark.
Let the light of the seven spirits,
Enlighten me, As Carfunkel,
That stand before Thy throne,
And go abroad in all lands.

Oh! I find myself so wretched,
That I can hardly tell Thee about it.
However, I will still seek Thee,
And lament my things to Thee.
Other souls adorn themselves.
But I am dark, cold and lazy.

My beloved, radiate to me,
The hot Love-Look.
Drive me on this Life's-Highway,
Refresh this languid spirit,
So that I can courageously,
Contend against all opposition.

Lead me with Thy Grace-Word,
So that with my entire soul,
I press can through the narrow gate. [sic]
Make Satan fail against me.
As he with his dark Power,
Strives to lead me away from the Light.

Oh! Bind me oh so well,
To Thee, Jesus, in love.
Thou art truly full of love,
Draw me, so that I cleave unto Thee.
Then flow into me, Thou Life's-Source,
Oh my God! Emmanuel.

This poem was published in the Brethren hymnbook printed in Berleburg, Germany in 1720. It was written in German. This is a translation to English by James Zaiger.[6] You can see that this poem is seven stanzas in length, a relatively short poem for the eighteenth century.

Knepper begins this poem with a call for Jesus' Spirit to flow its power into his soul. He is also asking to be taught how to live out of that filled soul. It is clear that Knepper sees his life as hopeless without his relationship with God. By stanza five, Knepper names the need for his "languid spirit" to be filled so he can "contend against all opposition." Stanza five also uses the words "My beloved," and "hot Love-Look." Knepper had an intimate spiritual relationship with Jesus. Knepper was imprisoned because of his Anabaptist faith. Few of us know the kind of oppression Knepper faced while he was imprisoned. The source of his strength was not will power; it was soul power. It is this deep love for God and relationship with God that helps Knepper "press…through the narrow gate."

In 1944 Brethren Publishing House published a devotional book, *Heritage of Devotion*, compiled by Lillian Grisso. A devotional titled "Spiritual Worship"[7] gives us insight into a Brethren understanding of spirituality. To compile the book, Grisso searched through periodicals and books for poems and devotional writing that would be helpful in meditation. The following are the words of Ira H. Frantz from the devotional "Spiritual Worship":

> God is a spirit and cannot be represented by an image or painting of any kind. True worship is an act of the spirit and could not be helped by a visual representation of God, even if that were possible. Our concept must be spiritual.

Ira Frantz wrote these words in the context of worship, corporate worship. At the end of Grisso's quote, she included the citation "(condensed)—Ira H. Frantz (T.M. 1938)." I decided that I wanted to read the complete article, but I did not know which periodical the letters "T.M." stood for. After a bit of research I learned that "T.M." stood for the *Teacher's Monthly*, or more specifically the *Brethren Teacher's Monthly*. Fortunately, there are a couple nearly complete sets of that periodical at the Brethren Heritage Center. I sat down and began to flip page by page through the 1938 volume. The quote Grisso used is from the October 1938 issue. On my way to finding that quote, another article by Ira Frantz caught my attention. In the September issue, I spotted a paragraph with the heading "Spirituality is not froth."[8] Frantz begins by noting that people have different understandings of the word "spirituality." He also gives this definition of spirituality:

> Spirituality may be identified not so much by emotional religious outbursts nor by long-faced piety as by the willingness of the indi-

vidual to yield his personal life, his business, his politics to the ordering of God. Whether you accept this view of spirituality or not, it would be well to determine just what you do mean by the word. Then you will know how eagerly you desire to see spiritual revival.

Frantz's words provide historical perspective on a Brethren understanding of spirituality. We will need to do further research to determine if there are any earlier uses of the word "spirituality." As we continue to read the words of our Brethren sisters and brothers, our spirits may resonate with their words or be challenged by them. Either way, this gives us an opportunity to grow in our understanding of spirituality and grow deeper in our own faith. Perhaps insight from reading the words of these poets will help us determine what we mean by the word spirituality.

A prose writer and poet, George Zollers (1841-1911), lived during the same time as Samuel Kinsey. However, Zollers made different choices in life than Kinsey. Kinsey remained nonresistant during the American Civil War. Prior to becoming Brethren, Zollers participated in the American Civil War as a member of the military band. He played the cornet. His story is quite interesting. He shared it in his book *Thrilling Incidents on Sea and Land*.[9] I have included one of his poems for our consideration today.

"Midnight"[10]

I love to ponder in the lone
 And silent midnight hour,
To bow before my Father's throne
 And feel his saving power.

Such midnight thoughts how calm and sweet,
 When daily toils subside;
And men have sunk profound in sleep,
 And no sad cares betide.

To view by faith God's smiling face,
 When all is still at night,
And triumph in his sov'reign grace,—
 This is my soul's delight.

Oh, may I fervent vigils keep
 In lonely nights to come!

> And o'er my sins and follies weep,
> Before my Father's throne.

In this short but profoundly meaningful poem, Zollers revealed who he was when he was alone. It is the end of the day; the chores are completed; and everyone else has gone to bed. Zollers takes this time to be with God. His spiritual relationship with God is what makes this time so sweet. This is not written as a prayer, nor does it state that during this evening time Zollers spent the time in prayers of petition or prayers of praise. This midnight time is spent pondering and enjoying his relationship with God.

Zoller's source of delight is grace. He delights that God's grace covered his sin and folly. Without his relationship with God, nurtured by such times as this midnight reflection, perhaps his sinful nature would control. Zollers mentions the silence of the midnight hour. Later in this paper, we will consider another poem that points to silence in relation to spirituality.

Let us move on to a poem from the eighteenth century written by Alexander Mack Jr., also known as Sander Mack. Sander was a prolific writer. Fortunately, more of his writing has been preserved than that of his father Alexander Mack Sr., giving us more depth of understanding as to Sander's faith and spirituality. Sander Mack would have learned much from his father. However, it was only a few years after arriving in the "New World" that Mack Sr. died. Sander, who lived to be ninety years old, was twenty-three years old at that time of his father's death. The writings of Sander had more influence on the early Brethren in Pennsylvania than his father's writing.

There is no date on this poem. The poem is included in the collection of Mack Jr. writings that Samuel Heckman published in 1910. Mack Jr. lived from 1712 to 1803 so this poem gives us a look at Brethren spirituality in the 1700s. I do not know if Sander wrote this during the time of the American Revolution, but stanza one mentions the world as "beset by terror and distress." Perhaps this refers to the unrest in the colonies prior to, during, or perhaps even following that war. This lengthy poem is untitled. It was originally written in German. The version included below is a translation to English by Samuel Heckman.[11]

> A soul which loves God
> Finds anguish in this world.
> What it loves outside of Jesus

Is beset by terror and distress.
Therefore Jesus calls to it
"Come, in me is joy and peace."

"I have overcome the world,"
Says Jesus Christ consolingly.
"I have bound its strongest man
Through the splendor of my light."
Therefore He calls ever and ever
"O dear souls come to me."

Let riches alone, and let them lie
Wherever they themselves wish to be.
Seek thou thy pleasures
Only where time and the world are forgotten.
My advice brings the riches of God to you
Although the devil ever mocks at you.

It is true, the world says
Christ's teachings are not to be understood;
That one is under obligation
To follow Him in all things
In poverty particularly.
This would be too unreasonable.

But Christ knows His own,
He is near of kin to them,
When they seem lost
He is often made known to them
As the good and faithful shepherd
Makes himself known to the lamb which has gone astray.

All the words of His teachings
Seem to them as sweet as sugar.
Their desire, even their adornment and honor
Are the steps of His feet.
He is their shepherd, they are His sheep
In spite of anyone's denial.

To meditate upon the words of Christ,
To follow all His deeds,

To trust alone Christ's counsel
Bring, of course, disgrace in the eyes of the world.
But this meditation on Heaven
Gains Heaven as a reward.

The lambs of Christ like to kiss
The feet of Jesus, their shepherd,
All that they learn from Him
Seems to them sweeter than honey.
The spirit and the word of Christ
Are always their freedom and their law.

All the flowers which give forth fragrance
According to the fear of the Lord,
Furnish them with great pleasure
Because they are their nourishment,
They desire no other sustenance
Save that which comes from the spirit and power of Jesus.

Whatever savors of Christ's love
Calls up His precious blood.
Whatever awakens the desire for virtue
Makes the timid heart courageous
Whatever disturbs the kingdom of satan
Remains a thing of honor forever.

It is clear that Sander has a spiritual relationship with God. His soul loves God and "finds anguish with the world" (stanza one). In the first two stanzas, Sander quotes scripture. When faced with the distress of the world, Sander turns to Christ as revealed in scripture. He understood Christ as his shepherd and he was the sheep. He also knew that his, Sander's, relationship with Christ, and thus his behavior in the world, would be misunderstood by the world. In stanza seven, he specifically notes that his meditation is on the words of Christ. By the end of that stanza, he is also meditating on Heaven. This poem gives evidence of the markers we identified in Kinsey's poem.

There is much more we could learn from both the eighteenth and nineteenth centuries, but time is limited and volumes of poetry are available from writers in the twentieth century. By 1900, the Brethren were dividing into different denominations. Theological differences and emphasis on the importance of various practices led us to part. The markers of spirituality which I named earlier in this paper are present regardless of what group a person identified with. We may find that even with these differences there are aspects of our spirituality that are similar.

Mary Skiles (1868-1925) would have been twenty years old at the time of the first major division. Many of her poems and writings were published in *The Vindicator*. In putting some facts together, I have come to the conclusion that she was a member of the Old German Baptist Brethren. Her husband and children published a book of her poetry after her death. That is the source for the poem *The Sigh of the Toiler*.[12] This poem is addressed to the "Heavenly Father" and reads like a prayer. Words spoken in prayers certainly speak to our spirituality. Skiles is praying this prayer at the end of the day.

> Heavenly Father, dear kind God, the day is done,
> I bring my burdens now and Thou canst count them one by one.
>
> The many vexing things that patience tried,
> The weary toil and care my strength have tried.
>
> And O, the many times I've failed to do my duty as I should.
> The many times I failed to do to others as I would have them do to me.
>
> And I am weak with striving day by day my own self will to crucify complete,
> O help me, Lord, with Thine own strength to see that sacrifice is sweet.
>
> I only ask for strength, my burdens still to bear,
> And hope to lift my heart to Thee where all is fair.
>
> For well I know this life will cease sometime,
> A better life begins in fairer climes.
>
> And if the way seems weary, Thou art near,
> With love divine Thou seest the penitential tear.
>
> Forgive me for my faults I humbly crave.
> O help me keep Thy law as I go onward to the grave.

I don't know about you, but many days I feel the same as Mary. I feel like I have failed to be a faithful witness for Christ and have allowed the stress of the day to control me. In the midst of the reality of stress and burdens, Skiles turns her heart to God. She knows her weakness and his strength. It is also clear that she is trusting in a future in heaven when the earthly trials and burdens will end. There is no date for this poem; so we do not know if this was written near the end of her earthly life or earlier.

Mary Stoner Wine (1885-1959) was a member of the Church of the Brethren. Since Wine was born in 1885, that makes her about twenty years younger than Mary Skiles. Mary Wine wrote many poems, some of which were set to melodies. Today we will consider her poem *Love of God, Eternal Love*. Before we look at the poem, we see from the title that she had an understanding of God as eternal, one of the markers we are using in this study today. The poem by Mary Skiles reflected thoughts in the evening. Mary Wine had a habit of morning devotions where she waited before God, surrendering herself to him for the coming day. The following words came to her during such a time, June 6, 1941.[13]

"Love of God, Eternal Love"[14]

Love of God, eternal love,
Reaching down from heaven above
To the hearts of all mankind,
Bless us with Thy grace divine.

Take away our guilt and pride,
Let no petty sin abide;
May unholy longings cease,
Give us inner joy and peace.

Love of God, O love divine,
Serve through us this world of Thine;
Reaching out in tenderness,
Touch and comfort, heal and bless.

Flowing from Thy heart to ours,
Quickening us with all Thy powers,
Till returning full and free,
Our devotion gladdens Thee.

The opening stanza of this hymn shares Wine's understanding of an eternal God and of heaven, my fourth marker when considering spirituality. The words "inner joy and peace" in the second stanza share Wine's understanding of the inwardness of a relationship with God. In the fourth stanza, she begins with the words "Flowing from Thy heart to ours," again showing us her relationship with God. Her soul is speaking to God, and God responds with comfort, healing, and blessing flowing back to her, and "us." Wine is writing this for the community at worship to sing. That is another marker I look for, unity with other believers.

As we consider poems written in the 1940s, we need to remember that World War II was in the headlines and on the radio. The various Brethren groups were impacted in different ways during the 1940s depending on whether they had taken a nonresistant stand and had chosen to refuse to serve in the military, or whether they had moved from that traditional Brethren stand. In the Church of the Brethren, many young men entered military service. Regardless of one's stand on that particular issue, 1945 brought the deployment and use of the atomic bomb and that event affected everyone.

Kenneth I. Morse (1913-1999) wrote the following poem in 1944. The date places it as written before the bomb was deployed, but the war would still have been heavy on Morse's thoughts.

"Morning Song"[15]

> Scarcely had the velvet clouds appeared
> Above the east, before the sun;
> Scarcely had shades of darkness cleared
> To say the new day had begun;
> When bursting from the hills around
> A hundred trees broke into song;
> A thousand voices joined to sound
> A hymn of praise serene and strong.
>
> If songbirds joining in the praise
> Of God's own creatures can invite
> Nature's whole symphony to raise
> A choral greeting to the light,
> Let us who know God's mercies, then,
> Be early in our morning prayer,
> And let us lift now and again
> Our songs of faith into the air.

There have been many times that I have heard the birds singing as I awakened from sleep. Sometimes the songs brightened my morning after a night of restless sleep due to responsibilities or grief or other worries. Their songs reminded me that the cares of the prior day could be washed away in the new day. Other times, the songs reminded me that even though praise was not quick on my lips, the birds could praise for me until I was ready to join the song. I can only imagine the concerns on Morse's mind the day in 1944 when he wrote those words.

The only marker of spirituality that may be clear in this poem is Morse's trust in God and his relationship with God. Morse was starting his day with thoughts of God regardless of other circumstances. His poem reminds us to begin each day with prayer.

We now turn to a poem by Irene Stout (b. ? –1991). Even though I do not know the date of her birth, a newspaper article states that she began writing poetry in 1981. An auto accident left her with time to write while she recovered from injuries. The poem appears in a book published in 1986; so she wrote it sometime between 1981 and 1986. It reminds me of the poem by Samuel Kinsey that we considered at the beginning of this paper. Her poem is titled "Meditation."[16]

> I want to be alone,
> With humble adoration,
> To listen to God speaking
> With solemn meditation.
>
> I listen very closely
> To learn of His great will.
> Then I put to practice
> What lingers with me still.
>
> We know that God is talking
> In many loving ways,
> Perhaps in answer to a prayer
> Or grateful words of praise.
>
> He tells me of His love
> He had for you and me,
> That he sent His only Son
> To die to set me free.
>
> He tells of the Holy Spirit
> He sent to guide me right.

> I'll sing praises to my Master,
> The giver of my life.

According to the obituary for Owen Stout, Irene's husband, he was a member of the Plevna Dunkard Brethren Church. I assume she also was a member and thus Dunkard Brethren. As stated earlier, my goal is to include a wide variety of Brethren voices. So I was glad to discover Irene's poetry.

As I try to find writers from a variety of Brethren groups, I am noticing that the words of the poetry do not clearly inform me as to which denomination they joined. In looking at markers of spirituality, my spirit resonates with the words of these brothers and sisters, regardless of their church affiliation. That also brings me to realize that we have not focused on any aspect of their writing that makes them clearly Brethren. Their words could easily speak for many Christians in many denominations. In that case I have not done research that sets Brethren spirituality apart from other faiths. Rather I am simply sharing examples of the spirituality of Brethren. I have been diligent to include only poetry written by Brethren.

Moving to the twenty-first century, I include a poem by Flora Williams. Flora also suffered injury from a vehicle accident. That accident left her with a serious injury to her arm. Many of us would not have been as gracious with God as Flora was and is. This poem shows a more modern form of poetry than many that we have read today. Flora wrote this poem in 2003.

"Be Still and Know that 'I AM' God"[17]

> Be Still, I was told,
> But I resented it.
> Couldn't sit still,
> Yearning to squirm.
> Wanting to run,
> Couldn't be still Aching to talk.
> Balking not talking,
> Couldn't be still
> Had to fight, get revenge, get even.
> Couldn't let God be in control.
> Couldn't let Christ show me the way.
> Couldn't be still and hear Christ.
> Couldn't be still and feel Christ.

Couldn't let the Spirit pervade
With love and calmness!
The Spirit finally prayed
With sighs beyond words.
I surrendered in stillness.
Strength, wisdom, and hope
Invaded my soul!
Power and peace
Invaded my stillness.

I did not include stillness or silence as a marker of spirituality. Perhaps it is implied in the marker about our relationship with God. Our relationship with God must include time when we are silent and allow God to speak, giving us time to listen. This poem reflects the restlessness I sometimes feel during times of prayer, when I already know how I want God to answer, but the answer doesn't come, or at least I do not hear it and I am left to sit in silence.

I have spent most of our time focusing on poetry. For early Brethren, the only books they most likely owned were the Bible and the hymn book. Through the hymn book, poetry became a significant part of their devotional reading. As the Brethren began publishing periodicals, the editors included poetry on a regular basis. For many of the Brethren groups, that practice continues to today.

The genre of writing we refer to as "devotional writing" is more recent. As early as 1942, the Church of the Brethren published devotional booklets. The devotionals were organized to provide a daily reading that included scripture, a brief paragraph to encourage or challenge, and closing words of prayer. Some devotionals include a line of two as a quote or thought for the day. This structure seems standard. The book by Lillian Grisso, mentioned earlier in this paper, was formatted in the "devotional style."

In preparation for the Brethren 300th anniversary, a devotional[18] was published that included daily writings by authors from all the Brethren groups. Brethren Press regularly publishes Advent and Lenten devotional booklets. There is not time to discuss the variations in style and approach of Brethren in writing devotional books. These quotes[19] shed light on the current understanding of spirituality in the Church of the Brethren. As I stated earlier, my approach to this presentation has been to let the devotional writing and poetry teach us about Brethren spirituality. Rather than discuss each of these, I will leave them as food for thought as you continue to discern Brethren spirituality, and your personal spirituality.

"Friendship with God means we must make an intentional effort to cultivate that friendship. Solitude, silence, meditation, and prayer are ways to do that."
Kenneth L. Gibble, "Journey to Jerusalem," Lent, Sunday, March 21, 2004

"Lent is a season for returning. It is a time to return to who we most deeply are—children of God desirous of a life with God."
Glenn Mitchell, "Returning," Lent 2005, Introduction

"Christ is forever breaking into our experience, calling us to see, to believe, and to follow."
Daniel M. Petry, "The Promise of His Coming," Advent 2005, Introduction

"Lent is a food time to consider fallow ground: a time to be rather than do, trust rather than control, contemplate rather than strategize or produce."
Sandra L. Bosserman, "A Time to Lie Fallow," Lent, 2006, Introduction

"Our faith is fully formed only when it is fully found in God."
Christopher D. Bowman, "Life to the World," Advent, Sunday, December 17, 2006

"Lent invites us to both inward piety and outward practice."
James L. Benedict, "He Set His Face," Lent 2008, Introduction

"Out of our joy and despair, we cry out to God. We seek God. We thirst for God."
Amy S. Gall Ritchie," Thirsting for God," Lent, Thursday, February 18, 2010

"There is something deep within us that yearns for God. There is an awareness of a deeper, more enduring reality that surrounds us and calls forth the better part of our human nature."
Edward L. Poling, "Emmanuel: God Is with Us," Advent 2010, Introduction

Brethren Devotional Literature and Poetry

There are many more poets whom I could have cited, and many more poems by the authors we have discussed that could have been included. Time has limited us to these few. Perhaps this has whet your appetite to read these poems again or to seek out other poems and writings. Maybe you will decide to include poems in your devotional time or write your own poems. Poetry can be a good voice to our spirituality because it has rhythm and patterns that can help the words sink deep into our spirit.

To close I will read once more "Blessed by Burdens."[20] After reading and discussing the selection of poems today, I trust that this poem may resonate in your spirit in a new way.

> Out of pain have come poignant poems;
> Out of problems, the sweetest songs;
> Out of suffering, the greatest spirits;
> Out of tears, the rights from wrongs...
>
> From adversity have come the most blessed lives;
> From harsh conditions, the most compassionate souls;
> From trouble, those filled with the greatest peace;
> From sorrow, those who console...
>
> Therefore, may I find comfort in my suffering Lord,
> Find peace in my pain;
> For from my trials of deepest testing
> Will come rich blessings of greatest gain.

Notes

1 Kay M. Bowman, "Blessed by Burdens," *Tears Within My Heart: A Modern-Day Psalms Collection* (Harrisonburg, VA: Prince of Peace Press, 2012), 30.

2 Samuel Kinsey, *The Pious Companion, containing a variety of original Essays and Hymns; Hymns adapted to the Worship of God* (Dayton, OH: Samuel Kinsey, 1865), 77.

3 Samuel Kinsey included an asterisk with the following note *By an eye of faith.

4 Kinsey, *Pious Companion*, 78-79.

5 This hymn text appears in *Pious Companion* published in 1865. The hymn text did not appear in an earlier publication, a collection of Kinsey's poems, 1858. The assumption is that the poem about spiritual desires was written between 1858 and 1865. The American Civil War lasted 1861-1865.

6 James Zaiger, *The First Songs of the Brethren* (Waynesboro, PA: James Zaiger, 2008): 65-66. In this book Zaiger has translated 99 hymns by Wilhelm Knepper that appeared in the first Brethren hymnal printed in Berleburg, Germany, 1720.

7 Lillian Grisso, *Heritage of Devotion* (Elgin, IL: Brethren Publishing House, 1944), 157-158.

8 Ira H. Frantz, "Lessons in Everyday Life," *Brethren Teacher's Monthly* 32, no. 9 (September 1938), 404.

9 George Zollers, *Thrilling Incidents on Sea and Land: The Prodigal's Return* 5th Edition (Mount Morris, IL: Kable Brothers & Rittenhouse, 1903). The first edition was published in 1892.

10 George Zollers, *Poetical Musings on Sea and Land* (Elgin, IL: Brethren Publishing House, 1905) 151-152.

11 Samuel B. Heckman, *The Religious Poetry of Alexander Mack, Jr.* (Elgin, IL: Brethren Publishing House, 1912. The poem I refer to appears on pages 36-41.

12 Mary H. Skiles, "The Sigh of the Toiler," *Peoms and Writings of Mary H. Skiles* (Compiled by her husband and children. Publication date unknown.), 14.

13 Statler, Ruth B. and Nevin W. Fisher, "88. Love of God, Eternal Love," *Handbook of Brethren Hymns,* The Brethren Press, 1959, 20. In the booklet, Statler and Fisher share stories about Brethren-authored and Brethren-composed hymns in *The Brethren Hymnal* published in 1951

14 Mary Stoner Wine, "Love of God, Eternal Love," *The Brethren Hymnal (Elgin, IL:* House of the Church of the Brethren, 1951), 88.

15 Kenneth I. Morse "Morning Song," *Listen to the Sunrise* (Elgin, IL: FaithQuest, a division of Brethren Press, 1991), 14.

16 Irene Stout, "Meditation," *Tree of Life: Poems of Meditation* (Winona Lake, IN: Light and Life Press, 1986?), 2.

17 Flora L. Williams, "Be Still and Know that 'I AM' God," *Renewal: Spiritual messages through a collection of Flora's Poetry* (Lafayette, IN: Arolf Publisher, 2011), 31. (Used with permission.)

18 *Fresh from the Word: Devotions for the 300th Anniversary of the Brethren* (Elgin, IL: Brethren Press, 2007).

19 All of these quotes are from Lenten or Advent devotionals published by Brethren Press, Elgin, IL.

20 Bowman, "Blessed by Burdens," *Tears Within My Heart,* 30. (Used with permission.)

Spiritual Formation Practices

Christy Hill

The rise in interest over spirituality in general and Christian spirituality in particular gives us the opportunity to consider what Christian spiritual formation is and how we engage in practices that nurture a relationship with God. Augustine articulated the deep hunger for relationship with God when he said, "Our hearts are restless until they rest in You." So what is this restlessness? How is spiritual formation part of the answer to the soul's craving for God?

We begin by defining spiritual formation by noted authors. Dallas Willard states that spiritual formation is the "Spirit-driven process of forming the inner world of the human self in such a way that it becomes like the inner being of Christ himself."[1] Anderson and Saucy provide a similar definition by saying that spiritual formation is growth "toward a destiny characterized by the fullness of Christ's life and character (see Colossians 1:28)."[2] The emphasis in both of these definitions is on the outcome of Christ-likeness.

As I worked on my doctoral dissertation, I focused on relationality and came up with my own definition: Spiritual formation is the ever-deepening relationship between God and his beloved that leads to an increasing sense of Christ being formed in us. I think that the emphasis on relationship is noteworthy, for if an individual tries to become Christ-like without intimacy with the Savior, it is more than likely going to be a performance-based spirituality and can degenerate into behavior-modification and not true life change. Relationship with God, union with him, is the goal, and Christ-likeness is the by-product of this growing intimacy. We will begin to see the world from his perspective as he promotes his life in us. Spiritual formation is being discipled by Jesus into his life.

In my quest for understanding spiritual formation and relationality, I realized that our relationship with humans provides a starting point for understanding intimacy and deepening bonds with God. What we experience on the horizontal level with humans develops capacities for relating to God as another Person.[3] A humorous, but telling, approach to thinking about our intimacy patterns with God comes as we ponder *Ten Rules to Avoid Intimacy* which were originally written by David Gershaw, Ph.D. and adapted for this workshop.

1. **Don't talk.** This is the basic rule for avoiding intimacy. If you follow this one rule, you will never have to be intimate again. If you are forced to talk, don't talk about anything meaningful. Talk about the latest episode of "CSI," your newest household upgrade, or the weather—anything but your feelings.

2. **Never show your feelings.** Showing your feelings is almost as bad as talking, because your feelings are a way of communicating. If you cry or show anger, sadness or joy, you are giving yourself away. You might as well talk, and if you talk, you could become intimate. The best thing to do is remain expressionless. (Although this is still a form of communication, it only says that you don't want to be intimate.)

3. **Always be pleasant.** Always smile; always be friendly, especially if something is bothering you. You'll be surprised how effective that hiding your feelings from others is in preventing intimacy. It may even fool them into thinking that everything is okay in your relationships. Then you don't have to change anything or become emotionally close to another person.

4. **Always win.** Never compromise; never admit that another's point of view may be as good as yours. If you compromise, that is an admission that you care about another person's feelings—which could lead to intimacy.

5. **Always keep busy.** If you keep busy with your work, you don't have to be intimate. Others will never figure out that you are using your work

to avoid intimacy. Because our culture values hard work, they will feel unjustified in complaining. Likewise, devoting yourself to work will give others the feeling that they are not as important as your work. In this way, you can make others feel unimportant in your life without even talking!

6. **Always be right.** There is nothing worse than being wrong, because that is an indication that you are only human. If you admit that you are wrong, you might as well admit that others are right—and that will make them look as good as you. If they are as good as you, then you may have to consider the other person. Before you know it, you will start to feel connected to another person!

7. **Never argue.** If you argue, you may discover that you and the other person are different. If you are different, you might have to talk about the differences to make adjustments. If you begin making adjustments, you may tell the other person who you *really* are, what you *really* feel. These revelations might lead to intimacy.

8. **Make others guess what you want.** Never tell others what you want. That way, when others try to guess and are wrong—as they often will be—you can tell them that they don't *really* understand or love you. If they did love you, they would know what you want without you telling them. Not only will this prevent intimacy, but it will drive others crazy as well.

9. **Always look out for number one.** Remember, you are number one. All relationships exist to fulfill your needs, not anyone else's needs. Whatever you feel like doing is okay. You're okay—the other person is not okay. If others can't satisfy your needs, they only care about themselves. (After all you are the one making the sacrifices in the relationship.)

10. **Be available to technology at all times.** Keep the TV, internet, and cell phone turned on at all times—during dinner, while you are reading, and while you are talking—especially when you are talking about something important. This rule may seem petty when compared with the others, but it is good preventative action. Staying distracted by technological interruptions keeps you and the other person from talking to each other, which leads us back to the #1 rule: don't talk.

As we consider our relational patterns, we may feel uncomfortable correlating our human emotional habits with intimacy with God. But research findings show a statistical correlation between attachment patterns (how we relate to other humans) and our spiritual intimacy patterns with God.[4] It seems that we have one relational wiring system that gets applied to all of our relationships, whether human or divine. Therefore, it would be helpful to ponder these strategies that prevent intimacy and see if there are some changes that we can make to remove barriers that thwart our desire for an ever-deepening relationship with God.

The Protestant reformers emphasized the idea of double knowledge when it came to growing in spirituality. John Calvin, one of the leading reformers, began his systematic theology treatise with this concept: "There is no deep knowing of God without a deep knowing of self and no deep knowing of self without a deep knowing of God." What this means is that the growing Christian must have a two-pronged approach to their spiritual formation. Knowledge of God without knowledge of self tends to form pharisaical religiosity, where information about God produces self-righteous pride. Knowledge of self without knowledge of God usually degenerates into morbid introspection and narcissism. It is important to have a balance of both types of knowledge. Most evangelical churches have tended to focus on knowledge of God exclusively. If this is the case, then we must balance this emphasis and equip people to learn to know themselves, "the good, the bad and the ugly." As we get in touch with the weaknesses and struggles, especially, we tend to have more appreciation and need for the knowledge of God.

In order to equip us more in this double knowledge, I have found Larry Crabb's basic principles of Christian growth helpful. These were given at a spiritual formation conference in Long Beach, CA in 2006. Crabb taught at Grace Theological Seminary in the 1980s and has gone on to be one of the leading voices in Christian evangelical spiritual formation circles. His emphasis on a relational spirituality, especially through his classic work, *Inside Out*, shook up the traditional perspective of spirituality being based on biblical knowledge or behavioral conformity to biblical standards. He approached spirituality as a cooperative relationship with God, who has a vision for us to be intimately united with him.

The first basic principle is: "God always reaches us where we are, never where we pretend to be." Thus, we need to have knowledge of self or, a more recent term, "self-awareness." One might question why self-awareness is a spiritual formation practice. The reason is that many barriers to self-awareness exist. The following is a brief list of these barriers: we don't value it (no one gets paid to do this); busyness; it's hard; we don't know how or where to start; we have never been confronted with the need to understand ourselves; we don't have support from others; pride and fear of what we might find. It is when we do the hard work of becoming more aware of what is really going on in our soul that we will take off the false pretensions of relating to God and start having real conversations with him about what we cannot fix in ourselves.

The second principle of growth: "It's God who reaches our hearts. He does the work. We cooperate by being real." The point here is that God is the one who sanctifies us; it is his job to bring this about. Sometimes we approach growing in our relationship with God as if it all depended on our own efforts to memorize Scripture, to attend Bible studies, to get our act together, and to be committed. While our efforts toward gaining knowledge about God have a role to play, our primary role is to yield and surrender to and relationally abide in Christ's Spirit. This requires brutal honesty with God as our flesh wrestles with the new life of the Spirit that has been placed within us.

The New Testament is replete with examples of the cooperative work that it takes to be transformed, but we will focus only on two passages here. Galatians 2:20 is Paul the apostle's spiritual formation road map. He states, "I have been crucified with Christ. It is no longer I who live, but Christ who lives in me. And the life I now live in the flesh I live by faith in the Son of God, who loved me and gave himself for me" (ESV). The self-life that was ruled by worldly conceptions of life is no longer seen as valid. Christ's life, his way of thinking now must take up residence in our lives. Similarly, Ephesians 4:17-24 gives the believer a clue as to the role of the surrendered will in spiritual formation.

> Now this I say and testify in the Lord, that you must no longer walk as the Gentiles do, in the futility of their minds. They are darkened in their understanding, alienated from the life of God because of the ignorance that is in them, due to their hardness of heart. They have become callous and have given themselves up to sensuality, greedy to practice every kind of impurity. But that is

not the way you learned Christ!— assuming that you have heard about him and were taught in him, as the truth is in Jesus, to put off your old self, which belongs to your former manner of life and is corrupt through deceitful desires, and to be renewed in the spirit of your minds, and to put on the new self, created after the likeness of God in true righteousness and holiness (ESV).

Embedded in these verses are important truths about God's work (he is the one who created the new self) and our work (putting off the old self and putting on the new self). This requires double knowledge and cooperating with God by being honest about the old self that still has residence in our lives.

The third principle of Christian growth is the evidence of relational growth with God. "One clear evidence (perhaps the strongest) that God is reaching our hearts is our discovery of a desire within us that wants to experience God more than we want our lives to go well." What Crabb means by this is that growth in spirituality must entail hating sin (all forms, even motives, attitudes and value systems that are opposed to dependence on God) more than just hating our pain and wanting God to make our lives go better. A consumer mentality of spirituality wreaks of selfishness and corrupted desires, which may not be observable from the outside, but can be seen for what it is when we take a deeper look at our motives, even our motives for trying to be more "spiritual." Relational spirituality is more concerned about getting God than we are about getting something from God.

The fourth principle of Christian growth states that "God's power is fully available to us to the degree that we fully pursue his purposes, not ours." Crabb shared that two motives are at work in the converted heart. The first power is a residue left over from the flesh or carnal nature: the desire to use God to get what we want. The second motive is a new power that the life of the Spirit gives us: the desire to be used by God to get what he wants. Understanding the propensity to live out of the flesh-life even as a Christian is where we need to grow in our self-awareness. Being honest with God when we see this ugliness woven into our lives is a first step toward growth. Repenting of this foundational paradigm out of which our observable sin patterns grow is a necessary part of yielding and surrendering and learning to abide in Christ on deeper levels.

The Spirit of God, who now resides in the heart of the believer, gives a new paradigm out of which to operate, due to now belonging to Christ.

Spiritual Formation Practices

The lack of intimacy is what causes our sin problem in the first place, trying to meet legitimate needs for security and significance in illegitimate ways. This new and growing attachment to the Spirit of God is what Paul says permits us to relate to God in intimately dependent ways.

> So then, brothers, we are debtors, not to the flesh, to live according to the flesh. For if you live according to the flesh you will die, but if by the Spirit you put to death the deeds of the body, you will live. For all who are led by the Spirit of God are sons of God. For you did not receive the spirit of slavery to fall back into fear, but you have received the Spirit of adoption as sons, by whom we cry, "Abba! Father!" (Romans 8:12-15, ESV).

Paul prayed for the Ephesian believers to experientially know God's power that was strong enough to raise Christ from the dead. Fittingly, Jennifer Kennedy-Dean has this to say about the believer's power that is at our disposal if we will but relinquish trusting in our own power, which she likens to being broken of the old life:

> True brokenness means losing all faith in your own abilities, abandoning all dependence on human resources, and disavowing all outward pretensions of righteousness to cling to the Spirit of God as if to a lifeline. The broken person—the person wholly dependent upon that indwelling life—will find that all the resources of heaven and all of the Spirit's power are now at his disposal and, unless heaven's riches can be exhausted or the Spirit's power can be found wanting, he cannot come up short.[5]

How does one grow in this type of relationship with God, where we are able to be honest and open in our dependence and where we are appropriating truth in our lives about who he is and who we are in him? Here are a few suggestions to consider:

1. **Seek out moments of silence and solitude throughout the day to become more self-aware.** Take inventory of what you have been thinking and feeling, much of which is beneath the surface of our busy lives. Learn to recognize patterns of behavior that betray your trust in the God of the Bible. For example, worry and anxiety should be brought to the Lord and truth about who he is can be appropriated to the particular issue that has been vexing us. This is called cognitive reframing.

2. **Keep a journal in these moments of silence.** As you grow in articulating what is going on beneath the surface, invite God to minister to you in your thoughts and feelings that are not grounded in the truth of his love and provision.

3. **Practice the presence of Christ.** Growth in spirituality is growth in appropriating the truth that God is always with us and that Christ's Spirit lives inside us. "God engineered your salvation not only for the purpose of cleansing you from sin but also for the purpose of filling you with himself. The work he is doing—the breaking, the crucifying, the cleansing—all has one purpose: to prepare his chosen dwelling place for his presence."[6] Some practical steps that you can take to practice Christ's presence are when you wake up, consciously invite Christ into your day. Think through your day ahead and invite him into the known activities that you will encounter. In the midst of your activities, find ways to be conscious of his presence with you. Remember to ask the Holy Spirit to help you become more aware of Christ's abiding presence and the help that he so lovingly wants to give.

Spiritual formation is a cooperative relationship between God and his beloved. We can engage in practices that enhance that relationship by growing in double knowledge, the knowledge of God and the knowledge of self. The knowledge of God becomes more experiential when we appropriate the truth of the Bible into our lives and learn to walk in step with his Spirit. In order for our walk to be authentic, though, we must also grow in our knowledge of self. As we become more self-aware, our need for all of who God is will be more desperate and real, thus creating an ever-deepening love relationship with the one who wants to be called Emmanuel, God with us.

Notes

1 Dallas Willard, *Renovation of the Heart* (Colorado Springs, CO: Navpress, 2002), 22.

2 Neil T. Anderson and Robert L. Saucy, *The Common Made Holy* (Eugene, OR: Harvest House, 1997), 18.

3 Klaus Issler, *Wasting Time with God* (Downers Grove, IL: InterVarsity Press Books, 2001).

4 See Christine Marie Morr, "The Role of Attachment Styles and Relationship with God among Evangelical Christians in Southern California" (Ph.D. dissertation, Biola University, 2003) and Judith K. TenElshof, "Attachment Styles and Spiritual Maturity : The Role of Secure Attachment in Predicting Spiritual Maturity among Seminary Students " (Ph.D. dissertation, Fuller Theological Seminary, 1998).

5 Jennifer Kennedy-Dean, *He Restores my Soul* (Nashville, TN: Broadman & Holman, 1999), 27.

6 Ibid., 68-69.

Worship Messages

Prayer

Roger D. Peugh

Jesus Christ lived in constant fellowship with the Father in heaven. Everyone who studies his life is struck by the intensity and the intimacy of his relationship with his Father. Regularly in quiet places, often early in the morning, often in the middle of a conversation with his earthly disciples he looked up and spoke with his Father. His ministry began in prayer; it was bathed in prayer; and he ended his ministry praying on the Cross.

Luke 6:12ff. Jesus prayed all night before choosing his disciples. In Luke 11:1 the disciples came to Him with a request: "Lord teach us to pray." Isn't it instructive that they did not ask him to teach them to preach? I see this as very instructive.

He carefully and repeatedly instructed his followers, especially Peter, to "watch and pray" lest they fall into temptation. The last night of Christ's life, the three leaders of the eleven (the "class president" and co-officers), slept–after specifically being instructed and admonished by the Lord to watch and pray with him in his greatest hour of need. They slept! Three times the Lord came, and rebuked them. Peter failed by denying our Lord Jesus Christ three times. I wonder if there is a correlation between the three failures in prayer and his three failures in denial of our Lord? But our Lord, with his exceptional grace came to Peter, and, as recorded in John 21, he restored this disgraceful failure, asking Peter three times: "Do you love me?" "Yes, Lord, you know I love you." And merely seven weeks after his disgraceful failure, Peter was anointed to preach the first sermon of the church age at Pentecost!

And apparently, I think, Peter, James and John finally GOT IT. Because Acts 2:42 records that the whole church continued steadfastly, faithfully, continually in prayer. After persecution in Acts 4, they immediately gathered for prayer, and the Holy Spirit shook the place. In Acts 6, the Apostles focused on "prayer and the ministry of the Word" rather than other good things which could be cared for by other fine leaders in the church.

In chapter 12 when Peter was arrested and then released by that angel, I think he knew where to go because he had trained them to do it. He knew he would go to that house and find them praying. He knocked on the door and they did not believe he could be there. Rhoda finally convinced them, and they listened to his report and then left.

Yes, the early church throughout the book of Acts, as well as in all of Paul's letters, demonstrated a commitment to prayer, which was derived from the practice and the instruction of our Lord. Prayer was practiced and taught by Christ, practiced and taught by the early church in Jerusalem, practiced and taught by the Apostle Paul and his ministry teams. Prayer was absolutely essential, crucial, to the ministry of the church. God said through Paul: "Pray without ceasing" (1 Thess. 5:17). "Be fervent in prayer" (Col. 4:2).

At this Brethren World Assembly, we ask ourselves: What has been our belief and practice, as Brethren, regarding the centrality of prayer in ministry? I cannot speak for all of our groups, but I can for my experience among the Grace Brethren. I am thankful that wonderful things have happened here and there as a copy of the prayer life of Jesus. I am indebted for my following comments about James Gribble to a student, James Momeyer, who did a research paper for History of Missions class. He drew from all of the writings about James Gribble his belief in and his practice of prayer.

James Gribble was born 130 years ago in Mechanicsburg, Pennsylvania; he died at age 40 in 1923, having been used by God to start a ministry in the Central African Republic (back then it was called Oubangui-Chari and later French Equatorial Africa). Gribble was a man of prayer. After serving a year with the Africa Inland Mission, he decided to celebrate his one year anniversary in Africa, November 29, 1909, with a night of prayer. His wife, Dr. Florence Newberry Gribble, wrote that this very night in late November should be considered the birth-night of the Mission Oubangui-Chari. God assured Gribble that night that there would be an evangelistic ministry in the area of Oubangi-Chari, though he was uncertain if he would have a part. He and Florence Gribble left the Africa Inland Mission in 1914, after six years, and began preparing for their ministry in Oubangui-Chari (today called the Central African Republic). They traveled the States three years (1915-1917), sharing their vision and seeking prayer support and co-laborers. In January 1918 they set sail; however, it was not until three years later, February 1921, that they were finally able to enter the country.

Gribble's Mother had taught him to pray. He regularly spent hours in prayer. "He was known to rise every morning at 2:00 o'clock to pray for members of his own family, many of whom were as yet unconverted. He was up again at 4:30 am for his regular devotions, which included all parts of the world."[1] He would spend at least an hour praying in the morning. And when he was sick and prevented from doing his other labors, "he simply added to his hours of daily intercession."[2] While being inundated with ministry in the USA prior to departure for Oubangui-Chari, he was very busy. Dr. Gribble records of her husband: "Then he was traveling, preaching, giving illustrated lectures, or writing letters and articles for publication, but never was he too busy to pray. 'Prayer is the greatest thing I have done today,' he often said in his daily letters to his wife."[3] It is said of him that out of desperation for the Gospel "he had prayed literally night and day for the opening up of this particular portion of Central Africa [Belgian Congo] to the Gospel!"[4]

They sailed in 1918, arrived at the entrance to the Central African Republic in 1919, but they were denied immediate entry. In what is well known, this little party of James and Florence Gribble, their daughter Marguerite, and two single missionaries waited on permission to enter Oubangui-Chari (French Equatorial Africa). They spent two full years waiting, but they did not just twiddle their thumbs and grumble. Gribble was not passive–he prayed–at what came to be called "Camp Wait-some-more" in order to get into the country. Two full years of prayer! Could it be that the miracles that God has worked in that Central African country are traceable to the two years of prayer foundation laid before they entered?

While in ministry in Africa he wrote: "These are busy days here, but we do not allow ourselves to be too busy to pray. Intercession, in spite of the pressure of other duties, is the greatest work that any missionary can do."[5]

I'd like to change that sentence. Intercession, in spite of all of the other duties that a housewife could do, is the greatest ministry that a housewife can do. Intercession, in spite of all the other duties, is the greatest ministry any pastor can do. The same goes for truck drivers, doctors, lawyers, farmers. It is the only thing which has and leads to eternal benefit.

Sometimes he would stop all his activities and devote a whole day to prayer. He writes in one of his letters: "Yesterday, I did nothing but pray. I literally spent the day in prayer, as I felt that we are facing a crisis in the work."[6]

During their last year with AIM, it is recorded that "There were whole days which Mr. Gribble and his wife spent in no other service than prayer."[7]

One last example is necessary to illustrate how his prayer life was also a great witnessing tool. In his last year with AIM while traveling through some dense jungles, he was in need of some canoes. At first they had trouble getting them, but after praying the canoes were given. Concerning this account it is written, "Without exception *every* request was granted immediately upon prayer, the people saying, "It is useless to refuse 'Jembo' [James Gribble]. He simply kneels in the sand and talks to the Unseen One, who *must* have power for we can no longer withhold our canoes!"[8]

James Gribble understood the vital importance of prayer support for this missionary ministry. The establishment of **"prayer bands"** throughout the United States was probably Gribble's greatest contribution to the field of Africa. He wrote: "The prayer bands will be the strong arm of the African work. We want a series of such bands stretching from the Atlantic to the Pacific."[9] He wrote further: "Humanly speaking, I look upon the prayer bands as being the bone and sinew of our work."[10]

An article outlining the responsibility of "Prayer Bands" was included in the "Constitution and Policy of the Ubangui-Shari Mission."[11] It reads: "Each member of a prayer band should be faithful in upholding the Mission and its need, the missionaries and their need, in daily prayer. At regular periods of time each prayer band should meet for united prayer. To these prayer bands there will be a monthly report sent, as the Lord may lead, so that they will be able to pray more intelligently."[12]

James Gribble died at age forty on June 4, 1923, only two short years after he was privileged to enter the country. He was buried on Bassai Hill.

Praying In Harrah

I personally became a follower of Christ sixty-two years ago at age eight through the ministry of the Harrah Brethren Church in my home town of

Harrah, Washington. My mentoring in prayer began as a child since my parents took us to prayer meeting, and we prayed for missionaries in cities of French Equatorial Africa and Argentina and Bill and Imogene Burk in Brazil. Missionaries who served there came to report in my church, and two young people from my church spent a lifetime in Africa as missionaries–the children of my parents' best friends. Twenty five of us from the Harrah Brethren Church, in a town of 300 in Washington State, went into full-time Christian ministry. We were scattered from Alaska to Africa. I am convinced it was because a number of people, possibly widows in the church, began praying for us to go into the ministry when we were infants. I believe they followed the directive of our Lord to "pray earnestly to the Lord of the harvest to send out laborers into his harvest" (Matt. 9:38). Is the Church praying today for harvesters to be sent?

GORDON BRACKER – PRAYER MENTOR

A week after graduation from Grace College, Nancy and I got married, and several months later began a ministry internship at the Elkhart, Indiana Grace Brethren Church while I studied at Grace Seminary. My mentor, Pastor Gordon Bracker, was a man of prayer. If it moved, he'd pray with it! He prayed all the time. He always said: "Let's pray about it right now." And we prayed anywhere. He instructed me that after shaking the hands of countless people after church, I should wash my hands before leaving to rid them of the countless germs! Often he and I would meet in the men's room by the wash basin to wash our hands. We'd share about people we had met during the morning services. He'd say: "Let's pray about it right now," so we prayed in the men's room. We prayed in the parking lot, on the lawn, in the car, we prayed everywhere. "Let's pray about it right now" is a sentence I pass on to others. By the middle of the semester, students are reporting that they are using this sentence and praying with people on the spot. I respond that they are grandsons and granddaughters of Gordon Bracker.

Within the first months of our ministry there, I was scheduled to meet Pastor Bracker on a Saturday afternoon at the church building. He arrived late, completely undone physically and emotionally. A man had taken a pistol and gone across the fields with the intention of taking his life. Pastor Bracker had searched for him for many hours, carrying this man's small child on his shoulders. He did not find the man that day, but to finish the story, he was found and lived many more years. As the pastor came into the church auditorium, he took only several moments to briefly explain what had taken place and then said: "Let's pray right now!" We fell to our knees at the front bench of the church, and he began sobbing as he prayed. I was twenty-two years old and estimated once that by that time I had attended at least 1000 prayer meetings–at the Harrah Brethren Church, Youth for Christ, Grace College missions prayer groups–but never one like this one. And kneeling beside him as he sobbed and cried out to God, I asked the Lord to teach me to pray like that. I spent three years at his side and a deep mark was impressed on my life by this man of God. He mentored me to pray. He passed away in 1987. I prayed with him the night before he died, leaning over him in his hospital bed. He went into heart surgery the next morning and did not survive the operation.

Mrs. Agnes Bracker

Three years at his side left a deep mark upon my life. When we went to Germany as missionaries in 1969, prayer was a growing practice, but I had so much to learn. His widow, Mrs. Agnes Bracker, took up his mantle of prayer upon his death–and this is her ministry to this day. Among others, she prays daily for us. I had the privilege of sitting beside this ninety-nine year old prayer warrior last month in Elkhart, Indiana. I don't want her to die–you could imagine why! She's 5 feet tall, weighs about 75 or 80 pounds, but she is a giant in my eyes. [She was promoted to Glory on October 22, 2013].

Lamar's Health Needs

We went to Germany in 1969 to serve in a church planting ministry. In January of 1976, our youngest son was born prematurely; he weighed 3 lbs., 4 oz. and nearly died at birth. We called the Mission office in Winona Lake and begged them to ask churches to pray. A call was issued across the Fellowship of Grace Brethren Churches–and thousands prayed. At three months, he got a gastro-intestinal infection and nearly died a second time. That son, Lamar, is now thirty-seven years old, working and serving the Lord in Taiwan. As recently as about five years ago, I had some ask me about his well-being. They said: "When the call came to pray for him as an infant, we prayed." It is probably no exaggeration to say that between 5,000 and 10,000 people prayed for him, since I know he was prayed for on Sunday mornings in a LOT of Grace Brethren Churches. Nancy and I attribute much of the blessing of God upon our family and children and grandchildren to the thousands of loving and faithful Christians who prayed for us.

Conflict

In May of 1979, the leadership team of the church we were establishing in Stuttgart, Germany experienced horrific conflict. I walked the streets of our suburb and wept and prayed much of the night. Early the next morning, I called Europe Team leader, Tom Julien, in France and begged him with tears for prayer support. He asked me and our co-worker to clear our schedules for the following Saturday. He came from France, and we found a quiet room in a friend's home–to spend the whole day in prayer. At about 6 pm, Tom turned to me and asked: "Roger, would you be willing to lay the Stuttgart church on God's altar and allow him to terminate its ministry, if he so desired?" With tears I replied that I was willing, but I came to see that this form of surrender of personal dreams can only happen with the help of God's Spirit!

Split

The tensions which began in May of 1979 culminated in a very ugly and painful split in May of 1980. Following that horrible rupture in the church, I suffered four months of deep depression–battling against suicidal thoughts daily. My Scripture study and prayer deepened exponentially. I am so thankful for God's grace that he delivered me in answer to prayer.

Support

My wife and I are not slick fundraisers. We would do our ministry presentation and simply ask the church to pray that the Lord would meet our needs. I often told them that if they, as a church, came upon hard times financially, God would supply our needs from another source, but I begged them never to stop praying for us. I told them that nothing could replace their prayers. Our support account remained in the black all during the twenty-two years of our mission. We believe this was in answer to the prayers of many.

One very meaningful visit to our home in Germany is worth mentioning. James and Dr. Florence Gribble had one child, Marguerite Gribble, who was born October 29, 1915. She sailed with her parents to Africa on January 8, 1915 as a 2 ½ year old. She waited with her parents at Camp Wait Some More and stood as a seven year old on Basai Hill at the grave of her father who died on June 4, 1923. When she went to French Equatorial Africa, there were no Christians in the country. She and her husband, Harold Dunning, served many years in Africa, starting in 1949. In 1985 they made their last visit to Africa and stopped to visit us in Stuttgart on their way home. During their 1985 visit they learned of hundreds of churches and over 100,000 believers. Picture that, in Marguerite Gribble Dunning's seventy short years, hundreds of thousands of Africans were won to our Lord because of the ministry begun, in prayer, by her father, James Gribble!

Euro-Missions Institute

In the 1980s, our European team of missionaries conducted training institutes each summer and later a pastoral institute. We invited young people interested in missions in Europe to come for eight weeks. We started with a two week training period in France. One day of the two week training period was set aside for fasting and prayer. We met for brief instructions at 8:30, and by 9 am they scattered out alone on the beautiful French countryside to meet God. In the late afternoon, we culminated the day with worship and sharing about what they learned. In their written reviews, a majority of the participants wrote that the day with God was their favorite part. Isn't it ironic that they could just as easily have had a day with God in Iowa or Indiana or California, but that they would report that their greatest experience in Europe was their day with God in France.

Pastor's Institute

Later we had a pastors' institute to which about twenty-five American pastors came. We also had a day of prayer and fasting during this institute. The program of those days was much like our mission field meetings: prayer before and after breakfast; before and after the meeting; before and after the next meeting; before and after lunch. One man who accompanied his pastor from California asked his pastor: "What's with all this prayer stuff?" His pastor replied: "I guess missionaries pray a lot." Shouldn't everybody?

Teaching A Prayer Class At Grace

And then in late summer 1989, Nancy and I and the family returned to Winona Lake so I could begin teaching missions classes at Grace. I was given freedom to re-shape the missions curriculum according to my vision. I learned that a class called Principles & Practice of Prayer had been taught on campus since 1980. So I went to the Professor, Pastor Ivan French, and told him that I wanted to make this class required in the Missions Curriculum. His face fell, and I was a bit surprised, knowing of his passion for prayer. We had been on his regular prayer list during our Germany years! Professor French said: "I was planning on teaching the Prayer Class this one last time and then retiring!" I quickly responded and said: "Well, how about if I take the class this semester from you and then begin teaching it myself?" So in the fall of 1989, I took the class and began teaching it the next year. Pastor French graciously gave me free and full use of his notes.

About half of the semester is spent on the Prayer Life and the Prayer Instruction of Jesus. I tell students: "If all we had were the prayer model of Christ our Lord, that alone should be enough to instruct and inspire every single one of us to pray without ceasing for everything!

Requirements

No skips because prayer is more caught than taught. The students have to be there! I had to be around Pastor Bracker. He showed me his life or prayer. What I've learned came from others, so I can pass it on to the students. So, no skips!

Prayer Partner: Students are asked to pray an hour a week with somebody–not ten minutes a day, but about an hour in one sitting. Many are overwhelmed at the thought of an hour at once, having never done it. But soon they realize the joy of extended fellowship with the Lord and an hour is just a good start! I require a half page report on what they learned. This assignment is ungraded. I do not grade prayer performance.

Praise Journal: 250 praises during the class, with a half page report about what they learned. I added something to this assignment a few years ago: No complaining about anything at any time, especially no complaining about food in the cafeteria! And they laugh, and after their laughter subsides, I tell them that at least several billion people in the world would switch places with them in a heartbeat to have access to the amount and quality of prepared food they get in the dining commons and they would never complain. It is the most revealing and life-changing assignment! They report that their whole outlook on life has been revamped through this assignment.

Pray for Missionaries, for **Enemies**, for **those in Authority**, for wisdom in **all financial decisions:** Again, I ask for a half page report about what they have learned. Some families have been completely changed and reunited as students have begun praying for their parents, who have become their enemies. God always changes the person praying, and sometimes the enemy being prayed for.

1200+ pages of reading: College freshmen are reading 1200 pages in eight weeks, which is a pretty heavy load!

Since I was asked to speak here about how we conceive and teach and practice prayer, I copied and brought along a set of my Prayer Class assignment sheets for each participant.

2001 – Taught Prayer Class In Africa

One of the great thrills of my life was to teach the Prayer Class to fifty-five African students and, during that time, to visit Basai Hill and stand at the graves of James and Florence Gribble. I wept for joy at what God has done in Africa through this courageous couple, even though James only got two years in country.

This week, I requested a historical search. As far as I can tell, Pastor Ivan French taught the Prayer Class at Grace Seminary from 1980 through 1989. I began teaching it in 1990. So for 33 years, it has been taught at Grace–now both semesters because it is required for all Seminary students and all Bible majors. However, of the 50-60 in each class, more than 50% are taking it as an elective. The Registrar's office reported that 965 students have taken the class since 1997. It would be safe to estimate that at least 1200 to 1300 have taken it over the last 33 years.

One of my greatest thrills is to learn from students who have taken the class that they keep praying with their prayer partners; they take the class notes and teach prayer in their churches and youth groups and Bible study groups; and they mentor others to pray. They encourage others to read the books and catch a vision for what it means to walk with God.

Prayer

A graduate of the class from about six years ago recently wrote me from Ft. Wayne, Indiana to report that she was mentoring her niece in prayer. This young girl had posed a very complicated question for which she wanted some outside input. How utterly exciting!

Some of the many prayer principles we have touched on today:

1. Christ prayed, and instructed his followers to pray.
2. The disciples finally GOT IT and began leading the early church to continue steadfastly in prayer.
3. Paul prayed and urged all Christians to pray continually.
4. The mother of James Gribble taught him to pray: PARENTS MENTOR THEIR CHILDREN TO PRAY. Do our children pray? This is a desperate need of our age. About halfway through the course this past semester, I went to colleague Dr. Christy Hill perplexed. My students were reporting that they had never prayed like this. I asked her what the church is doing to teach young people to pray. Apparently not very much prayer instruction is being given to young Christians in our youth ministries.
5. James Gribble was never too busy to pray. PRAYER IS A CHOICE TO EXPRESS OUR UTTER DEPENDENCE ON CHRIST!
6. James Gribble prayed full days and full nights – AFTER THE MODEL OF CHRIST!
7. Gordon Bracker mentored me in prayer: THE BEST TEACHING OF PRAYER IS DOING IT WITH SOMEBODY. Whom are we mentoring in prayer? May I make it personal? Whom are you mentoring right now in prayer?

8. In 1921, there was not one single African believer in French Equatorial Africa–AND TODAY THERE ARE 4.4 MILLION LIVING IN THE CAR– WITH OVER 2,000 GRACE BRETHREN CHURCHES–AND OVER 200,000 BELIEVERS in those churches–NOT TO COUNT THE MANY OTHER CHRISTIAN DENOMINATIONS WHICH ALSO HAVE WONDERFUL CHURCHES THERE. THE JOSHUA PROJECT WEB SITE REPORTS THAT 74% OF THE POPULATION IS "CHRISTIAN" AND 32.3% EVANGELICAL CHRISTIAN!!! THIS IS NOTHING SHORT OF PHENOMENAL.

GOD HAS WORKED IN ANSWER TO THE PRAYERS OF MANY AND A WHOLE NATION HAS BEEN TOUCHED WITH THE LIVING GOSPEL OF CHRIST!!! GOD HEARS AND ANSWERS PRAYER.

In 1985 when we were living in Germany, we had an amazing privilege. Harold and Marguerite Dunning came back from their last ministry trip to Africa. Remember, she is the daughter of James and Florence Gribble. On their way back to California, they stopped in Germany to visit us. I pondered her life. When she stood on Bassai Hill at her father's grave as a six-year old, there were no Christian believers among the Africans in the CAR. By 1985 there were hundreds of thousands of Christian believers in the country. Isn't that amazing and thrilling–because of prayer. A whole nation has been touched with the living Gospel of Christ because many prayed and some praying missionaries went–and God acted in grace toward this precious country!

9. It is the responsibility of parents and Christian leaders of every generation to mentor the next generation to be praying men and women of God.

Scratch The Surface

I was a student at Grace College when Dr. Alva J. McClain concluded his ministry. I remember hearing him say in a sermon while I was in college: "After more than fifty years in full-time Christian ministry, I feel like I have only scratched around a little bit on the surface–of all there is to know about God and his Work." I remember thinking: "Wow, where does that leave me?"

Dr. McClain's words certainly express my sentiment today about prayer. I tell students this every semester: "I feel like I have finally graduated from Kindergarten and entered grade school when it comes to knowing and practicing all the Lord intended for our prayer lives." There is so much more to know and learn. But this much is certainly clear: Our Lord prayed intensely, regularly, in every physical position and setting about everything. And he instructed us to watch and pray lest we fall into temptation. After the horrific failure of Peter, James and John, the early church was led to pray at all times about everything–continuing steadfastly in prayer. And the Western church in general treats this incredible privilege and honor of prayer with significant disinterest. God's blood-bought children are able to speak anytime from anywhere with the Creator of the universe–and few take advantage of this privilege. Many forget to pray. Our hectic lives keep us too busy to pray. We have dishonored his royal invitation.

In my youth, I heard that Billy Graham was supposed to have said: "Take the Holy Spirit out of the church and 90% of the activities would go on uninterrupted." Could we re-formulate that sentence for today and say: "Take prayer out of most churches and 90% of the activities of that church would continue on without interruption." Most of them are being done by most churches now without much more than token prayer–a prayer at the outset asking God to bless our meeting and our plans. There's little sense of desperation in most churches.

The reality is that we live in perhaps the most crucial age of human history since the crucifixion and resurrection of Jesus Christ! Worldwide moral breakdown has never reached this level. Over 50% of families are either divorced or severely eroded so that few young people are growing up in a secure and safe and healthy environment. Our job is enormous, and this is not the time to twiddle our thumbs. This is a time for us to pray. Whom are we teaching to pray? About what are we praying all night?

The church will have no meaningful effect against the erosion of society simply by holding more programs and polishing better sermons. Someone said: "The devil does not fear our preaching, but he is terrified when dedicated Christians pray."

We have a little time and I'd like to suggest that we pray. If you'd like to kneel, facing the bench, or if you'd like to pray standing, or sit, please, let's gather in small groups of two or three and pray for the next ten minutes or so, and I'll close at the end of our time.

Notes

1 Gribble, *Stranger than Fiction,* 1949, p. 85-86).

2 Gribble, *Undaunted Hope: Life of James Gribble* (Ashland, Ohio: The Brethren Publishing Company, 1934; reprint, Winona Lake, IN: BMH Books, 1984), 42.

3 Gribble, *Undaunted,* 171.

4 Gribble, *Undaunted,* 47.

5 Gribble, *Undaunted,* 318.

6 Gribble, *Undaunted*, 300.

7 Gribble, *Undaunted*, 102.

8 Gribble, *Undaunted*, 86.

9 Gribble, *Undaunted*, 114.

10 Gribble, *Undaunted*, 172.

11 James S. Gribble and Florence N. Gribble, *Notes on Africa and the Ubangi-Shari Mission* (Ashland, Ohio: The Brethren Publishing Company, n.d.), 47-53.

12 Gribble and Gribble, *Notes*, 50.

Missions and Evangelism as Brethren Spirituality

Fred Miller

Good evening, brothers and sisters of the fifth Brethren World Assembly. I praise God and thank you for the honor to share with you on the topic, *Brethren Spirituality: Evangelism and Missions*. As I read from Luke 19:1-10, I pray that the Holy Spirit will use me to bring words of encouragement.

When my oldest son, David, was four years old, he had a dramatic encounter with the Lord. I had picked him up at the babysitter's house, and we were on our way home. He was looking out the window of the car when I heard him say, "Dad, I see Jesus." Startled at this revelation, I asked him where he saw Jesus, and he said, "In the clouds." I began to look frantically into the sky because, as we all know, Jesus is coming with the clouds. After a fruitless search, I asked David, "What is Jesus doing?" He responded, "He's talking to me." Now my curiosity was peaked. I concluded that the Lord had a message for me through my son. So I pulled the car off to the side of the road, looked my four year old son in the eyes, and said, "Tell me, David, what is Jesus saying?" He said, "Go to Pizza Hut." Although it was not what I wanted to hear, it gave me great joy to know that at the age of four my son was thinking about Jesus. As we look at the history of our church, the Brethren like to think about Jesus; we like to talk about Jesus; and we like to teach about Jesus.

If I am a person standing on the outside of our church history, looking at our church signs, what is one of the first things I will notice and what will that tell me about the evangelism and mission of our church? I would

Brethren Spirituality

see a sign that says, "Old German Baptist Brethren Church." Another says, "Old German Baptist Brethren Church, New Conference." The third says, "Church of the Brethren." The fourth says, "Dunkard Brethren." The fifth says, "Brethren Church." The sixth says, "Fellowship of Grace Brethren Churches." And the seventh says, "Conservative Grace Brethren Church, International."

Look closely. A person standing outside of our history would notice the word, Brethren. Listen closely. A person standing outside of our history would hear words like "brother" and "sister." They would hear words that highlight relationship because relationship is at the core of who we are. It is at the core of every attempt of evangelism and mission. From the first Bible study held in the home of Alexander and Anna Mack, to Passing on the Promise, to planting churches in the villages of India or Nigeria, every attempt at evangelism and mission is an effort to restore a lost people to a loving God through faith in our risen Lord, Jesus Christ.

In our passage from Luke this evening, we see the Master Evangelist restore a person's relationship with God and pave the way for the restoration of other relationships in his life. We will see that Jesus was looking where no one else was looking; seeing what no one else was seeing; and doing what no one else could possibly do.

Jesus was entering the city of Jericho which was historically known for its walls. More specifically, it was known for walls that came tumbling down. Little had changed since Joshua led the people of Israel through Jericho. The walls that surrounded the city now surrounded the hearts of the people. The people of Jericho were about as fond of the "sinner" Zacchaeus as the religious leaders in Germany were of the Dippers. Neither antagonist had any trouble voicing displeasure at their target.

When Jesus reached the sycamore tree whose branches now held a man of small stature, he looks where no one else is looking. He sees what no one else can see. And he does what no one else can do. "Zacchaeus, come down immediately. I must stay at your house today." No one was looking for fruit from that tree. In the book of Genesis, Eve looked into a tree that she should have avoided. In the Gospel of Luke, the people of Jericho avoided a tree into which they should have been looking.

Jesus was always looking "to seek and save what was lost." He was always looking to restore the relationship between lost people and a loving God. We see Jesus looking at two boats and seeing what others could not see, fishers of men. We see Jesus looking at a tax collector behind his tax booth and seeing what no one else could see, a collector of souls. We see Jesus looking at a cave occupied by two of the most violent, unbridled men you would ever meet and seeing what no one else could see, someone who could tell others about the goodness of God.

As we search our history books, we see people who followed in the footsteps of Jesus by looking for those who would respond to the call, "Repent, and be baptized for the forgiveness of sins and you will receive the gift of the Holy Spirit." We see people who responded to the command, "Go, make disciples of all nations, baptizing them in the name of the Father, and of the Son, and of the Holy Spirit, and teaching them to obey everything I have commanded you." We see Alexander Mack and other Brethren leaders looking for those who would respond to that call up and down the Rhine Valley. We see evangelists and teachers in our churches who would look for people to respond to that call at tent meetings, revival meetings, camp meetings, VBS meetings, youth conference meetings, service projects, disaster responses, and anywhere in Jerusalem, Judea, Samaria and to the ends of the earth where God would lead us into a harvest.

Reggie McNeal spoke at the General Conference of the Brethren Church in 2011. He challenged us to be more missionally minded, to look for opportunities where we had not looked before at developing relationships. He personally made it a habit to visit the same restaurant each week and eventually he became the resident pastor to the staff that served him there.

I decided to take up his challenge and look for an opportunity at the restaurant where I most enjoy lunch. All we were instructed to do was inform the waitress that we were going to give thanks to God for our meal and ask, "How can we ask God to bless you?" The waitress informed us that her two-year old son was deaf in one ear and going deaf in the other ear. He had another test coming up in two weeks, and she wanted us to pray for his hearing, that it would not be totally lost. She stood there as we prayed over the meal and heard our request for her son. One month later, sitting in the same restaurant, the same waitress ran up to us and said, "Your prayer was answered. My son can hear, out of both ears." Her praise to God filled the restaurant. What had been no more than a dining hall a moment earlier, now became a house of worship and praise.

Another waitress, who had recently graduated from a nearby university, asked that she be blessed with a job. She came up to me at a funeral service two months later and said, "Do you remember me?" I did not. "I served as your waitress and you prayed for me to get a job. I want you to know that I got the job." Another waitress asked that her son, who had been searching for months, could find a job. One week later she informed us that he had a job. Who would have thought to look in a restaurant for a harvest? Who would have thought that at the age of fifty-three this teacher could still be taught? Our call is to look for hearts where seeds can be planted. Our call is to look for hearts where seeds can be watered. Our call is to look for God to do his great wonder of salvation.

Jesus looked where no one else was looking, and he saw what no one else could see. The people of Jericho looked at Zacchaeus and saw a sinner. They spit at the sound of his name. Jesus looked at Zacchaeus and saw what no one else could see, "a son of Abraham." The people of Jericho looked at Zacchaeus and saw a thief. Jesus looked at Zacchaeus and saw what no one else could see, one of the most generous givers that you would ever meet in your life. The people of Jericho looked at Zacchaeus and saw a callous heart. Jesus looked at Zacchaeus and saw what no one else could see, a heart ripe for the harvest. The people of Jericho wanted nothing to do with Zacchaeus. Jesus wanted a relationship and offered the ultimate sign of acceptance, "I must stay at your house today."

I read that a major denomination in the United States did a study of their membership. They wanted to know how often their members invited other people to join them in worship, how often they invited someone to the house of the Lord. The discovery was startling. The typical member in this denomination invites someone to join them in worship once every thirty eight years. "Where there is no vision the people perish." Where we do not see opportunity, we lose opportunity.

I spoke to a taxi cab driver in Indianapolis. He was from Ghana and he drove the taxi to make a living. But his mission was to reach the people of Ghana who had moved to that area of the country. That is the vision I see when I read the web sites of our churches and see our leadership development classes in Nigeria preparing people for ministry. That is the vision I see when I get my newsletter from Tony and Cathy Webb concerning church planting in Ohio. We are asking God to help us see what we could not see.

Jesus looked where no one else was looking, saw what no one else could see, and did what no one else could do; he changed hearts. "Zacchaeus stood up and said to the Lord, 'Look, Lord! Here and now I give half of my possessions to the poor, and if I have cheated anybody out of anything, I will pay back four times the amount." All of my life I have heard a saying, "You can't teach an old dog new tricks." Don't tell that to Jesus. If you are going to buy into that idea, you may as well just lay your Bible down and walk away. We may have seen people sink deeper and deeper into their bad habits as they grew older, but Jesus can do what no one else can do. He can create in us a new heart. We may have seen people whose minds were hardened beyond our repair, but Jesus can change and renew a mind with His great power. "For with God, all things are possible."

In 2004, I was asked to go on an overseas mission trip to Argentina. All of my life I believed that missions was for missionaries, for people who had been called overseas. I loved to hear stories from Prasanth Kumar in India when he would visit our church and sit down with my family for dinner. I loved to hear him talk about visiting villages where the gospel had not been preached and seeing the village come to Jesus. I loved to receive news from missionaries like Larry Bolinger who spent an entire day with a friend in Nigeria baptizing people in a small river. Those people had been in class for a year getting ready for their big day. One by one, they came throughout the day, more than one hundred in all. I would tell these stories and urge people to support our missionaries overseas with their prayers and money. I was even willing to sit on the Missionary Board of the Brethren Church and give my stamp of approval on those who had been called to go overseas. I recognized the great sacrifice and danger that each of them faced.

Then I was asked to go to Argentina to help build a counseling center at our Seminary in Colón and speak to the congregation in that city. Dr. Fred Finks, one of my life mentors, encouraged my wife and me to accompany the Seminary on this trip. After twenty-two years in the ministry, I made my first short term mission trip overseas. It changed my life forever. The moment of transformation occurred when we were feeding the children at the Milk Station. On Tuesday and Thursday we gathered in a building called the Milk Station to prepare a meal for the children in the neighborhood. For the majority of the children, it would be the most substantial meal they ate all week.

On Tuesday, thirty-five children came to dinner. On Thursday, it was seventy. I remember watching a young boy, thirteen years old, walk up to the door with his younger brother and sister. The look on their faces was priceless. The look on his face was haunting. As his brother and sister entered the room, the thirteen-year old boy turned, with his shoulders slumped, and walked back down the road. I asked a member of the church in Colón why the boy had left the building. She informed me that they could only afford to serve so many children, so the cut-off age was twelve. That young man had come to the Milk Station for years and enjoyed the company and food of the Brethren. Now he could only hear how good it was from his brother and sister.

I cannot get that picture out of my mind. It changed me. My message has changed from "Support" to "Go!" It has been my joy to watch it change the lives of people at Mount Olive who have gone to serve others in Israel, Mexico, New Zealand, Australia, Mongolia, Honduras, Sierra Leone, and Peru. I have had the opportunity to visit the jungles of Peru three times now. I never saw myself in the jungle, but Jesus can see what we cannot see. What I have discovered is that the people you work with on a mission trip capture your heart. My wife has accompanied me on two of those trips. We just had a team return home from Peru this past Sunday.

We have worked for the past six years with other Brethren congregations to build an orphanage in the Amazon jungle of Peru. In Puerto Maldonado, God had us looking where we had not looked, seeing what we had not seen, and preparing for God to do what only God can do. Five children have now moved into the building. A year ago, people would have looked at three-year old Carlitos and said that he did not stand a chance in life. He had been abandoned by his mother and left as a two-year old to fend for himself. The only place they could find to place him was a home for girls, and his time there was limited. People would have seen a two-year old orphan who was going to be a burden to society. Carlitos would have grown up thinking about how unfair life had been. He would have been talking about his loneliness and fear. All of that changed when Italo and Rebecca Abuid opened their door to Carlitos and said, "Come, live with us, and we will make you a fisher of men." It is my dream that Carlitos, or Anthoni, or Mirian, or Kelly, or Maria will one day visit Mount Olive, like our brothers from Nigeria are visiting us this week, and tell us what they are thinking about Jesus, talk to us about Jesus, and teach us about the difference Jesus has made in their lives. It will be a powerful story. It will be good news.

The name of Zacchaeus will live on because Jesus was looking where no one else was looking. Who is Jesus looking at in your life, in your church, in your community, along your path? The generosity of Zacchaeus will live

Missions and Evangelism as Brethren Spirituality

on because Jesus could see what no one else could see. Who will be the next great giver along your path? There is no question that Jesus came to seek and save what was lost. The question is: Will we continue to participate in that mission? Will we continue to see the lives of lost people changed in the name of Jesus?

Brethren Spirituality for the Future

Robert Earl Alley

What a wonderful Brethren World Assembly! For the past three days, we have listened and explored Brethren spirituality. We have shared, and we have questioned each other. We have surveyed a broad plain of that spirituality—across three centuries, in love feast, music, family, worship, prayer, mission, separation from the world, and more. Yet, we confess that we have not fully defined Brethren spirituality. However, in singing, prayer, preaching, fellowship, and lectures, we have experienced that spirituality. So, as we come to the close of this Brethren World Assembly, it is appropriate for us to ask "Now What?"

The disciples of Jesus had listened and experienced the presence of the Holy in being with Jesus. They had shared and they too had questioned. They had encountered the death of their Master and even witnessed the mystery of his resurrection. They looked around and asked "Now What?" In the Gospel of John, Simon Peter responded in saying, "I am going fishing." Six other disciples with him responded, "We will go with you." After the excruciating event of Jesus' crucifixion and the mysterious encounter with his resurrection, they were asking "Now What?" And so they responded—by returning to their former vocation—fishing.

Several weeks later—"when the Day of Pentecost had fully come"—in the gathering of a hundred and twenty of Jesus' disciples, some must have still been asking "Now What?" Then, they heard and saw; they witnessed the response of the Holy as the wind or breath, the *ruach*, of God moved through their assembly. In the variety of languages and with the anointing of the Holy Spirit, they discovered that God was calling them to a present awareness and mission that transcended their former vocations and continued their walk with Jesus beyond his crucifixion and resurrection. Those on the Day of Pentecost in Acts 2 did ask "Now What?" when they responded to Peter's sermon with the question "Brothers, what should we do?" Many of us can quote Peter's answer: "Repent, and be baptized every one of you in the name of Jesus Christ so that your sins may be forgiven; and you will receive the gift of the Holy Spirit. For the promise is for you, for your children, and for all who are far away, everyone whom the Lord our God calls to him" (Acts 2:38-39). But that didn't close their Pentecost event or complete the answer to "Now What?" Acts records, "So those who welcomed his [Peter's] message were baptized, and that day about three thousand persons were added. They devoted themselves to the apostles' teaching and fellowship, to the breaking of bread and the prayers" (Acts 2:41-2). Here in simple form is their Pentecost response to "Now What?"

Brethren originally assembled for their annual meetings at Pentecost, believing that the Holy Spirit is present in that assembly together for the discerning work of the body. Some among us still do. However, are our annual meetings, whether at Pentecost or at another time, occasions when we ask with anticipation "Now What?"

The future is always intriguing, especially when we ask "Now What?" Some generations have lived with an obsession for the future, and some have simply ignored the inevitable. Others have followed the counsel of the writer of Ecclesiastes: "I know that there is nothing better for them than to be happy and enjoy themselves as long as they live; moreover, it is God's gift that all should eat and drink and take pleasure in all their toil. I know that whatever God does endures forever; nothing can be added to it, nor anything taken from it; God has done this, so that all should stand in awe before him. That which is, already has been; that which is to be, already is; and God seeks out what has gone by" (Ecclesiastes 3:12-15). Financial advisors help us to address the future. Recently, my financial advisor mentioned that when we seek to know the future, what we are really trying to do is "to predict the unpredictable." The writer of Ecclesiastes seems to predict the unpredictable within the context of faith in the Holy One whose providence embraces the future.

Brethren Spirituality for the Future

Alexander Mack and the other Schwarzenau Brethren were already Christian, being members of Reformed and Lutheran churches. They were seeking a more authentically genuine expression of their Christian faith than they were finding in those official churches. In meeting together and centering in the study of scripture, they discovered fresh resources to understand and to express their convictions of faith. Some of what they found resulted in concrete formations for church and Christian living: the mode of believer's baptism, communion through love feast, anointing for healing, nonresistance, nonconformity to the world, no oath-taking, a disciplined church community, and more. All of these continued giving shape to their newly formed expression of church into the future. Yet in moving into the future, Mack and those who followed him would return again and again to the power in meeting together and studying scripture to gain the energy of the Spirit to respond to prevailing cultural trends around them. One sees this displayed in minutes of early Annual Meetings as those Brethren encountered the challenges of slavery, war, ecumenical connections, and more. Indeed the power of meeting together and the study of scripture would even create dynamics for separations among the Brethren into the seven bodies (U.S.) we have today, as well as into some other bodies that came and went through the generations.

Scholars identify a dynamic tension present in the Brethren DNA—a tension inherent from the beginning as early Brethren wrestled with how to integrate their Radical Pietism with what they discovered in their New Testament studies calling them to visible expressions of church. Every generation of Christians has faced a similar scenario in wanting to integrate spirit with form. Spirit without form is like a fire without boundaries; it can become very destructive. Form without spirit may become cold and lifeless. As my father once remarked to me, "If you do not have the spirit, you have little or nothing." Form for the early Brethren became inherent in their association with Anabaptism through Mennonites. This interrelated tension of spirit and form, Pietism with Anabaptism, has been both life-giving and life-altering for the Brethren. When the chapel on the Oak Brook, Illinois campus of Bethany Theological Seminary, the Church of the Brethren seminary, was constructed in the 1960s, the roof took on a strange shape. Some said it resembled a chicken house. The sides of the roof did not meet together at the comb. Instead one side was higher than the other requiring a wall of windows to connect the top two roof lines. It looked like an architectural error. When asked, the architect noted that the two roof levels with windows forming a connecting wall symbolized the nature of the church received from Anabaptism along with the openness to new light received from Pietism. While that expressed a Church of the Brethren understanding of this interrelated tension, other Brethren bodies would need to decide if it expresses their understanding of the Anabaptist-Pietist tension.

The Pietist movement of the late seventeenth and early eighteenth centuries carried with it responses to "Now What?" Indeed the movement itself was an effort to gain insight into "Now What?" After decades of war and famine, people influenced by Pietism began to anticipate a new age—an age of the Spirit where love and peace would be embodied more effectively in human life. Some even set dates for a second coming of Christ. When those predictions failed to materialize, Mack, the Schwarzenau Brethren, and others turned their energy from messages about the second coming of Christ to searching for how they should be living in the current time. Their passion materialized in being obedient to Christ through baptism and the creation of a new community called *Neu-Täufer*. Brethren writings continued to carry apocalyptic views, especially in hymnody, but their focus centered more in this new community as a passionate realization of God's future reign. Brethren recognized this approach from the beatitudes of Jesus' Sermon on the Mount where each beatitude combines some wisdom teaching for living with an apocalyptic promise.[1]

"Now What? Brethren Spirituality for the Future" challenges us to both recognize the lure of the future and the bait of the future—to use fishing terms. Future not only intrigues us; it is a certainty. One moment leads into another. Future may easily be assumed to be "out there," but Brethren have generally shared a view of the future, an eschatology, that centered on Jesus' reference to the Kingdom of God/Heaven in the near time. In several instances, Jesus said, "The Kingdom of God has come near." He taught his disciples, including us, to pray: "Your kingdom come, your will be done on earth as in heaven." And in numerous parables, Jesus gives vision to Kingdom concepts as if it is current, not just imminent.

Jesus' language brings us to a vision of future that invites Brethren to live as if the future has come. The Brethren New Testament image for this has been the ordinance of Love Feast expressed with feet-washing, meal, and communion. Its companion eschatological image has been the Marriage Supper of the Lamb in Revelation 19. Love Feast has been viewed by Brethren as a foretaste of the Marriage Supper of the Lamb. Carl Bowman in *Brethren Society* quotes James Quinter as saying, "This feast of love may be regarded as a representation of the great Marriage Supper of the Lamb, which is to take place when the Savior comes, and his people shall gather themselves together . . . and sit down in the Kingdom of God."[2] Bowman continues:

> While communion was considered a commemorative institution that pointed back to the cross, the Lord's supper was a forward-looking rite that anticipated the coming Kingdom. "Take away the Lord's supper," one brother wrote, "and there remains not a single institution in the Christian economy of grace that points forward to that great nuptial feast and the reunion of the blessed in heaven." The supper dramatically anticipated a future time when Christ's church (the 'bride') would sit down with the Lamb (Christ) in a grand marriage banquet, based upon Christ's promise that "I will not any more eat thereof until it be fulfilled in the kingdom of God." (Luke 22:15-16)."[3]

Areas of church life among the Brethren supported this connection between Love Feast in the contemporary context and the future context of the Marriage Supper of the Lamb.

In the nineteenth century, Peter Nead took the format of the beatitudes as a guide and offered this admonition to Brethren: "'Brethren, recollect we are pilgrims, not children of this world; let us therefore live like pilgrims.' To live like pilgrims," according to Church of the Brethren historian and theologian Dale Brown, "was to live out the ethics of the future kingdom way in the present, to live as if the kingdom has already come."[4] To ask "Now What?" in the context of Brethren spirituality challenges us to remember and to recover this identity as pilgrims. Pilgrims are present in the now so as to be present to the yet to be. In more contemporary terms, this concept has been named "realized eschatology."

So much for the lure and certainty of the future. What about the bait of the future—what is it that brings the future among us in the present? Let me offer several crucial points as questions to help us assess "Brethren Spirituality for the Future."

1. How will Brethren journey and continue to journey as pilgrims? One contemporary hymn phrases it, "We are pilgrims on a journey, we are trav'lers on the road."[5] Inherent even in our separations, such interrelated connections and care have fueled our passions. Being pilgrims on a journey together connects Brethren desires to be both a discipled and gathered community—both an asset and a tension for our Brethren bodies. Above all, we are connected through the light given in Jesus Christ. Lesslie Newbigin, former bishop of the Church of South India, relates the effect of this common light in an experience from India.

   > When we have to go to a distant village in our pastoral duty we try to start very early in the morning, so that we do not have to walk in the heat of the day. And it sometimes happens that we have to set off in total darkness; perhaps we are going towards the west so that there is no light in the sky and everything is dark. But as we go, a party of people travelling the opposite way comes to meet us. There will be at least a faint light on their faces. If we stop and ask them: "Where does the light come from?" they will simply ask us to turn round (do the U-turn) and look towards the east. A new day is dawning, and the light we saw was just its faint reflection in the faces of those going that way. They did not possess the light; it was a light given to them. The church is that company which, going the opposite way to the majority, facing not from life towards death, but from death towards life, is given already the first glow of the light of a new day.[6]

   In sharing that light, we are common pilgrims living into the future as we live to the risen Christ.

2. How will Brethren journey and continue to journey together? Pilgrims, plural, journey in common. The contemporary hymn referenced above has a phrase, "We are here to help each other walk the mile and bear the load." Throughout our history, this common journey has been a vital element of our identity, even when we have chosen to separate, perhaps like bees swarming to create new hives. After all, Paul and Barnabas chose to go separate ways in fulfilling their missionary task. We journey together—whether in congregations, regional gatherings, or our annual meetings and conferences. The role, power, and influ-

ence of that togetherness vary among us and have contributed to our separateness, but they have not diminished the fellowship and discernment that is crucial for being Brethren in each of our Brethren bodies and even when we are together. Separation does not need to create a permanent gulf between us.

3. Will Brethren journey and continue to journey as people who study and embody scripture as the Word of God? Remove scripture from our heritage and all of us will find our Brethren body without any mooring or guide for the future. Here I would challenge us to recognize the relevance and understanding of scripture, but as a means to cultivate our love for Jesus. Was not this of vital importance for the early Brethren as Pietists? All of us Brethren hold the scriptures to be the Word of God. How we understand, interpret, and focus those scriptures will vary among us. But the reading and study of scripture will be paramount for any spirituality of the Brethren into the future. At the same time, that reading and study will find its greatest effectiveness in the gathered community of the church whether in weekly worship, in smaller study groups, in families, or in larger regional and national gatherings.

4. Finally, how will Brethren journey and continue to journey as people living out the future of God's Kingdom as envisioned in the Love Feast—service and cleansing in feet-washing, fellowship in meal and greeting, and faith centered in the bread and cup of Christ's communion? When our planning team for this assembly was meeting together, some of our conversation began to indicate that all our Brethren bodies still share the three ordinances of three-fold baptism by immersion, love feast, and anointing for healing. I asked whether that was so, and each responded yes. These have been central for identifying who we are as Brethren. As Todd Scoles quotes from Don Durnbaugh in *Restoring the Household*, "Brethren 'considered the New Testament ordinances *in their original form* a visible sign by which Christ's true church could be recognized.'" The format may vary but the reality continues. In that reality, we embody a future spirituality—anticipating the yet-to-be-in-the-present being, anticipating the Marriage Supper of the Lamb as we celebrate Love Feast.

To ask "Now What?" at the close of an assembly centered in the theme of "Brethren Spirituality" anticipates that spirituality will continue to empower our particular bodies. Spirit gives life to our forms and even helps to shape the forms. So may the closing which Alexander Mack gave in *Rights and Ordinances* give blessing to our deliberations together and invite us to pursue the passion of spirituality.

"Now, may the Lord Jesus bless our soul, and strengthen your faith, and let this simple instruction grow within you and bear fruit which will remain for life eternal. We will together praise and glorify our God forever. Amen."[7]

Notes

1 Dale Brown, *Another Way of Believing,* Elgin, Illinois, Brethren Press, 2005, 179-180.

2 Bowman, Carl F. *Brethren Society*. Baltimore, Maryland: The Johns Hopkins University Press, 1995, 63.

3 Bowman, Carl F. *Brethren Society*. Baltimore, Maryland: The Johns Hopkins University Press, 1995, 63.

4 Bowman, Carl F. *Brethren Society*. Baltimore, Maryland: The Johns Hopkins University Press, 1995, 46.

5 "Will you let me be your servant", 307 in *Hymnal: A Worship Book.*

6 Lesslie Newbigin, *Mission in Christ's Way*, 21.

7 William Eberly, ed., *The Complete Writings of Alexander Mack,* 103.

Bibliography

Bowman, Carl F. *Brethren Society*. Baltimore, Maryland: The Johns Hopkins University Press, 1995.

Eberly, William R., editor. *The Complete Writings of Alexander Mack*. Winona Lake, Indiana: BMH Books, 1991.

Newbigin, Lesslie. *Mission in Christ's Way*. New York: Friendship Press, 1987.

Scoles, Todd. *Restoring the Household*. Winona Lake, Indiana: BMH Books, 2008.

Slough, Rebecca, managing editor. *Hymnal: A Worship Book*. Elgin, Illinois: Brethren Press, 1992.

The Holy Bible (New Revised Standard Version). Nashville, Tennessee: World Publishing, 1989.

Youth Panel

Michael Miller, Convener

Michael and Sondra Miller gathered a group of 12 youth from the Church of the Brethren, Grace Brethren, Old German Baptist Brethren- New Conference, Conservative Grace Brethren and Dunkard Brethren. For close to a year, periodic gatherings, often around pizza and singing, invited sharing about being youth and young adults in their churches, communities and world.

Two key questions were addressed:
What is your church doing right to keep the youth involved?
What could your church do better to keep the youth involved?

On Saturday afternoon, July 13, 2013, these twelve youth shared their responses with the Brethren World Assembly gathered at Brookville, Ohio. Presented here are the written responses submitted by seven of the twelve participants. [Panel members had not been asked to submit written statements, but in the following months, those that were able, did assist the editor with notes and remembrances. For that "extra mile" effort, we thank all members of the youth panel.]

The best way to experience the youth addressing these crucial concerns for our church, is to go to "YouTube" to see a 55 minute replay captured by Joy Miller. *https://www.youtube.com/watch?v=JvH-7VdWwZE*. At the end of these printed comments you will find a summary report from one of parents.

Brethren Spirituality

Rachael Laux. *(Castine Ohio, Church of the Brethren)*
One of the best things our churches are doing for our young people is in the area of missions. I come from a church with an excellent missions program that goes to six places of vastly different cultures and types of people to serve for a week. Some of the greatest experiences I have personally had in my walk with Christ have been on those mission trips. There is great power in getting out of your comfort zone and serving someone in their home and becoming a part of their lives. It opens up opportunities to see Christ in a way that isn't possible within the familiar walls of our own homes and churches; and it stretches you to become increasingly like Christ by developing the heart of a servant.

What I think our churches could do to keep our young adults as active and influential part of the church is to let the "student become the teacher". Many of us have grown up in church all our lives. We have listened and studied under your expertise and your wisdom. We have learned from you and ingrained your lessons on our hearts. Now however, we want to give back. We want to share with those around us the lessons we have learned. We want to feel we are an integral and contributing force in our churches. Being able to teach a younger generation has matured me in ways I could not have done through simple study. When our generation feels respected and valued enough to not only be filling the chairs and being the hands of Christ, but to also be trusted to teach and share all we have learned and experienced to help those around us, that is an excellent place to start in making a place for our young adults to belong.

Aaron Oswald *(Brookville (OH) Church of the Brethren)*
My name is Aaron Oswald and I attend the Brookville Church of the Brethren. I was raised in a very sound Christian family that raised me in the ways of Christ from a very young age. My parents, siblings and my church family were extremely influential in my decision to follow Christ. This is the principal blessing in my life.

I received a telephone call from Mike Miller several months ago concerning sitting on this youth panel and he explained that he was looking for youth who would be willing to share with you some things that our denominations are doing well and things that they could improve upon.

I find that my observations for these questions are related. Within the past several years, the Church of the Brethren has seen the lack of attendance in the age groups post high school to post college. My church sees this as a significant problem as an entire generation ends up missing within the church. The Church of the Brethren has started seeking out ways to reverse this trend and they are seeking out new ways to minister to this age group.

However, several of our churches have taken on a policy of "acceptance" in order to reach out to this young age group. Young people bring in new ideas and theologies which at times are revitalizing for the church but at other times create a detrimental effect on the church community. Churches have compromised the true word of God in order that it may be more appealing to a new generation. This has destroyed our Biblical foundations as we have forgotten the concept of hating the sin while desperately loving the sinner. This leaves a young Christian or an unbeliever no better off and possibly in a worse spiritual state after they have had exposure to a church community than before they heard the message of Christ. I have often summed up this observation in this way: "In our attempt to become relevant to a younger generation, we have become completely irrelevant in our culture." Unfortunately, we have a very limited amount of time so I cannot say more, but I pray that you found something in my sharing that moved your heart that might broaden your understanding and draw you closer to our Lord Jesus Christ.

ANDREW PETERS *(Salem Old German Baptist Brethren New Conference, Brookville, OH)*

Though I speak with the tongues of men and angels and have not charity...

HOW I HAVE COME TO KNOW THE LORD:
- Teaching in a godly home (God's Word is true) I am blessed to say, "from my youth I have known the holy scriptures…"
- 3 years ago I accepted God's call on my life and began to walk with Jesus at 19.
- Prayers and intercession of my family and others.
- Holy Spirit convicting me of my lost state without the blood of Jesus, and gently leading me to Him.
- God has been faithful in showing me areas of my life that I haven't given to Him and helping me grow in my relationship with Him.

MY FELLOWSHIP:

Encouragements that have blessed and helped me in my Christian walk
- *A godly home* is such a blessing, and none of my own doing. Why was I placed here? Can this be emphasized too much? Is this not the Foundation of the church?
- *Brotherhood (Friends across the nation)* –blessing to attend congregations in other states. Blessing to form relationships in various locations-verse memorization?
- *Leaders* standing for biblical truth and preaching them-areas like morality, finances.
- A minister at New Year's gathering challenging the youth to read through the Bible in a year. *–accountability* throughout the year.

Desires for my fellowship
- More teaching emphasizing practical living of the Word of God. What should this look like in my daily life?
- Accountability – especially among the local congregation. Areas like daily time with God and the use of technology. I desire openness about practical areas of our lives and to be real with each other.
- Also more teaching and practice of spiritual disciplines. Such as prayer, fasting, tithing.

General Thoughts regarding youth
- Hypocrisy has a crippling effect in the church. While growing up, if youth see the older ones saying one thing but living another, they aren't going to buy into it.
- As youth, we want to be part of something that's real! The Kingdom of God is very real, but so is this world and its pleasures.
- If I see that those older than me are not sacrificing for the Truth of God's Word and His Kingdom, I get the idea that it's not worth it.
- Example of an older brother liquidating a valuable collection in order to invest in the Kingdom of God. Things like this are an encouragement to me!
- Should a lack of youth surprise us, if, in the church, there is a lack of the power of the Holy Spirit and obedience to the Word of God?
- In general, we have plenty of head knowledge of God, but what about heart knowledge? We can know much about God and His Word. We can fill our minds with knowledge of the Bible and theology and historical facts. We can memorize great portions of the Bible and in general in-

crease our head-knowledge of God. We study and know so much about God, but do we know Him?
- It's very encouraging when our leaders are living the Word; allowing it to truly change them.
- Shows me that this Christian walk is real and worth it.
- And that's something I want to be a part of.
- "We don't speak great things; we live them," Justin Martyr.

JAMIN TURNER *(Shiloh Old German Baptist Brethren New Conference, Pitsburg, OH)*
I have been blessed by being a part of the Old German Baptist Brethren in many ways. I especially appreciate the sense of community that we experience as a body of believers. It has been good to be a part of a wide-reaching community during my growing-up years. A godly family and this sense of community are the chief reasons why I am a part of this church.

There are other facets of our fellowship that I believe could be strengthened. Primarily, I think we could use a little less luxurious lifestyle and a little more ministry to our communities (both local and global communities). As a general perspective on the Brethren Churches and their declining or missing youth population, I would affirm that the youth are in search of something genuine. Solid biblical teaching and clear truth are more appealing than entertainment and watered-down truth. We are not in search of an entertainment facility, social club, or weekend hangout. We desire genuine transformation and healing! May God give us grace to follow him!

MEGAN TURNER *(Shiloh Old German Baptist Brethren New Conference, Englewood, OH)*

1. Conversion
I committed my life to God and was baptized 3 years ago at the age of 16. Growing up in a Christian home I was taught about Jesus, which contributed much to my choice to follow Christ. My many godly friends also encouraged me in my relationship with God.

2. Assembly's Strengths
In our assembly, there are many opportunities to fellowship with the brothers and sisters that we worship with. We get together frequently with the youth, as well as having Bible study and other functions with a mix of ages.

I have been encouraged when the youth get together with older believers and hear their wisdom and testimony of God's faithfulness.

3. Assembly's Weaknesses
I have been blessed to be a part of this group of believers, but there are a few areas that could be improved that would benefit the youth. One suggestion is to have more practical Biblical teaching from the older to the younger, such as meeting one on one, to learn how to stand as a bright light in a dark world.

JOSHUA STEINER *(Orrville Conservative Grace Brethren, Orrville, OH)*
My name is Joshua Steiner and I have the privilege of representing the Conservative Grace Brethren Churches International. A couple of things that I think our fellowship as a whole is doing to keep and encourage young people to stay is to provide them with different opportunities for ministry and spiritual growth. One of those opportunities is an Evangelism Team that assembles every summer for two weeks. The group focuses on presenting programs that include singing, puppets and drama. There is also a large emphasis on evangelism through many different means.

Another avenue that our fellowship offers that could be seen as a way to encourage young people to stay in our churches is what is called *Practorium*. Basically it is a school of theology managed by Pastors for the purpose of training the future leaders of our fellowship. Some choose to take these classes right out of high school; while others, like myself, use these classes as graduate work upon receiving an undergraduate degree. There is much more that can be said about this unique and purposeful program, but I want to quickly press on to what I think that we can be doing better.

As I look at the situation, I can definitely see the problem. I have "friends" who faithfully attended during high school, but then faded away and no longer attend. As I reflect on this problem my conclusion is that it is a heart problem. In my eyes many of the things that have been suggested so far, while they are good ideas, do not address the deeper problem. You see unless a person has truly given their heart to the Lord and desires to serve Him with their life, as they grow older they are going to get busy with everything that the world has to offer and slowly drift away.

The solution is a heart change. There is not any of us here that can change another person's heart, only God can do that, so the first step is prayer, and lots of it, praying that God will change their hearts!

Second, I would submit to you that the major responsibility of pointing a young person to the Lord and giving them an opportunity to give the Lord their life lies heavily on the shoulders of parents. God has given parents the duty to raise their children to seek after the Lord.

There is so much that can be said about this, but I would just like to summarize it by referring us to what God says in Deuteronomy 6: "Hear, O Israel! The LORD is our God, the LORD is one! You shall love the LORD your God with all your heart and with all your soul and with all your might. These words, which I am commanding you today, shall be on your heart, You shall teach them diligently to your sons and shall talk of them when you sit in your house and when you walk by the way and when you lie down and when you rise up...."

This must begin from the time the child is young. If the parents wait to do this until their child is a teenager, it may be too late.

In summary: (1) The problem is a heart problem, (2) only God can change the heart, (3) parents have a huge responsibility to teach their children the truths about God and lead by example.

JOY MILLER *(Orrville Conservative Grace Brethren, Orrville, OH)*
My name is Joy Miller and I had the awesome privilege of growing up in a Christian home. It has been said before, and can't be emphasized enough, how important that is in the growth of young people.

At the age of six, I was listening to a radio dramatization by Pacific Garden Mission called "Unshackled." It was a weekly tradition at our house to listen to that program on the radio. After listening to the story, that night, I went back to my bed and couldn't fall asleep because I knew that, like the man in the story, I had sinned against the Lord and because of that, my penalty was spending eternity in hell. That night in my bed I prayed and asked Jesus to come and be the Savior of my life. But as I went through my junior high/high school years, I slid away a little, because I still wanted to do what I wanted to do, even though we were still very heavily involved in our church. It was when I was seventeen that I finally rededicated my life to the Lord and I said I would serve Him and do what He wanted me to do.

As I said, the role of my family has been huge in my spiritual growth. One thing that I think my church has done very well has been encouraging the family to step up and be the spiritual role model. Not the pastor, not the youth pastor, but the parent really needs to be the role model. There is nothing wrong with the other two people being there with them, but the parent needs to be there to step up, not just expecting the church staff to take care of spiritual growth.

Joshua Steiner mentioned the Evangelism Team that we both have had the opportunity to be on. That has also been a huge stretching experience for me and has helped me grow closer to the Lord. The Evangelism Team is something our fellowship has been doing the past 7 years.

I think one of the big problems in the church of America is that we are very entertainment oriented. Everything needs to be fun. You can have a blast serving the Lord! This last week we were at a church serving with the Evangelism Team and we had two floods in two days. We mopped water for hours both days and we had a blast because we were serving the Lord, not because it was fun, but because we were serving the Lord and that's what He wanted us to do. That is a big thing we need to remember. We need to build service into our young people. The tendency these days is to walk into church thinking, "who is going to talk to me today" or "what am I going to get out of the service today." Not, "who can I minister to today" or "what can I do to help the church today." I think we need to build the service mentality into our children when they are young, not starting when they graduate from high school.

An idea that we have done at our church is slowly trickling into other churches in our fellowship. We started having a youth Sunday where the whole Sunday service is led by the youth. I think when we first started people thought, "We are going to turn the whole service over to the youth?" But it has really been a neat thing to have. At the beginning it started kind of small. The youth weren't able to do everything, so we had people with more experience preach or maybe lead the singing. Now we are to the point that the entire service is led by the youth and young adults. The pastor doesn't have to do anything in the worship service that day. I think it is really neat to teach the young men to step up and lead in the church when they are young. Then they are comfortable doing that when they get to the age where they need to take the lead. We are the next generation and we need to fill that spot. In conclusion, I would urge you to encourage your children/grandchildren or people around you to serve the Lord now and not to wait until they're older.

Youth Panel

Summary Notes from Youth Panel Discussions
(provided by a parent of one of the youth panelists)

What is your church doing right to keep the youth involved?
- Get youth involved with mission activities.
- Give youth meaningful work in the church and outside.
- Provide funding for meaningful youth activities.
- Be sincerely loving and welcoming.
- Focus on discipleship as there is less time spent with families today.
- Connect sermons to the Gospel each time.
- Being "real." Be open and communicate when dealing with sin.
- Repeatedly it was mentioned that the godly home was of most importance for godly youth. (just meeting at church on Sunday is not enough).
- Encourage youth relationships with other congregations.
- Ministers should preach practical lessons.
- Ministers should live what they preach. No hypocrisy.
- Expect and practice accountability with the youth.
- Teach on basic disciplines like prayer, fasting, and tithing.
- Several said that adult mentorship should be encouraged.
- Adults should be interested in the youth.
- Study to know God and not just have head knowledge of Him.
- Provide an alternative culture for the youth (as opposed to the world).
- Offer the full Gospel. Don't wrangle, just do it!
- The youth want transformation.
- Take scripture at face value.
- Get the children's heart at a young age. Support the parents and pray for the children.
- It has got to be the responsibility of parents and not the ministers.
- Instill serving with joy. Focus outward instead of inward. Start young.
- Host a youth Sunday where the youth lead the whole service. This will encourage involvement and leadership. The first few won't be so good.
- Teach the truth unapologetically.
- Include the youth in general church activities. Don't separate them into a youth culture within the church.
- No youth culture, have a Christ culture.
- Don't entertain the youth, equip them. Entertainment is easily obtained elsewhere.
- Be Bible-based; not culture-based.

What could your church do better to keep the youth involved?

- Don't compromise our beliefs.
- "Acceptance" of seekers can lead to accepting sin in the church.
- Being relevant can lead to being irrelevant.
- Hypocrisy in adults.
- Letting youth that are not as involved slip through the cracks. Care for them.

Participants in the Youth Panel at Brethren World Assembly,
Brookville, Ohio, July 13, 2013

Rachel Laux; *Castine Church of Brethren, Castine, OH*
Kelsey Limbert; *Happy Corner Church of Brethren, Clayton, OH*
Aaron Oswald; *Brookville Church of Brethren, Brookville, OH*
Colt & Lyndsey Stout; *Westbrook Grace Brethren, Brookville, OH*
Andrew Peters; *Salem Old German Baptist Brethren New Conference, Englewood, OH*
Megan and Jamin Turner; *Shiloh Old German Baptist Brethren New Conference, Painter Creek, OH*
Joshua Steiner; *Orrville Conservative Grace Brethren, Orrville, OH*
Joy Miller; *Orrville Conservative Grace Brethren, Orrville, OH*
Maddy Brock; *Pleasant Ridge Dunkard Brethren, West Unity, OH*
Joni Rolle; *CornerStone Dunkard Brethren, Covington, OH*
Convened by Michael and Sondra Miller

www.ingramcontent.com/pod-product-compliance
Lightning Source LLC
Chambersburg PA
CBHW060112170426
43198CB00010B/866